A Real Taste for Fairy-stories

A Real Taste for Fairy-stories

Essays by Verlyn Flieger

2025

Cormarë Series No. 54

Series Editors responsible for this volume:
Thomas Honegger & Doreen Triebel

Library of Congress Cataloguing-in-Publication Data

Verlyn Flieger
A Real Taste for Fairy-stories. Essays by Verlyn Flieger
ISBN 978-3-905703-54-2

Subject headings:
Tolkien, J.R.R. (John Ronald Reuel), 1892-1973
Middle-earth
The Lord of the Rings
The Hobbit

Cormarë Series No. 54

First published 2025

Set in Adobe Garamond Pro and Shannon by Walking Tree Publishers

Cover design by Stefan Honegger

Acknowledgements

All of the essays published herein were originally presented in other venues or publications. In some cases, I have tweaked or updated the contents, but their appearance here is substantially unchanged from the originals. My thanks go to the following for permissions to re-publish:

Janet Croft, editor of *Mythlore* and original publisher in that journal of 'A Note on a Name' (*Mythlore* 36.1); 'The Arch and the Keystone' (*Mythlore* 38.1); 'Tolkien's Lúthiens' (*Mythlore* 40.1); 'A Lost Tale, a Found Influence: Eärendel and Tinúviel' (*Mythlore* 40.2); 'The Dragon and the Railway Station' (*Mythlore* 41.2); and 'A Fearful Weapon' (*Mythlore* 42.1).

Michael D.C. Drout, David Bratman and Yvette Kisor for 'Tolkien's Great Tales', which first appeared in *Tolkien Studies* XX (2022).

Stuart Lee, volume editor, and Nicole Allen, commissioning editor for John Wiley and Sons Ltd. for 'The Lost Road and The Notion Club Papers: Myth, History and Time-travel' from *A Companion to J.R. Tolkien*, Wiley Blackwell, 2014.

Catherine McIlwaine and Samuel Fanous for 'Listening to the Music' which first appeared in *The Great Tales Never End*, Bodleian Library Publishing, 2022.

Maria Portaencasa and the Spanish Tolkien Society for portions of 'The Fate of Free Will in Tolkien's World', first given as an address to the Society in 2023.

Alan Sisto and Shawn Marchese for 'The Scouring of Frodo', first given as a talk on their Prancing Pony Podcast, October 23, 2022.

Anders Stenström and Nils Ivar Agøy for 'Whose Myth Is It?' from *Between Faith and Fiction*. Arda Special 1. Proceedings of the Second Northern Tolkien Festival, Oslo Norway, 1997.

Professor Isamu Takahashi of Keio University, Tokyo, Japan for portions of 'Tolkien's Doom of Choice', included in a Festschrift for Professor Yoko Hemmi to be published in Japan in 2025.

Christopher Vaccaro and Yvette Kisor for 'Putting Words in Their Mouths', which first appeared in their volume *Tolkien and Alterity*, Palgrave Macmillan, 2017.

Table of Contents

Acknowledgements vii
Series Editor's Preface xi
Prologue xiii

Prolegomenon

Essay 1: The Arch and the Keystone 1

Part I – Tales

Essay 2: Tolkien's Great Tales 17
Essay 3: A Lost Tale, a Found Influence: Eärendel and Tinúviel 39
Essay 4: Tolkien's Lúthien(s) 55
Essay 5: The Scouring of Frodo 63
Essay 6: The Dragon and the Railway Station 73

Part II – Myths

Essay 7: Whose Myth is it? 81
Essay 8: "A Fearful Weapon" 89
Essay 9: 'The Lost Road' and 'The Notion Club Papers': Myth, History, and Time-travel 97
Essay 10: Defying and Defining Darkness 115
Essay 11: Listening to the Music 129

Part III – Words

Essay 12: Words, Words, Words 143
Essay 13: Putting Words in Their Mouths 161
Essay 14: The Fate of Free Will in Tolkien's World 177
Essay 15: A Note on a Name 189
Essay 16: Credit Where it's Due 193

Postscript 199
List of Abbreviations 201
Bibliography 202

Series Editor's Preface

If we had to vote on who gets the sobriquet 'godfather of Tolkien studies', my money would be on Tom A. Shippey. If we had to do the same for 'fairy godmother of Tolkien studies', it could be no other than Verlyn Flieger. It is therefore a great honour to be given the opportunity to publish the aptly named collection of Dr. Flieger's collection of essays *A Real Taste for Fairy-stories.*

Flieger's books and papers have accompanied me for decades, yet it was only during my research stay in Oxford in 2006 that I finally met her in person. I had been working in the Bodleian on Tolkien's academic manuscript for what would become my 'The Homecoming of Beorhtnoth: Philology and the Literary Muse.' (published in *Tolkien Studies* 4 (2007): 191-201) when Verlyn joined me in the reading room for final checks on her and Douglas Anderson's transcriptions of Tolkien's 'On Fairy-stories' manuscripts (to be published in 2008 as *Tolkien 'On Fairy-stories'*). We soon started to chat with each other during the tea-break and the next day she asked me to take a look at a tricky passage (Tolkien's handwriting can be very hard to read) which she had deciphered as 'Augustine said …'. This seemed to me, too, the most likely reading, and we tried to figure out which 'Augustine' was meant – presumably Saint Augustine of Hippo – and which of his many 'sayings' Tolkien was referring to. By the end of the week, however, we knew that the passage correctly reads 'Ancient tales said …' – and had a good laugh at our initial self-deception.

Almost two decades later I found myself once more 'in conversation' with Verlyn, but this time as one of the series editors in charge of seeing her essays to publication. In this I could rely on the support of my colleague Doreen Triebel, the help of Larissa Zoller for the layouting, Matthias Maar, Nina Murre, and Emely Sobroß for careful proofreading, Peter Buchs for managing the legal and administrative aspects, Andrew Moglestue and Johanna Schön for the quality control checks at the end of the process, Ted Nasmith for allowing us to use one of his stunning pictures, and Stefan Honegger for the cover design. My heartfelt thanks to all of them.

Thomas Honegger Jena, May 2025

Prologue

"A real taste for fairy-stories" wrote J.R.R. Tolkien in his essay on the subject, "was wakened by philology on the threshold of manhood, and quickened to full life by war" (*MC* 135). Philology and war are not traditional partners, and at first glance his juxtaposition appears not just incongruous but inharmonious. It was probably meant to be both, a way to startle his audience into skeptical attention. More compellingly, Tolkien seems to be saying that the two ostensibly unlike experiences provided him with similar mind-changing encounters. He was explicit that philology taught him about the altered state of enchantment he called 'faërie', insisting that the word 'faërie' did not denote a sprite with gauzy wings but named a country of the mind, a condition of being. His philological expertise would certainly have taught him the derivation of the word 'fa-er-ie' (compare 'cook-er-y') from Old French *fae* 'fairy' from Latin *fatum* 'fate', past participle of *fari* 'to speak', hence 'spoken'. "Small wonder," he declared, "that *spell* means both a story told, and a formula of power over living men" (*MC* 128). The power of the word, here as always, was paramount for Tolkien.

Contrariwise (as Lewis Carroll's Tweedledum would say), he seems to have learned from war – he was on the Somme in 1916 – that a hostile environment could be just as effective as an enchanting one at producing an altered state of mind and condition of being. Sam's feeling in Lórien that he is "inside a song" stands in dramatic contrast to Frodo's zombie-like trance in the Dead Marshes, where he is hypnotized by the dead faces that stare up from below the surface of the mire. The enchantment of faërie is no more powerful – but also no less – than the numbing effect of war. One of these conditions was light, the other dark, but they were two sides of the same coin. A similar alternation between war and faërie shows up in Tolkien's two great essays. 'On Fairy-stories' extols the Happy Ending, while '*Beowulf*: The Monsters and the Critics' places the monsters at the heart of human existence. This duality, this two-sidedness, is a hallmark of the man himself as well as of his fiction.

It is to highlight this persistent duality that I have chosen to open my collection with 'The Arch and the Keystone', an essay about the opposing sides of Tolkien and his work, and his role as the middle-man, the separator-cum-uniter of them both. The keystone that by its interposition creates and holds the arch.

Prolegomenon

Essay 1

The Arch and the Keystone

It's strange to remember now that when I first encountered *The Lord of the Rings* back in the nineteen-fifties, I was reading a book that seemed to have come out of nowhere. True, its author, one J.R.R. Tolkien, had written a popular children's book called *The Hobbit*, but aside from that he was pretty much an unknown quantity. When in the winter of 1956 a co-worker lent me the three volumes with the red cover, I had never heard of it, and I venture to guess that 99 people out of 100 had never heard of it either. I therefore had an experience impossible now not just for me but for anyone who hasn't been living in a cave for the last seven decades – the thrill of discovering *The Lord of the Rings* by myself, unburdened by other opinions, uninfluenced by hype, criticism, interpretation or imitation. Like the man in Tolkien's own allegory of the tower in his essay on *Beowulf*, I could climb to the top of Tolkien's tower and gaze out upon a hitherto-unimagined sea.

Looking backward is an exercise in nostalgia. Moving forward is more challenging. Like Alice's Red Queen, we have to run faster and faster just to keep up with all the adaptations, spinoffs, and television franchises that have engulfed Tolkien's original work. The growing body of writing both by and about Tolkien ensures that not only can we no longer read the same book I discovered in 1956, we can't even all read the same book in the present day. We have too many opinions based on too much information from too many sources to come to a consensus. In spite of its fame, in spite of its position at the top of the heap, in spite of its status as the fantasy that established the genre, the world has and probably will continue to have trouble agreeing on exactly what it is.

That's not for lack of trying. We have pasted labels on its author, saying the book makes him a medievalist, a modernist, a post-modernist, a royalist, a fascist, a misogynist, a feminist, a racist, an egalitarian, a realist, a romantic, an optimist, a pessimist. He's been variously characterized as homophobic and homo-social in both work and life. His fiction has been interpreted as Boethian, Manichean, Augustinian and Aquinian. He's been typed as a radical and a conservative, a Christian apologist and a closet pagan, a Catholic who believed in Fairyland, a monarchist who exalted little people, a Tory who supported anarchy (*Letters* 63). The fact that all these labels can find a fit only adds to the confusion.

It is in that confused situation that we now find ourselves, confronting evermore narrow and discrete paths of investigation, all of which lead – where? What exactly is the goal? Is it the tremendous body of work? Is it the man himself? And how do you – or even *can* you – tell the difference? With the enormous proliferation of fantasy, sword and sorcery, science fiction, urban fantasy, 'to-pias' of all sorts from *u* to *dys* to *eco*, what is it that sets Tolkien apart from the others? We've all read the books. We've all seen the photographs, the scholarly professor at his desk with his pipe, the venerable grandfather figure posed next to an equally venerable tree. He towers over modern fantasy like one of the Pillars of the Kings at the Argonath. But who exactly is this guy? What is it that makes him still, after sixty-five years and a lot of competition, the premier author (not just fantasist) of the 20th century. Who is J.R.R. Tolkien?

That he is a literary icon I think most would agree. But *icon* just means 'image' and that is part of my problem. Much of the Tolkien scholarship is devoted to creating the image by finding the man in the work, by exploring the fiction for clues to his thinking, his beliefs, his opinions on everything from sexuality to the green movement to social order to industrialization by, in short, constructing an image out of what can be found in his writings. But therein lie pitfalls for the unwary and dungeons for the overbold. There are so many and various things to be found in his writings that we make the inevitable mistake of confusing the image with the man.

In spite of (or perhaps because of) all that has been written about him, and all that he himself has written, the essential J.R.R. Tolkien still eludes us. What he really thinks, what he really believes, is still and undoubtedly will continue to be a matter of conjecture and (of course) of lively debate. That is partly because his work is so various, but also because when we look at Tolkien, we are likely to see ourselves, and thus to find in his work what we want to see. This is as true of his most devoted fan as of his nastiest critic. It is as true of me as it is of Edmund Wilson or Germaine Greer or, I dare say, of Peter Jackson. But the result is that the more I read about Tolkien the less homogenous a figure I find. What I discover instead is increasing fragmentation and polarization. Everybody has their own private Tolkien – more Tolkiens than you can shake a stick at.

I have to admit that Tolkien himself makes it easy, because so much of the primary evidence – that is to say, his writing – seems to toggle between diametrically opposite positions. He's been accused of writing about 'good and evil' or 'black and white' and maybe that's where the trouble starts, because his good guys do bad things, and his bad guys do good things, and black and white get blended into grey, and their inventor has to answer for all. The man who betrayed Frodo at the Cracks of Doom also arranged to make it Gollum who actually saved Middle-earth. The author who brought Frodo home to the Shire is the same one who made it impossible for him to live there. The writer who sent Frodo in sight of the 'far green country' pivoted 180 degrees to write 'The New Shadow', a futuristic sequel about the Fourth Age so "sinister and depressing" in its outlook that he couldn't bring himself to finish it (*Peoples* 410).

The immediate response by the reader to such contradictory positions is bewilderment. The subsequent response is the desire to reconcile the contradictions – which, of course, cannot be done, because if they could be reconciled, they wouldn't be contradictory. In what follows, I'm not going to tell you anything you don't already know. Instead, I'm going to cover old ground in the hope that it will at least get us up to the starting gate. What I intend to do this morning is to explore some examples of contradictions and see if we can find a way to allow them to live together, to be in opposition yet representative of their creator. If it works, this will – fingers crossed – allow us to see Tolkien less as 'either-or' and more as 'both and' – the center between two points, a center that defines them by keeping them apart.

Like a good politician, I'm going to give you old news as new revelation and try to persuade you to rediscover it.

'*Beowulf*: The Monsters and the Critics' and 'On Fairy-stories'

Let's look first at two outstanding examples of his academic work, the two great lecture-essays, '*Beowulf*: The Monsters and the Critics' (1936) and 'On Fairy-stories' (1939). I am going to assume that everybody has some acquaintance with these two essays, so I won't go over them in detail or give their histories except to say that they are both dense, erudite, and scholarly. They were written by Tolkien the professor, not Tolkien the master-fantasist, and I only want to make one point that their contrasting subject matters and Tolkien's treatment of each stand as philosophical bookends to his fiction. Opposition – in fact contradiction – between two important works by the same scholar is perplexing, as we expect writers to be reasonably consistent in thought and work. Yet, opposing viewpoints are what I find here. The *Beowulf* essay extols a worldview that faces death with courage and accepts it as finality, the end. The fairy-story essay exalts the Escape from Death that brings the Happy Ending. Simple juxtaposition of the two shows the contrast between them, a contrast not just in subject but in Tolkien's attraction to each. Rather than trying to close the gap and reconcile the two, I'll let each speak for itself, starting with *Beowulf*.

Beowulf, writes Tolkien, is a poem written by a Christian looking back at a heathen time, and it is the death-embracing worldview of that heathen time that both the poem and his essay explore and praise. In particular, Tolkien defends two of the poem's central characters, the humanoid man-eating monster Grendel and the fire-breathing dragon, finding them not the irrelevancies they were judged to be by scholars in his day but central embodiments of some of the darkest elements of human existence. The first monster, Grendel, epitomizes greed, possessiveness, bloodthirstiness, wholesale destruction, mayhem and murder. The second monster, the dragon, is death, the lurking, prowling, pouncing monster we all live with.

Of course there are human monsters as well, who plunder and betray and burn and kill. That they parallel but do not outshine the actual monsters is one of the *Beowulf* poet's most brilliant strategies. "For the monsters do not depart, whether the gods go or come," Tolkien wrote, "and within Time the monsters would win" (*MC* 22). The poem's closing phrase is, "until the dragon comes"

(*MC* 34), as he does for everyone sooner or later. It is a heroic vision but also a hopeless one.

One of its most memorable lines is a sentence in Anglo-Saxon: "*lif is læne: eal scæceð leoht and lif somod,*" "life is [a] loan [i.e. fleeting]; all perishes, light and life together" (*MC* 19). So powerful is this statement that first-time readers of the essay not infrequently mistake it for a line from the poem itself. It is not. In his note on 'A Spliced Old English Quotation' (Drout 2006), Michael Drout has shown that this particular sentence does not occur in this form anywhere in Anglo-Saxon literature. It is Tolkien's own invention, made by combining two related ideas that do appear in some form or other in early English poetry. The first idea, *lif is læne*, is a commonplace that pops up in various forms in such poems as *The Wanderer* and *The Seafarer* and *Beowulf*. The second comes from the Anglo-Saxon poem *Widsith*: *oþþæt eal scæceð leoht and lif somod* ('until all departs, light and life together'). Both are typical of what Tolkien called the Northern theory of courage (*MC* 20), but it was Tolkien who put them together.

Combined, these two sentences are greater than the sum of their parts. They proclaim the message that Tolkien found in *Beowulf* and restated a few pages later as "man, each man and all men and all their works shall die" (*MC* 23). He called it a "theme no Christian need despise" (*MC* 23). Clearly, the Christian Tolkien did not despise it. Instead, he espoused it. What Tolkien says about *Beowulf* can with equal truth be said about Tolkien. Though his essay reiterates that *Beowulf* is the work of a Christian looking back at a pagan time, his interest and his focus are nevertheless on the pagan, 'Northern' ethic that death is the end of life.

I think it worth noting that it is also in the *Beowulf* essay that on two separate occasions Tolkien laments the lack of information about pre-Christian English mythology. "Of English pre-Christian mythology we know practically nothing" (*MC* 21) and a few pages later and even more strongly, "we may regret that we do not know more about English pre-Christian mythology" (*MC* 24). Given Tolkien's later description to Milton Waldman of his ambition to write a mythology "for England," I suggest we should read these two statements in that context and thereby see his regret as a motive to action rather than a static state of mourning.

Turning now to 'On Fairy-stories', we find there not just a contrast to the *Beowulf* essay but its opposite pole in both content and strategy. 'On Fairy-stories' is equally learned but less focused, more wide-ranging, not an analysis and defense of one poem but the re-valuation of a time-honored (and to Tolkien a much-misunderstood) genre. Less an argument than an investigation, the essay winds from the power of language to enchantment to fantasy to the sub-creation of another world. Tolkien covers a lot of ground, but today I want to focus on one particular element which he finds in fairy-stories and which offers a direct contrast to the *Beowulf* essay – that is escape, especially and most importantly Escape from Death. This comes about, says Tolkien, through the one element central to the fairy-story genre, the *eucatastrophe.* A word of his own coinage combining Greek *eu,* 'good' and *catastrophe* 'downturn', it describes the last-minute escape that turns the story from sorrow to joy, the turn that brings Snow White back from death or awakens the Sleeping Beauty with a kiss. That brings the Happy Ending. It is the combination of *eucatastrophe* and Happy Ending that characterizes the fairy-story. A pretty big contrast to the Beowulfian acceptance of death as the end.

But Tolkien does not stop there. He goes on to propose a thematic link with Christianity that further divides the two essays. The Gospels, Tolkien says, "contain a fairy-story" (*MC* 155) except that this one is true. Instead of the Beowulfian tragedy of human life "within Time," fairy-stories, says Tolkien, "open a door on Other Time, and if we pass through [...] we stand [...] outside Time itself, maybe" (*MC* 129). And in that context, the whole of the essay is preamble to its 'Epilogue'. Here, he proposes the birth of Christ as the eucatastrophe of Man's history and the Resurrection as the *eucatastrophe* of the Incarnation. Redemption is the Happy Ending.

What is noteworthy here is that the same man wrote both essays and espoused both positions. I believe this contradiction comes less from without, from the subject matter of the two essays, than from within, from the author's own inclinations, his personal gravitation toward what to speak and write about. I will return to this later, but for now I want to further explore the dichotomy I find in Tolkien's work and thought that makes him the powerful author that he is.

Murray vs. Resnick

Turning now from what Tolkien wrote for publication to what he said on more informal and spontaneous occasions, I want to look at statements to individual people. It is of course not unusual to find contradictions among someone's letters and interviews. We all say different things to different people in different circumstances at different times, and a lot depends on what they say or have said to us. I am going to cite two examples of contradiction in Tolkien's non-fiction, his letters and interviews, and relate them to the disparity I find between the two essays.

In 1953, Tolkien wrote to Fr. Robert Murray SJ, an old friend who had read a proof copy of *The Lord of the Rings*, that it was "fundamentally religious and Catholic" (*Letters* 172). Yet, in 1966, he gave a quite different response to the interviewer Henry Resnick's question about the meaning of the Company's Dec. 25 departure from Rivendell and the identification by some of Frodo with Christ. Tolkien's answer was, "you don't have to be Christian to believe that somebody has to die to save something" and furthermore that [*The Lord of the Rings*] "was not a christian [sic] myth anyhow" (Resnik 1967: 42-43). What are we to make of such a blatant contradiction by one statement of what another has to say on the same subject?

There is, of course, a distinction to be made between *Catholic* as a religion and *Christian myth* as a type of story. *Catholic* refers to a particular system of belief, a specific doctrine; *Christian myth* describes a genre, a type of story which expresses and illustrates that belief. Tolkien's statement to Resnick rejects the notion that *The Lord of the Rings* is a specifically Christian myth. He may have been thinking of C.S. Lewis's Narnia books, which are intentionally Christian and which Tolkien was on record as disliking for their bad sub-creation. His rejection of Christian myth as a template for his *The Lord of the Rings* could easily be read in that context.

In a more general sense, however, it seems inarguable that *fundamentally Catholic* and *not a Christian myth* are incompatible terms when applied to the same story by the same man. If *The Lord of the Rings* is Catholic, then it is Christian. If it is not Christian, then it is not Catholic. That each statement negates the other is obvious – less so my point, which is rather that Tolkien was comfortable saying each at a different time to a different person. Either he is a hypocrite, which I do not believe, or he is more comfortable with paradox than are some of his readers, who would rather find him on one side or the other.

To be fair, Tolkien's later (1965) explanation in a letter to W.H. Auden was that he "intended [*The Lord of the Rings*] to be consonant with Christian thought and belief" (*Letters* 355). Nevertheless, 'consonant with' is a long way from 'fundamentally', and the difference is noteworthy.

In a more general sense, we can find evidence of the same dual perspective, the same apparent contradiction in some of his shorter fiction.

Niggle vs. Smith

Here, I want to pair two of Tolkien's short stories, the two most famous as well as the two best examples of my thesis. These are 'Leaf by Niggle', the most clearly allegorical of his shorter works, and *Smith of Wootton Major*, the purest example of what he meant by fairy-story. As with the essays, I'm going to assume that this audience is acquainted with both. 'Leaf by Niggle' was written in 1938-39, just a few years after his *Beowulf* lecture, at about the same period in which Tolkien gave the lecture that turned into 'On Fairy-stories'. *Smith of Wootton Major* was begun in 1964 and published in 1967. Tolkien was in his late seventies, retired from academia, and had written in 1965, "I find it difficult to work – beginning to feel old and the fire dying down?" (*Bio* 236). His great work was behind him. *Smith of Wootton Major* was the last story he wrote and the last of his work to be published in his lifetime.

I want to make a case that these two stories move in opposite directions and take their protagonists – Niggle and Smith – to two quite different ends. One man, Niggle, goes from troubled human life through what is unmistakably purgatory and thence to a succession of higher and more fulfilling visions that invite interpretation as heavenly. The other man, Smith, is expelled unwillingly from the enchanted otherworld of Faërie to go back to ordinary human life. Tolkien is the arbiter of fate for both these protagonists.

'Leaf by Niggle' is easy to read as allegory and indeed lends itself to that approach more easily than almost anything else Tolkien has written. It is the story of a man, Niggle, who knows he must go on a journey but is preoccupied in the meantime by his efforts to paint the essence of a tree or even a leaf and is hampered in so doing by day-to-day demands and obligations. We have all felt Niggle's frustration when the ordinary – all the things we have to do – gets in the way of the extra-ordinary – the thing we really want to do. The story is a moving and lyrical exploration of the struggle of human life, presenting Niggle as a Tolkienian Everyman striving to create while constantly being deflected by the chores and demands of the everyday world around him. As a short story, it is near perfect in its brevity, compression and compassion. As an allegory, it invites sympathetic comprehension. Niggle goes through stages from earthly life to an afterlife where his art is fulfilled and extended, and the story by implication (allegory, by its nature, has a message beyond its subject matter) holds out that vision to its readers.

Smith of Wootton Major, though it can be (and has been) read as allegory, is in tone and treatment a fairy-story, a genre which, while open to interpretation, is not agenda-driven as is allegory. Its protagonist Smith, whom many readers also identify as a Tolkien figure, is given access to Faëry, but in contrast to Niggle's final progress toward the Mountains and his laughter with Parish that ends the story, Smith is told he has to give up the star that grants him entry and "come back to hammer and tongs" – that is to say, to surrender his passport at the end of his holiday and get back to work. It is worth noting that while Niggle is an artist, Smith is an artisan, a blacksmith who works with iron, traditionally an element inimical to Faëry. That Tolkien should have chosen this medium for his central character I find quirky and perplexing. But then, nobody ever said Tolkien was an easy read. (I certainly never did.)

Smith of Wootton Major was written in response to George MacDonald's *The Golden Key*, whose vision of fairyland Tolkien found too sugary for his taste. It is probably Tolkien's best and most honest portrayal of his idea of Faëry, a world of enchantment that yet is remote, even severe, standoffish with strangers. In Faëry, Smith enters a world he does not fully understand and is witness to events – some beautiful, some daunting – that go beyond his experience and his comprehension. He sees warriors marching on their way to an unknown destination to fight a battle whose cause is unrevealed and whose outcome he will never know. He sees maidens dancing, and one invites him to dance with her, but he doesn't know till afterward that she is the Queen of Faëry. He is guarded from the "Greater Evils", and the "Lesser Evils" avoid his star so that he is "as safe as a mortal can be" (*Smith* 24). But that there are evils is not in doubt.

I want to make clear that I am not equating Niggle's Heaven with Smith's Faëry or promoting Faëry as a kind of Heaven. I am simply contrasting them as two different otherworlds to which in Tolkien's fiction and his imagination the human traveler – or the human experience – has access. What I do want to point out is that the two protagonists Niggle and Smith are projections, as well as competing aspects of Tolkien. He himself made no bones about the autobiographical element in 'Leaf by Niggle', attributing its inspiration to the tree outside his bedroom window (*Letters* 321), referring to *The Lord of the Rings* as his "own internal Tree" (*Letters* 321), and describing the story as "part apologia, part confession" (*Letters* 113). In Priscilla Tolkien's article on 'Leaf by Niggle' written for the Tolkien Estate website, she cites her father's endless professional academic duties "which left him little time for creative work" (Tolkien Estate.com), so we are in good company with both Tolkien and his daughter in reading Niggle as Tolkien and Tolkien as Niggle.

It is equally possible to read Smith as Tolkien and Tolkien as Smith. As with 'Leaf by Niggle' and its image of the tree, Tolkien made no bones about what his biographer Humphrey Carpenter described as his "farewell to faery," calling it "an old man's story filled with the presage of bereavement … written with deep emotion, partly drawn from the experience of … advancing age" (*Bio* 243). Carpenter wrote of Tolkien that "like Smith […] [he] had, in his imagination, wandered for a long while through mysterious lands; but now he felt the approach of the end, and knew that he would soon have to surrender his own star, his imagination" (*Bio* 243).

The contrast between the two stories is not the epic contention I've described between *Beowulf* and fairy-stories nor is it the flat-out contradiction between what Tolkien wrote to Murray and what he said to Resnick. But it is a change of dynamic, an altering of perspective that produces a draconian difference in outcome for Tolkien's two heroes. One knows what he really wants and gets it. The other knows what he really wants and is forced (I don't think that's too strong a word) to give it up.

The Lord of the Rings

So far, I have offered examples from scholarly or personal or minor works, but I would be fudging if I didn't also apply my approach to *The Lord of the Rings* itself. As it set out upon its adventure in the 20th century, the fairy godmothers at its birth christened it fantasy, and it has since been called a myth, a fairy tale, an epic, and juvenile trash. I have not been so diligent in my special walk as duly to read all that has been printed on this work. But I have read enough to venture the opinion that Tolkien studies, while rich in many departments, is surprisingly poor in one. It is poor in understanding it as tragedy, as a story that, not unlike *Beowulf*, is concerned above all with fall and failure, with the ultimate victory of the monsters.

It would not be Tolkien's first such story. Both his Kullervo and his Túrin Turambar are tragic heroes who fail, both more relentlessly if less precipitously than Frodo. Nevertheless, what Tolkien does to Frodo is worse than what he does to Kullervo or Túrin or what the poet did to Beowulf, for while these heroes' lives ended in death – two of them by suicide – Tolkien forces Frodo to live with the knowledge of his moral failure at a job he never wanted to do in the first place. It is Sam Gamgee, not his master, who lives happily ever after. The tragic hero's failure brings about the fairy-story hero's Happy Ending. Frodo and Sam, at the Cracks of Doom and in the aftermath, embody between them the final tension and opposition that characterizes Tolkien's masterwork.

As he is for Niggle and Smith, Tolkien is the arbiter of fate for the two heroes of *The Lord of the Rings*, and their contrasting fates are not unlike those of Niggle and Smith, though the harshest is reserved for Frodo. Sam gets the *eucatastrophe*: the destruction of the Ring, the restoration of his beloved master to sanity, the return to the Shire and Rosie and the Happy Ending. It is Tolkien's most supreme irony that Frodo gets these selfsame things and cannot keep them. Destruction of the Ring, which saves the world, is to Frodo irreparable loss. He is rescued from madness only to awake to the bitter knowledge of his moral weakness and his downfall. His return to the Shire is equally bitter, for not *it* but *he* has changed. Sam heals the Shire, but he cannot heal Frodo. Instead of Sam's Happy Ending, Frodo gets the tragic hero's *peripeteia*, reversal of fortune. Instead of coming home to

Rosie, he has to leave Bag End and the Shire and Middle-earth for an unknown future.

I know what you're going to tell me: The Grey Havens, the ship, the Straight Road, and of course the far green country. My point is – we never get there. Tolkien doesn't take Frodo that far, so he doesn't take the reader either. He shows it to Frodo and therefore to the reader from a distance, in contrast to the immediate power of Frodo's heartbreaking farewell speech to Sam about the inevitability of loss. Moreover, in his letters, Tolkien makes it clear that though he sends Frodo to Valinor, to be healed "if that could be done, *before he died*" (*Letters* 328) that healing is by no means a foregone conclusion, whereas death is. *lif is læne.* Here are some of the things he wrote to inquiring and concerned readers who wrote to him about Frodo.

"The Quest [...] was bound to fail" (*Letters* 234). "Frodo indeed 'failed' as a hero [...] he gave in, ratted" (*Letters* 326). "He saw himself and all that he done as a broken failure" (*Letters* 328). And here's the kicker. "The power of Evil in the world is not finally resistible by incarnate creatures" (*Letters* 252). That seems pretty unequivocal. Also pretty pessimistic; also pretty Beowulfian. Just as he saw Beowulf's contention with the monsters as ultimate inevitable defeat, Tolkien has stacked the cards against his hobbit hero to make it "quite impossible" that Frodo could resist the Ring (*Letters* 251). Like Beowulf, Frodo cannot win. His Quest cannot succeed. And then in the twinkling of an eye through Gollum's treachery, it does succeed, and the reader is thrown out of epic tragedy back into fairy-story to experience the most stunning *eucatastrophe* in modern literature.

The Murray Letter

Such conflicting testimony, all of it straight from the horse's mouth, re-invokes but does not answer my original question: Who is J.R.R. Tolkien? I said earlier that Tolkien carried a contradiction within himself, and in this context I'd like to return to Father Robert Murray, the man to whom Tolkien wrote the "fundamentally religious and Catholic" statement about his work. Murray was a longtime friend, having become a Catholic through his close friendship with the Tolkien family and knew Tolkien firsthand in a way not accessible to scholars and critics today, however much they may study his work. That being the case, his comments are worth taking seriously.

In 1980, Murray wrote a letter to a graduate student whose dissertation on Tolkien he had been asked to read. Concerning the 'fundamentally Catholic' statement, Murray wrote, "Tolkien was a very complex and depressed man and my own opinion of his imaginative creation [i.e. *The Lord of the Rings*] is that it projects his very depressed view of the universe at least as much as it reflects his Catholic faith" (West 2019: 135).

I have to agree with Murray, especially in light of the fact that the statement in question was written to Murray himself, who, it seems safe to say, knew the writer of it better than I do. I too find in *The Lord of the Rings* a powerful pull toward the dark that's equal to his desire for light and is even more narratively effective. That pull goes a long way toward accounting for the dichotomies and contradictions I have also found elsewhere. It throws light on not just the two great essays with their competing worldviews but also the diametrically opposing trajectories of the two short stories, 'Leaf by Niggle' and *Smith of Wootton Major*. It deepens and enriches the complexities of *The Lord of the Rings*. It's what gives Tolkien's work its curious power to capture and hold not just the imagination but the spirit. In fact, Murray's summation can stand for the whole arc of Tolkien's work from the very early 'The Story of Kullervo' and 'The Fall of Gondolin' through a lifetime spent on *The Silmarillion* and *The Lord of the Rings* to that book's abandoned sequel 'The New Shadow'.

In the same letter, Murray wrote further that, "There <u>is</u> a case to be made about Tolkien the Catholic, but I simply could not support an interpretation which made this the key to everything" (West 2019: 135-36; underlining in the original). Perhaps the problem lies in the student's implied assumption that there is a key. I would like to offer in place of a key that will unlock everything, a key*stone* that will hold everything together, a central element that will sustain and bridge in opposition two sides that do not meet.

Back at the beginning of my talk I asked: 'Who is J.R.R. Tolkien?' Now, I will offer an answer to my own question, not with a *who* but with a *what*. Tolkien is the keystone in the great arch of his work, the element that divides and at the same time bridges the divide.

He is the center held in place by the two sides of his own nature. That nature yearns for the Happy Ending but anticipates the dragon. It can see his work as Catholic yet describe it as not Christian. It can walk toward Heaven with Niggle's joy and walk away from Faërie with Smith's regret. That nature can with ruthless compassion engineer the separate destinies of both Frodo and Sam. These oppositions are the sources of Tolkien's power and the tension between them is the energy that unites it. They are what after sixty-five years still sets him apart from the others and makes him the icon, the image, the towering figure that he is.

I want to emphasize that it is not two-sidedness per se that distinguishes Tolkien. Lots of fantasy authors – Stephen Donaldson, Neil Gaiman, Ursula K. le Guin, H.P. Lovecraft, Mervyn Peake, to name just a few – have used their fantasy to explore good and evil, light and dark, the power of the dark side. But Tolkien wasn't using his fantasy so much as his fantasy was using him.

Here's how: What holds a keystone in place is not cement but friction, the grinding of the two sides that only the presence of the middle prevents from abrading each other. It is the pressure of competing forces not against each other but against what keeps them separate – the keystone that holds the arch. It is these same forces that generate the curious power of Tolkien's work. And it is these same forces creating this friction that invite the disagreeing and debating Tolkien scholars and critics to find in Tolkien's work what they are looking for. I am not saying they're wrong. I'm saying they're right. What they see is there, even when they're seeing contradictory things. So instead of wrestling with Tolkien's contradictions, instead of trying to reconcile them or harmonize them, I propose that we take them *as* they are for *what* they are, two opposing and conflicting sides of one person whose contention makes him *who* he is as well as *what* he is, the keystone that creates the arch. Without it, there's just a pile of bricks.

Part I
Tales

Tolkien's Great Tales

In 1951, with *The Lord of the Rings* not yet published, J.R.R. Tolkien wrote to Milton Waldman, a representative of Collins Publishing, describing the story as one part of the mythology he once dreamed of dedicating it "to England, to my country." He wrote, "I would draw some of the great tales in fullness, and leave many only placed in the scheme and sketched. The cycles should be linked to a majestic whole" (*Letters* 145). He was more specific about the Great Tales in a 1964 letter to a reader, Christopher Bretherton, where amid a six-page answer of printed text, the tales again featured prominently:

> The germ of my attempt to write legends of my own to fit my private languages was the tragic tale of the hapless Kullervo in the Finnish *Kalevala* [...] though as 'The Children of Húrin' it is entirely changed except in the tragic ending. The second point was the writing 'out of my head', of 'The Fall of Gondolin', the story of Idril and Earendel [...] during sick leave from the army in 1917 [...] and by the original version of the 'Tale of Lúthien Tinúviel and Beren' later in the same year. (*Letters* 345)

The notion of particular stories that would be the foundation stones of his burgeoning mythology was already in Tolkien's mind when he began to write the first of the tales on sick leave in 1917 and the second soon after, "in the same year." Though over the ensuing years, they were endlessly rewritten, neither the tales named – 'The Children of Húrin', 'The Fall of Gondolin', and 'The Tale of Lúthien Tinúviel' (better known as 'Beren and Lúthien') – nor the "majestic whole" to which they were to be linked ever got finished to Tolkien's satisfaction before he died in 1973.[1] And one more, the tale that grew in the telling of the other three, intended to connect and round out the picture, was never written.

His third son Christopher became his literary executor, left with a stack of unpublished manuscript material and the hopes of Tolkien fans the world over

1 I give dates of composition wherever I can find them, with the caveat that many are more probable (or even conjectural) than certain. One can only sympathize with Christopher, who unlike me, didn't have him to rely on.

that he would finish the job. He did. It took him a little over forty years and produced seventeen hard-cover volumes. Less than a year before his own death in January 2019, he brought out his final segment of the "majestic whole" his father had hoped to sell to Collins.[2] This was *The Fall of Gondolin*, the third and last of his stand-alone editions of the three great tales named in the opening paragraph. *The Children of Húrin* was published in 2007, *Beren and Lúthien* in 2017, and *The Fall of Gondolin* in 2018. It is these volumes on which I wish to concentrate, exploring the value and significance of their stories both to Tolkien's life and to his work, as well as their specific and individual editorial treatments by Christopher.

Biographical Elements

Aside from their centrality to the *legendarium*, all three tales have particular relevance to Tolkien himself, touching – each in its separate way – on one or another of the most compelling and formative elements in his personal life. *The Fall of Gondolin*, an epic account of war and exile, was the first to be written in 1916-17. It arose directly from his brief but intense war experience in France in 1916 when he saw combat on the Somme. This was one of the most destructive battles of World War I in terms of human life and cost Tolkien two of his closest friends,[3] one killed by machine-gun fire on the first day of the assault, July 1, a second hit by stray shrapnel in November of that year. Their loss, and the war itself, affected Tolkien deeply and had a profound effect on the themes of his fiction, which focus, as with the Ring and the Silmarils, on the consequences of destruction and irretrievable loss.

The death of boyhood friends was not the first of his losses. The deeply tragic *Children of Húrin* erected a fictional framework around what Tolkien called the "dreadful sufferings" of his childhood (*Letters* 421). These began with the loss of his father when he was not yet four. Three-year-old Tolkien, his mother Mabel, and his younger brother Hilary had left the country of his birth, South Africa (or, to be more precise, the Orange Free State) for

2 Ironically, it was published by HarperCollins, which took over Collins and combined it with Harper & Row in 1989.

3 Members of the King Edward's School T.C.B.S., the boyhood fellowship that was also to shape his life and his fiction.

what was called "home leave" for English citizens abroad. In Tolkien's case this separation was further marked by the death of his father in Africa, whose loss left his family stranded in England. That would be enough trauma for any one child, but these shocks and displacements were followed by others equally stressful. Mabel Tolkien's recent conversion to Catholicism resulted in her alienation from the extended Protestant family that might otherwise have given her support and shelter as the widowed mother of two very young boys. While she struggled to raise her sons and send them to school, these sad circumstances were followed by Mabel's unexpected (by her sons) death from untreated diabetes when Tolkien was twelve, leaving him and ten-year-old Hilary as orphans. Although they were left in the care of Father Francis Morgan, their mother's spiritual guide, the boys were nevertheless robbed of their home, becoming unwanted poor relations shunted from household to household and finally put up in a boarding-house.

The love story of *Beren and Lúthien* was neither epic nor tragedy, but it too touched something personal to Tolkien. This was his forced promise to Father Francis when he was nineteen that he would neither see nor communicate with his girlfriend Edith Bratt[4] until he was twenty-one. Concerned that he would neglect his studies and jeopardize his chance for an Oxford scholarship,[5] Father Francis did not realize that he had pushed his young ward to make, as Tolkien himself later put it, "a boy-and-girl affair serious" (*Letters* 52). In fact, he made it more than serious. He made it his personal fairy tale (and thus rounded out the genres of the three great tales) of lovers thwarted by cruel fate who endure separation to triumph in the end. In so doing, he made *Beren and Lúthien* the central story of both his *legendarium* and his life. On the day he turned twenty-one, Tolkien wrote to Edith. When she wrote back that, tired of waiting, she was engaged to someone else, he went straight to see her, talked her out of the someone else and into marriage with him. Writing to Christopher many years later, Tolkien declared that "she [Edith] was, and she knew she was, my Lúthien" (*Letters* 420). Whether he was her Beren, the story does not say. Both storial names are on the tombstone in their shared grave, hers put there

4 Tolkien and Edith, both bereft of home and family, had first met while staying at the same boarding-house. He was sixteen, she was nineteen. See 'Privat lang. and Edith' (*Bio* 38-43).

5 Which actually happened. Tolkien failed his scholarship exam. He passed the second time.

by Tolkien, his by their children. The available evidence suggests that the fairy story was more his than hers.

Literary Antecedents

Personal circumstances are only part of the picture. Each story also has a formal antecedent in externally existing myths and legends. *The Fall of Gondolin* is in the direct tradition of Homer's *Iliad* and Virgil's *Aeneid*, an account of the siege and fall of a great city. *Beren and Lúthien* is a gathering of standard fairy tale motifs (love at first sight, the quest, the fairy marriage, the magical object, the impossible task) and recognizable character types (the oppressive parent, the animal helper, the resourceful princess). *The Children of Húrin* transforms a tragic episode in the Finnish Kalevala into the equally tragic story of Túrin Turambar, whose life – cursed by Morgoth and mesmerized by the dragon Glaurung, but marred also by other people's mistakes and his own blunders and bad decisions – is one long sequence of errors and wrong choices leading inevitably to his death. It is notable that while the latter two stories are named for their protagonists, the first of the tales, *The Fall of Gondolin*, is named for a city. Although it has other titles, 'Of Tuor and his Coming to Gondolin', 'The Exiles of Gondolin', the emphasis is on the city rather than the individual.

Christopher's Treatment

In their latest publications, the tales must be viewed as being almost as much the product of Christopher's efforts as those of his father, since they rely heavily on the son's extensive knowledge of both the author and the works in question, on his dedication to his father's vision, his persistence in the face of an overwhelming mass of material, and his finely-honed editorial skills. Without Christopher as editor, we would not only not have the great tales, we would hardly even know they existed except for a few references in *Letters*.

The decision to present the tales as separate entities rather than threads in a tapestry meant that Christopher had a textual tangle to unsnarl. All three arose in the earliest years of Tolkien's work on his *legendarium*; all three were subsequently re-written numerous times and in varying forms over almost the entire course of Tolkien's creative life. This oscillation back and forth started as early as 1916-17 and was still in process as late as 1951. It gave Christopher the problem of how to trace an exterior chronology of development while still managing to present an internally coherent story. He used different methods for the different tales, letting the nature, form, and state of revisions determine both his process and the final product.

The Children of Húrin (2007) was assembled by Christopher from extant versions of the Túrin story – the short version presented in *The Silmarillion*, the much longer *Narn*[6] given in *Unfinished Tales*, and elements from *The Annals of Beleriand.* Omitted entirely was the alliterative 'Lay of the Children of Húrin', begun in 1918 but abandoned by 1925 (*B&L* 88). It contained some of Tolkien's finest verse in this form but would have been a poor fit with Christopher's strategy, which was to create one seamless and continuous narrative that followed the headlong trajectory of Túrin from his deprived childhood to his final, utter ruin and death. Offering a minimum of editorial notes and commentary, this allowed the reader to experience directly the full arc of the story, to meet the characters face to face without editorial interference.[7]

This worked well for the Túrin story, but when Christopher came to the other two tales, he discarded synthesis in favor of historical analysis, tracing the development of each story through its successive overlapping and sometimes competing versions. This anatomized the process but at the cost of sacrificing the whole vision. It had the combined effect of bringing the reader as close to Tolkien's creative process as could be accomplished short of telepathy, while at the same time interrupting again and again both the story arc and the reader's suspension of disbelief, as each version broke off at one point or another, to be re-started in a new attempt. It was this authorial practice that Christopher chose

6 The term *narn* deserves some explication, for its use here can be confusing. It is a Sindarin (Grey-Elven) word that can be roughly translated as 'lay' and which, as Tolkien explained, signifies among the Elves "a tale that is told in verse, but to be spoken and not sung" (*UT* 146.) The *Narn* referred to was the work of a Mannish poet, Dírhavel, but done in the Grey-elven tongue. We are therefore safe in regarding all the versions we have as translations by one or another transmitter, be it Eriol/Ælfwine, Pengoloð, Findegil, or Bilbo, into the "common speech" [i.e. English] of a hypothetical Sindarin poem of which there is no record. Strictly speaking, we have no original "narn", only the presumed translations. For a fuller discussion see Flieger (2005: 109-110).

7 For Christopher's painstaking explication of this delicate and intimate process of diving into, severing and reattaching essential components of the story, the reader is referred to his 'Introduction' and 'Notes on the Composition of the Text' in *The Children of Húrin.*

to showcase in his two later editions. But as the stories are different in shape and content, the re-writing process for each was guided by these factors – and by Christopher's method as well.

The first great tale to be given this analytical treatment was the second to be published as a stand-alone, *Beren and Lúthien*. Christopher described his method as "twofold." It was first, to separate out the story from the "slowly evolving 'Silmarillion'" and second to show "how this fundamental story evolved over the years" (*B&L* 12) in a way that revealed his father's "apparently eccentric mode of composition." This enabled Christopher (and the reader) to "discover the sequence of stages in the development" (*B&L* 11), moving from the highly mannered and somewhat ironic voice of the narrator in 'The Tale of Tinúviel' to the impersonal reportorial passage from the 'Sketch of the Mythology' which is followed by a long extract in rhymed couplets from 'The Lay of Leithian', itself interspersed by paragraphs from the 'Quenta Noldorwina' and ending with a passage from *The Silmarillion*. Again, both authorial and editorial processes guided the edition. While this seems cumbersome, it is hard to imagine how Christopher could have interwoven such disparate texts into the kind of coherence he achieved with *The Children of Húrin*. That said, it must also be acknowledged that the end result is less than the sum of its parts and is qualitatively different from the unified text of *The Children of Húrin*.

He faced much the same problem with *The Fall of Gondolin*, which he called a "complex narrative of many strands in various texts" (*FG* 9). He explained that he arranged the contents so that the texts appear first, followed by an account of the evolution of the story with discussion of its abandonment in the last version at the crucial moment when Tuor passes through the last gate (*FG* 17). Even more than with *Beren and Lúthien*, this fragments the story and deprives it of inner coherence. How well each method serves its particular story is a matter for debate and may depend as much on the audience as the editor. Certainly, the unbroken narrative of *The Children of Húrin* is the most satisfying for anyone looking for a good read and best serves the catharsis that is tragedy's hallmark. Textual scholars, on the other hand, as concerned with process as with product, may prefer the more historical-analytical methods of *Beren and Lúthien* and *The Fall of Gondolin*, whose strategy gives readers not just the story but the story of the story and how it grew, or didn't.

An important aspect of Christopher's treatment of *The Fall of Gondolin* and *Beren and Lúthien* is the growing importance of the Silmarils, which increased over time. At the 'Conclusion of the Sketch' in *The Fall of Gondolin*, he pointed to "wholly new features, among which is the emergence of the fate of the Silmarils as a central element" (*FG* 246). That this emergence is "wholly new" will come as a surprise to readers familiar with Tolkien's work from the other end, where the fate of the Silmarils is clearly laid out, and "Silmarillion" is the generic name for the whole *legendarium*. Such new information is justification for Christopher's piecemeal method. He adds further that "it may well be said that the very existence of the Silmarils was of far less radical significance in the original conception of the mythology than it was to become" (*FG* 247). Indeed, he writes "That it was the Silmaril wrested by Beren and Lúthien from Morgoth in Angband that Eärendel wore and became the Morning and the Evening Star had not been achieved at this stage, though when achieved it seems a necessity of the myth" (*FG* 147).

The mention of Eärendel introduces perhaps the most potent yet most perplexing name in Tolkien's mythos and points to a missing piece of the "majestic whole," the story of the half-elven Eärendel who makes his first appearance in Tolkien's early (in fact pre-Middle-earth) poem, 'The Voyage of Éarendel the Evening Star'. Written in 1914, some three years before the mythology first took shape, before any of the great tales existed, this poem was nevertheless flagged by Humphrey Carpenter as "the beginning of Tolkien's own mythology" (*Bio* 71) and by John Garth as "the very first beginning of the matter of Middle-earth" (Garth *Exeter* 33). However obscure his beginnings, however complicated the logistics of his trip, Eärendel was to develop from a mystery-voyager into one of the most significant figures in the matter of Middle-earth, the lynchpin that locks into place the other parts of the story. Yet, his tale was never written.

The Unwritten Tale

In Christopher's 'Conclusion' to *The Fall of Gondolin*, wherein Eärendel as a character makes his first appearance, he quoted his father's last words in *Beren and Lúthien* about "the great tale of Eärendel" (*FG* 140), adding with implicit regret that "the Lost Tale of Eärendel was never written" (*FG* 241).[8] If it had been, there would have been four Great Tales, and the Silmarils would have had a clearer and more traceable story arc from the Two Trees to the Evening and Morning skies.

Tolkien first encountered Earendel while a student at Oxford in 1913, in two lines from the *Crist*, a medieval poem by the Anglo-Saxon poet Cynewulf (*Letters* 385):

> *Eala Earendel! Engla beorhtast*
> *ofer middangeard monnum sended.*
>
> Hail Earendel, brightest of angels
> above middle-earth sent to men. (*Bio* 64)

He transferred his response to his time-travel hero Alwyn Lowdham in 'The Notion Club Papers', who told his fellow Club members,

> When I came across that citation in the dictionary I felt a curious thrill, as if something had stirred in me, half wakened from sleep; There was something very remote and strange and beautiful behind those words, if I could grasp it, far beyond ancient English. (*SD* 236)

The voice of Lowdham and "the dictionary" notwithstanding, the vivid immediacy of the description makes it clear that Tolkien was describing his personal experience. He showed the lines in question to his T.C.B.S.[9] friend G.B. Smith, who asked him what they were about. Tolkien's reply that he didn't know but that he would try to find out (*Bio* 75), was typical of his creative process, suggesting that he thought the answer was waiting not to be invented but discovered.

It is a tempting oversimplification to speculate that Tolkien's entire vast *legendarium* might have grown out of his need to find the answer to Smith's question as to what the Anglo-Saxon lines were about, to "find out" who Earendel was, what he was doing, and why he was doing it. He later wrote:

> I was struck by the great beauty of this word [...] it at least seems certain that it belonged to astronomical-myth, and was the name of a star or star-group.

8 See Christopher's discussion of 'The Tale of Eärendel' in *LT II*, 252-277.

9 Initials standing for Tea Club Barrows Store, where Tolkien and his closest school friends would meet to study and talk. The T.C.B.S. lasted until the Somme in 1916, when between July and December two of its four founding members, G.B. Smith and Rob Gilson, were killed.

> To my mind the Anglo-Saxon uses seem plainly to indicate that it was a star presaging the dawn (at any rate in English tradition): that is what we now call Venus: the morning star as it may be seen shining brilliantly in the dawn, before the actual rising of the Sun. That is at any rate how I took it on first encountering the word, in 1914. (*Letters* 385)

Over time, Tolkien would find out more about Earendel. He would learn that his Old Norse name was Aurvandil and his Danish name was Horvendil; that various versions of his story went back to proto-Germanic myth so ancient it was untraceable; that he had a ship called Vingilot in which he voyaged through the skies.[10] But history, philology, and astronomy were only ports of call for Tolkien, way-stations along his own voyage of discovery. What he found out about Earendel led him to write his 1914 poem, 'The Voyage of Éarendel the Evening Star'. This was followed by other longer Earendel poems, each expanding on the one before but all describing "the star-ship's voyage across the firmament [...] until the morning light blots out all sight of it" (*Bio* 71).[11] Here's the first version:

> Earendel sprang up from the Ocean's cup
> In the gloom of the mid-world's rim;
> From the door of Night as a ray of light
> Leapt over the twilight brim,
> And launching his bark like a silver spark
> From the golden-fading sand
> Down the sunlit breath of Day's fiery death
> He sped from Westerland. (*Bio* 71)

The language here is vivid but confusing. Earendel springs "up" but speeds "down." So where is he going? And how does he get there? In point of fact, Earendel is not rising, as the first line suggests, but setting, moving apparently from west to east in opposition to the rest of the night sky. As the Evening Star, Venus/Earendel follows the setting sun into the west only to reappear in the east before the rising sun as the Morning Star. All this is difficult to convey poetically and without laborious astronomical explanation of orbits and apparent retrograde movement. Tolkien was trying to say without saying that Earendel's path takes him beneath

10 For more on this see Hostetter 1991 and, more recently, Honegger (2023: 110-126).

11 For a full discussion of Tolkien's early work on Earendel, see Christopher Tolkien's 'The Tale of Eärendel' (*LT II*, 252-277).

the earth,[12] where his voyage, unobserved by human eyes, will bring him to the eastern horizon as the Morning Star. Even more important than *where* and *how*, is *why*? What is going on? Unexplained from a mythological point of view is the reason for this journey. Tolkien would have to "find out" more about Earendel, who he was, where he was going, and why.

His answer was laid out in the first two of the great tales, *The Fall of Gondolin* and *Beren and Lúthien*.[13] Both were written after the 1914 poem yet in Tolkien's fictive world of Middle-earth, they are the antecedents and proximate causes of Eärendel's portentous voyage.

References to Earendel are scattered throughout the *legendarium*.

The Children of Húrin

Christopher Tolkien has called the Túrin story his father's "dominant story of the end of the Elder days," and "the chief narrative fiction of Middle-earth after the conclusion of *The Lord of the Rings*" (*CH* 281). Several versions of the story exist, the early, dragon-centered 'Turambar and the Fóalokë' (c. 1919), the brief synopsis drawn from the 'Sketch of the Mythology' (1926) published in *The Silmarillion*, the longer but incomplete account given as the 'Narn' in *Unfinished Tales*, and the alliterative poem included in *Lays of Beleriand* (c. 1918-25). In his Appendix to the stand-alone version, Christopher gives an account of how he cut and pieced together elements of the shorter versions to augment and supplement the base text of the 'Narn' published in *Unfinished Tales*.

Unlike the other two tales, this tale has one specific source not just generic precursors. In the quote cited at the beginning of this essay, Tolkien credits the Finnish *Kalevala* as the "germ" of his efforts to write legends of his own, though

12 One of the earliest known (or at least earliest-published) maps of the earth, titled *I Vene Kemen*, "The Shape of the Earth" or "The Vessel of the Earth" is reproduced in *The Book of Lost Tales I*, 84. According to Christopher, it is "closely associated with the cosmology of the *Lost Tales*." It is Tolkien's drawing of the earth as a ship and represents a (more or less) flat plane floating on water. The much later bending of the earth in Tolkien's Númenórean cataclysm assumes that it was originally flat, in which case the quickest way for Eärendel to get from West to East would be like the bottom tread of an escalator loop to double under and reverse his path to come out again at the top.

13 Though as discussed above in Christopher's 'Conclusion' to *The Fall of Gondolin*, they were not as fixed as later versions of the *legendarium* have made it seem.

he concedes that as *The Children of Húrin* the story is "entirely changed" except for the ending. Close examination will show more similarities than Tolkien was willing to admit. In his 1951 letter to Milton Waldman he described Túrin Turambar as "derived from elements in Sigurd the Volsung, Oedipus, and the Finnish Kullervo" (*Letters* 150). The sources and their referents are easily identified. Túrin's dragon-slaying episode comes from Volsungasaga, the story of Sigurd the Volsung (which Tolkien later put into verse as *The Legend of Sigurd and Gudrún*, published in an edition by Christopher in 2009). From the tragedy of Oedipus, Tolkien took Túrin's desperate search for identity, not the oedipal incest that first comes to mind. Just about everything else of any significance comes from the Finnish Kullervo, who gave Túrin his brooding, stubborn disposition, his loss of family, his wanderings, his unknown sister for incest, and his death when his own sword agrees to kill him.

Tolkien's interest in Kullervo began while he was a student at King Edward's School in Birmingham, where he first read Elias Lönnrot's Finnish *Kalevala*[14] in Kirby's English verse translation. He later called Kirby's a "poor" translation and made an effort to learn enough Finnish to read it in Lönnrot's original. While his attempt at Finnish was unsuccessful – he described it as "repulsed with heavy losses" (*Kullervo* 102) – he was, in fact, so taken by this story that he tried to turn in into his first serious attempt at fiction. In a letter to Edith Bratt dated by Humphrey Carpenter to 1914, he mentions *Kalevala* and tells her he is "trying to turn one of the stories – which is really a very great story and most tragic – into a short story somewhat on the lines of Morris' romances with chunks of poetry in between" (*Letters* 7).

This was 'The Story of Kullervo', Tolkien's own adaptation/retelling of the Kullervo *runos* (songs) from *Kalevala* about the Finnish anti-hero he called "Kullervo the hapless" (*Letters* 214), whose uncle murders his father and whom he kills in revenge (also recognized by scholars as the prototype of Hamlet).[15] A bitter, vengeful youth pursued by ill-fortune and creating disaster for all whose

---

14 With the Grimms' German *Kinder- und Hausmärchen* (*Children's and Household Tales*, published 1812), Lönnrot's 1835 collection of Finnish folk-songs, called *Kalevala*, ('Land of Heroes') was among the earliest examples of the 19th century's enthusiasm for collecting and enshrining ethnic folklores.

15 The story was apparently widely known in several loosely associated versions by northern European writers. See Snorri Sturluson's Prose Edda, Saxo Grammaticus' *Gesta Danorum*, Israel Gollancz's *Hamlet in Iceland*, de Santillana and von Dechend's *Hamlet's Mill.*

lives he touches, Kullervo is a kind of hard-luck Everyman, a role model for all the world's losers. Tolkien never explained his attraction to this character, but we can infer from the traumas of his own childhood the sympathy he might have felt. While we should be careful not to assign too much agency to these traumas – Tolkien survived them to live a full and productive life – neither should we overlook the effect on his future life of what Tolkien himself called "a sad and troublous time" (*MC* 135).

Kalevala creates similar circumstances for Kullervo, son of Kalervo, before he is even born. His uncle Untamo kills his father, forcibly marries his mother, and subjects the newborn Kullervo to a series of torments designed to get him out of the way, preferably by death. When these attempts prove unsuccessful, Kullervo is handed over to a foster-father, the smith Ilmarinen, in whose care he consistently fails by overdoing the tasks set him. When Ilmarinen's wife mistreats and abuses him, Kullervo vows to take revenge on her and on the world that does not understand him. He has her torn apart by wolves and bears magically transformed out of cattle. Rediscovering his family (inexplicably resurrected owing to Lönnrot combining two different versions of the story), he learns that he has a long-lost sister. He later meets a girl whom he seduces, only to have it revealed that she is the lost sister. Mutual discovery of the incest leads both siblings to take their lives, the girl by throwing herself under a waterfall, Kullervo by inviting his sword to kill him, which it declares it will gladly do.

While there are substantial differences between Tolkien and Kullervo – we know of no incest, fratricide, parricide, magical shape-changing or suicide in Tolkien's life – there are also clear parallels, moments when in grief and despair the young Tolkien might have seen in Kullervo's circumstances a reflection of his own. It is not hard to see a reflection of the young Tolkien in the youthful musing he gives his Kullervo in his "Story":

> "Wherefore have I been created?/ Who has made me and has doomed me/ [...] Others to their homes may journey [...]/ But my home is in the forest." He goes on, "Never Jumala [God] most holy/ in the ages of the ages/ Form a child thus crooked fated/ With a friendless doom forever/ To go fatherless 'neath heaven/ And uncared by any mother" (*Kullervo* 33).

Some lines seem particularly apropos: "I was small and lost my ~~mother~~ father/ I was young (weak) and lost my mother./ All my mighty race has perished" (*Kullervo* 34).

Tolkien's unfinished story breaks off after the seduction, when the girl tells Kullervo who she is but is followed by extensive notes outlining the rest of the story wherein the death of the girl by suicide awakes "old knowledge [presumably some buried memory of her] in his heart" (*Kullervo* 39). Kullervo's reactive rage sends him on a killing spree which ends with him "drenched in blood" (39) after having slain Untamo and all his kin. His mother's ghost appears and tells him the girl he seduced was her daughter and thus his sister. It is this "old knowledge" that sends him to the falls where she died, there to drown himself but where instead he asks his sword if it will kill him. When the sword agrees, Kullervo uses it to kill himself and find "the death he sought for" (*Kullervo* 40).

Biographical elements aside, the literary line of descent from the Kullervo of *Kalevala* to Tolkien's own 'Story of Kullervo' is clear, as is the subsequent, much fuller but still direct descent from both of these to his Túrin Turambar. Shared similarities among the three include loss of a father (Túrin's through war rather than death), separation from a mother (though Túrin leaves home at her behest), a somber disposition (Túrin is "not merry"), a tendency to brood on slights or perceived wrongs, and most significant, unwitting incest with an unrecognized sister, her consequent suicide in the waterfall and Túrin's by his own hand with the willing sword.

That said, the differences between Kullervo and Túrin are substantial. The Túrin story as it evolved became not just a formal tragedy but a study in character against the backdrop of war. Of all his Middle-earth stories, apart from *The Lord of the Rings*, Tolkien's story of Túrin is the most complete and the most compelling, as well as the most unrelenting.

Unlike his early Kullervo, who is "swart and ill-favoured", Tolkien's Túrin is handsome and attractive, loved by Thingol, Beleg, Gwindor, Finduilas, Brandir and Nienor. He is also humane. A central incident in Túrin's life is his treatment of the knife given to him by his father. In *Kalevala*, the knife that is the young

Kullervo's only legacy from his father is broken on the stone that in a cruel trick Ilmarinen's wife bakes into his lunchtime bread. The ruin of the knife proves to be the final straw that unleashes his revenge. In Tolkien's hands, in contrast, the knife, as in *Kalevala* the gift of his father, becomes Túrin's spontaneous gift to the lame thrall Sador and thus the emblem of Túrin's instinctive sympathy, his humanity and feeling for those less fortunate.

We are to remember this when we read of Túrin's tormenting of Saeros, of his proud refusal to accept Thingol's pardon, read even of his sojourn among the outlaws. Tolkien sets Túrin's humanity against his manipulation by the dragon, his failure to save Finduilas, his disastrous decision about the bridge at Nargothrond, and his final, shamed request of his sword that it kill him. The story of Túrin is as tragic a tale as that of Oedipus or Orestes, or Othello: the headlong descent from light into darkness of a man whose good intentions lead only to his self-destruction.

While his Kullervo sought outsize revenge on the whole world, Tolkien's Túrin, although he has a chip on his shoulder the size of a Yule log, means always to do the right thing. He's just tragically inept at figuring out what that is. Túrin's trajectory of honest mistakes, errors of judgement, willful contrariety and stubborn refusal to acknowledge error is almost too much to bear. If Tolkien was looking for an example on which to model errors of human nature, he picked the right one in Kullervo, whom he transformed into Túrin and made his poster child for stumbling humanity. But Túrin operates under more malign forces than his own nature.

Even knowing of its antecedent in *Kalevala*, we can see overkill in Tolkien's treatment of Túrin and his family. Morgoth's curse, the dragon's spell, Túrin's own nature, his childhood circumstances, of separation from home and parents, the perpetually warlike state of Middle-earth, the poor choices of others, such as Morwen and Niniel, or even Saeros – any one of these would be enough to explain the tragedy of Túrin's life. Such a piling-up of influences prompts the question why. Why has Tolkien so loaded the dice? I suggest that this is a deliberate strategy on his part intended to reflect the state of the world as he saw it, as flawed and fallen and subject to error. It was the prime illustration of the notion Tolkien expressed in his '*Beowulf*' essay that within Time the monsters would win (*MC* 22).

His choice of *The Children of Húrin* as the story's overall title, with its rather impersonal reference to Túrin and Niniel, suggests another parallel, secondary to *Kalevala* but equally apposite. This is the biblical story of Job, whose innocent (and unnamed) children are the victims of God's wager with Satan about their father. They are killed without ruth as part of God' effort to tempt Job into cursing God, the sin he will not commit. Just so, Húrin's son and daughter, Túrin and Niniel/Nienor are the victims of Morgoth's curse against their father that he be forced to witness their tragedies and be powerless to stop them. The curse is unrelenting and all-encompassing. No one hears it but Húrin and the reader, yet the shadowy knowledge of it hides in the consciousnesses of all his family from the moment Morgoth pronounces it:

> The shadow of my purpose lies upon Arda, and all that is in it bends slowly and surely to my will. But upon all whom you love my thought shall weigh as a cloud of Doom, and it shall bring them down into darkness and despair. Wherever they go, evil shall arise. Whenever they speak, their words shall bring ill counsel. Whatsoever they do shall turn against them. They shall die without hope, cursing both life and death. (*CH* 64)

It hardly needs pointing out that this is exactly what happens. But it does need pointing out that it does not happen by accident and that the last of Tolkien's three Great Tales is also the most realistic, the most doom-laden, and the most clearly indebted to its source. While it may be Morgoth who pronounces the curse, it is Tolkien who both invents and implements it, Tolkien who engineers the tragedies one by one, Tolkien who designs and orchestrates the tragedy and destroys the lives of Húrin and Morwen and Túrin and Niniel/Nienor – not to mention a host of secondary characters he may have borrowed the template from *Kalevala* and put the curse in the mouth of Morgoth, but the final product is his own. As is the final choice to create this tragedy as a chance to show, within his sub-created world as in the real one, that within Time the monsters will win.

Beren and Lúthien

The fairy story genre Tolkien chose (or that chose him) for *Beren and Lúthien* was a mode that he knew and wrote about, most notably in his essay "On Fairy-stories."[16] Here, he defined this eponymous genre as stories not about fairies but

16 Expanded from his 1939 Andrew Lang Lecture 'On Fairy-stories'.

about *Faërie*, "the realm or state in which fairies have their being", and about "the *aventures* of Men in the Perilous Realm or upon its shadowy marches" (*MC* 113). A re-write was required for Tolkien to conform *Beren and Lúthien* to his own standard, for in the earliest version, 'The Tale of Tinúviel', Beren was not a Man but a Gnome, one of Tolkien's early and early-abandoned names for his Elves. Recast as a Man in the next version, the rhymed 'Lay of Leithian', Beren wanders into Thingol's Hidden Kingdom (a fairy realm if ever there was one) where at first sight of Lúthien dancing he falls in love. The whole rest of the story unfolds from this moment. Although he had already used it in *The Fall of Gondolin*, the meeting of Beren and Lúthien is perhaps Tolkien's clearest and most explicit treatment of a fairy tale trope, the fairy marriage, the romantic union of a mortal and an otherworld being.[17] Tolkien's own description in a letter to Christopher of seeing Edith dancing in the hemlock wood at Roos begs for comparison and adds to the secondary fairy tale superimposed by eager fans for whom Beren and Lúthien are interchangeable with the life of their creator.

Another essential element of fairy story, Tolkien declared in his essay, is the Happy Ending. In *Beren and Lúthien* this rule is both followed and transcended. The lovers meet and fall in love only to be cruelly parted; they undergo ordeals and overcome trials, finally to be reunited by the *eucatastrophe* of Lúthien's song before Mandos pleading for Beren's life. It is granted but not necessarily happily ever after, for it is here that Tolkien goes beyond the formula. His ending, wherein Lúthien relinquishes elven immortality for human mortality and eventual death, is only partly – and even then, only temporarily – a Happy Ending.

The story both conforms to and transcends its type in other ways as well. In true fairy tale fashion, Tolkien's Lúthien is surpassingly beautiful, not just the most beautiful woman in Middle-earth, but in all the history of Middle-earth. As Cinderella outshines her stepsisters, so Lúthien outshines all other women. Like Snow White, she is "fairest of all." And like her counterparts she pays a heavy price for her beauty. Lúthien's imprisonment in a tree cannot but recall Rapunzel's in the tower, and her escape using a rope of her own hair is a clear re-purposing of the hair motif in the Rapunzel story. Lúthien's father,

---

17 These include the union of Beren (son of Barahir) with Lúthien, who is the daughter of Thingol, an Elf, and Melian, a Maia, and that of their distant descendants Aragorn and Arwen. Parts of the same pattern occur in the rumored marriage of Bilbo's Took ancestor with a fairy wife.

Thingol, lord of Doriath, may be one of Tolkien's High Elves, but he is also like Rapunzel's sorceress imprisoning her in a tree, or even more like the grim giant Ysbaddaden of the Welsh 'Culhwch and Olwen' folktale in the *Mabinogion*, an impossibly demanding parental figure who will go to murderous lengths to keep control of a daughter.

What sets Lúthien beyond the standard fairy tale princess is her courage and resourcefulness, her willingness to take risks and face foes of greater strength (though not greater magic) than hers. Tolkien's Beren does not fare as well. He is brave and resourceful but that too is standard for a fairy tale lover and does not distinguish him from his type. We take for granted that he is handsome, though his looks are not as essential to the story as are Lúthien's. It should be admitted, however, that Beren does manage to get off a couple of highly individual, un-fairy tale-like zingers in his exchanges with Thingol, his putative father-in-law. His response to Thingol's request of a Silmaril in exchange for Lúthien, that "for little price to Elven kings sell their daughters," is an unanswerable put-down to which Thingol has no reply. Beren's loss of a hand, bitten off by the wolf Carcharoth, is a borrowing from Norse mythology, not fairy tale, the incident in the Icelandic *Edda*s where the god Tyr sacrifices his hand to bind the Fenris wolf. Tolkien's re-use of this motif enables Beren's dramatic gesture when Thingol asks to be shown the Silmaril – wordlessly holding up first his empty left hand and then his handless right arm – transcending fairy tale formulas and lifting him into the realm of genuine myth.

Beren is not the only character in the story who can transcend as well as conform to type – all the characters do, to a greater or lesser extent. We have seen how Thingol can still conform to the archetype of a fairy tale parent without relinquishing his status as King of the Sindar, the Grey-Elves. Huan the hound has the gift of speech, though he uses it on only three occasions and thus is a classic Animal Helper like Puss in Boots. Yet, his battle with the wolf Carcharoth is epic in its proportions, taking hound and wolf beyond their fairy tale types. The story's too-briefly appearing villain, Tevildo, Prince of Cats (he didn't make the final cut), is not a denizen of Middle-earth like the fox who sniffs at the sleeping hobbits but a character drawn straight from British folklore, the old tale of The King of the Cats.[18] When Tolkien adapts, he does it with relish. Tevildo is a magnificent, albeit temporary creation, suave and menacing. In his brief appearance, Tolkien has created a personality out of a type, improving upon and individualizing the folklore model.

Even without a Prince of Cats among the cast of characters, a major aim of *Beren and Lúthien* is the creation of wonder, the enactment of the marvelous in a secondary world where magic is not just possible but necessary to the plot. Tolkien does not disappoint. The vision of Beren and Lúthien in animal disguise, Lúthien as bat fluttering and wheeling and Beren as werewolf leaping and "howling under the moon" (*S* 179), is unforgettable not just because of its visual impact but equally because of its eerie contrast with the conventional "good guy" roles of the two characters. The use of singing magic, both in Finrod's contest with Sauron and Lúthien's songs before Morgoth and Mandos, are borrowings from *Kalevala*, where the power of song can cause the earth to grow green, sing your enemy into a bog, or turn his sleigh into a willow tree.

The Fall of Gondolin

Following his treatment of *Beren and Lúthien*, Christopher chose "the same curious form" (*FG* 13) for his edition of *The Fall of Gondolin*. First to be written, last to be published as a single volume, 'The Fall of Gondolin' in its earliest version post-dated the Earendel poem by some three years yet derived directly from it in that it introduces Eärendel as a character. It was begun in 1916/17 (the precise date is indeterminable), almost immediately after Tolkien's return from France where he had seen combat in the bloodiest battle to date of World War I, the Somme. Not surprisingly given these circumstances, it is a story about war and the effects of war. "You ought to start the epic," Tolkien's surviving T.C.B.S. friend Christopher Wiseman wrote to him when he came back from France (*Bio* 90, 92) – and Tolkien did. John Garth calls *The Fall of Gondolin* "One of Tolkien's most sustained accounts of battle" (Garth 2003: 218), and it

18 The King of the Cats is a British fairy tale in which, according to one version, a domestic tomcat is given the mysterious message, "Tell Balgeary that Balgoury is dead." "Then I'm the King of the Cats!" he cries on hearing the news, revealing himself to be Balgeary, whereupon he rushes up the chimney and is never seen again.

cast its shadow over the developing mythology, making the whole thing a saga also about war and the effects of war.

The overall story falls into two parts, the long, landscape-descriptive journey of Tuor to Gondolin and the events in the city after and in part caused by his arrival: his marriage with Idril which arouses the jealousy and treachery of Maeglin, the birth of Eärendel, the siege of the city and its downfall, and the escape from the city that preserves Eärendel to become the standard-bearer and fulfillment of Tolkien's early poem. The earliest version of the story is called in manuscript 'Tuor and the Exiles of Gondolin' but titled in the published volume 'The Tale of the Fall of Gondolin'. While this is the least fleshed out in terms of detail, it yet includes the complete arc of the story that fits that tale into *The Silmarillion*. By this time, Earendel the Evening Star had become an actual person, the son of Tuor and Idril, and thus the first of Tolkien's half-elven. His star-status now derived from the fact that he carried aloft the last of the three Silmarils,[19] the jewels of light from Valinor whose name Tolkien bestowed on the entire *legendarium*.

The Fall of Gondolin also features the first of Tolkien's direct uses of the fairy tale tradition of fairy marriage we have already seen with *Beren and Lúthien*, a supernatural union between a human man and an elven princess. In this case, it is the union of Tuor of the house of Beor and Idril daughter of Turgon the Noldorin king of Gondolin. This is essential to Tolkien's growing vision, for it also includes, as far back as the earliest, "original" version, the birth to Tuor and Idril in Gondolin of their child Eärendel, and thus is both retrospective to 'The Voyage of Earendel' and predictive of the Quenta Silmarillion "the majestic whole" not yet in being. The presence of Earendel (now spelled 'Eärendel') in the story of Gondolin clarifies, justifies, and provides a context for his flight through the sky in the earlier poem, though its importance and relevance to the fate and significance of the Silmarils was apparently still in the process of formation as the poem took shape.

---

19 It would be easy also to oversimplify the connection between Eärendel and the Silmaril, or even which Silmaril, which took many revisions to achieve final form. For a fuller exploration see Christopher Tolkien's discussions in *The Shaping of Middle-earth*.

More than any other of the Great Tales, *The Fall of Gondolin* illustrates the effect of style upon substance. The earliest 1916/17 version is the most derivative, a formal echo of the faux-antiquated, pseudo-historical, oral-imitative style of the authors of Tolkien's childhood like Sir Walter Scott and William Morris, in which such locutions as "Now" to begin a sentence, noun-verb inversions, and paratactic 'and-and-and' sentence structure are used to give the story an air of great age and solemnity. Yet conversely, as a story it is distinguished from the other Great Tales by its highly modern level of violence, which links it not just to Homer's Iliad but to modern war novels such as *All Quiet on the Western Front* and *A Farewell to Arms*. Its explosive and flame-throwing devices, its metallic dragons that move like tanks with orcs inside, all are derived, scholars agree, from the mechanistic, inhuman war machines that Tolkien saw on the Somme in 1916.

In style and substance, the original version stands in contrast to what in the 2018 volume Christopher called "The Last Version" (and dated to 1951 (*FG* 145)) but which in *Unfinished Tales* he called 'Of Tuor and His Coming to Gondolin'. The years from 1917 to 1951 had matured Tolkien's prose but left him with diminished energy, impetus and leisure to use it, leading to what is perhaps the greatest buildup to a letdown in all of Tolkien's unfinished writing. The story as it stands is less an epic than an exercise in frustration. Tuor's dramatic meeting with Ulmo, his encounter with Voronwë and their arduous journey, the build-up of tension in the measured stages of their approach, the final vision of Tuor looking at Gondolin and Gondolin looking at Tuor (*UT* 51) all lead up to and culminate in – nothing. For there the story breaks off.

I venture to guess that I was not the only reader of *Unfinished Tales* in 1980 who got to the last paragraph in 'Of Tuor and His Coming to Gondolin' and felt as if I had fallen off a cliff. Or even more dramatically, as if I were one of those Looney Tunes cartoon characters who runs headlong off a cliff but does not immediately realize it and scrabbles for footing on thin air before plunging into unpictured depths. It was no consolation to me that note 31 appended to the last sentence of the published story – a note which went on for four paragraphs – mentioned "hasty jottings" about the future course of the story in which Tuor was to enter Gondolin, meet Turgon, Maeglin, and Idril, and carry the story forward. I knew all that. I wanted to see it. Perhaps there was no way, as with

The Children of Húrin, to blend the versions of the story to make a coherent whole. I sympathize with his dilemma. Christopher's scholarship, as always, was meticulous and I am grateful for the care he took. But I found (and find) myself wishing he had been a little less scrupulous and given me a whole story.

Conclusion

It seems clear that for Tolkien the Great Tales were the ones that brought him closest to his own life. His work is in a very real sense what he once implied as biographical, saying that "only one's Guardian Angel, or indeed God himself could unravel the real relationship between personal facts and an author's work" (*Letters* 288). He described the story of Beren and Lúthien as a "beautiful and powerful heroic-fairy-romance" and "receivable in itself" as well as a "fundamental link in the cycle" (*Letters* 149) and called *The Children of Húrin* and *The Fall of Gondolin* "equally independent and yet linked to the general history" (*Letters* 150). But the Great Tales have another "general history", that of their author and the time in which he lived. They are stories of war, of displacement, of hope deferred and not infrequently disappointed, of dreadful sufferings and irretrievable loss as well as some "glimpses of final victory" (*Letters* 195).

The Great Tales in the final and definitive form Christopher has given them to us are also the work of an editor whose scholarship and integrity made him uniquely qualified for the job. That job, the real task of all scholars, was to work with what he saw on the page and stay true to what he found. In working with an author whose formidable imagination stayed true to itself while his tale grew in the telling, he faced no easy task.

A Lost Tale, a Found Influence: Eärendel and Tinúviel

In this essay, I propose to fit together two examples of J.R.R. Tolkien's storytelling art. United chiefly by their difference, each is a trial venture into the art of mythmaking: one an experiment in omission, the other in commission. Each offers a different window into the workshop where the artist practiced his craft.

In his 1951 letter to Milton Waldman, J.R.R. Tolkien mourned what in light of his knowledge of other cultures he saw as England's lost pre-Christian mythology. "There was Greek," he wrote, "and Celtic, and Romance, Germanic, Scandinavian, and Finnish [...] but nothing English" (*Letters* 144). He went on to describe his ambition to fill in the gap:

> Once upon a time [...] I had a mind to make a body of more or less connected legend [...] which I could dedicate simply to: to England, to my country. I would draw some of the great tales in fullness, and leave many only placed in the scheme, and sketched. The cycles should be linked to a majestic whole [...]. (*Letters* 145)

A point to remember is that Tolkien was writing with hindsight. The long perspective of "once upon a time" gives the impression of a *fait accompli*, whereas the "more or less connected legend" he referred to was actually in a constant flux of revision and was still unfinished when he died in 1973. Christopher Tolkien's *The Silmarillion* (1977) was a condensation of this unfinished opus that compressed the arc of the overall narrative into one volume. While this gave the world its first view of the "majestic whole", it nevertheless blurred Tolkien's explicit distinction between tales drawn "in fullness" and tales "only placed [...] and sketched" by appearing to give equal weight to all the tales.

Christopher Tolkien's *The History of Middle-Earth* (1983-1996), with its painstaking unpacking of his father's constantly revised material, did much to undo this impression, and his publication in separate volumes of *The Children of*

Húrin, *Beren and Lúthien*, and *The Fall of Gondolin*, presenting from 2007 to 2018 the great tales from earliest to latest, also illustrated what Tolkien meant by "placed" and "sketched." The following discussion will examine an example of each separate treatment, the "only placed" tale of Eärendel and the very early and drawn in full 'Tale of Tinúviel'. I'll start with Eärendel.[1]

The 'Lost' Tale of Eärendel

Braided into his work on the great tales, Christopher has given us evidence for a tale that cannot be found, the only evidence for which is the empty spaces where it should have been. The Tale of Eärendel is established through poems about him, by references to the tale in other tales, by outlines, and by what seem to be consciously contrived omissions where it ought to have been. Just as the excavators of the ship burial at Sutton Hoo were able to infer the presence of the ship by the impression it left in the earth, or those at Pompeii could reconstruct from the hollows in hardened ash the shapes of bodies once entombed therein, so references in other narratives to the Tale of Eärendel create the impression of a 'great tale' outlined by the tales that surround the empty spot where it ought to have been. It is 'placed', but the 'place' is empty.

That there ought to be a Tale of Eärendel to go with the other three now seems obvious, yet Christopher commented more than once that it "was never written" (*LT II* 252; *FG* 241). Tolkien's description to Waldman of a "majestic whole" containing tales "only placed in the scheme, and sketched" suggests a conscious contrivance of loose ends, a mythology with built-in gaps. That concept may have had its beginning even before the tales, when Tolkien first came across Earendel. This was at Exeter College in Oxford back in 1913, where Tolkien encountered *Crist*, a poem by the medieval Anglo-Saxon poet, Cynewulf (*Letters* 385). Two lines in particular stood out to him.

1 Let me make clear here my rather arbitrary distinction between "tale" in the sense I take Tolkien to be using it – that is with a capital 'T', a "great" tale on a par with those of *Beren and Lúthien* and *The Children of Húrin* – and the more generic and general sense of a story told. We have the general outline of the story of Eärendel in its various poetic versions from Tolkien's earliest attempt to Bilbo's recitation in the Hall of Fire at Rivendell. We do not have a Tale comparable to the other three.

Eala Earendel! Engla beorhtast
ofer middangeard monnum sended.

Hail Earendel! Brightest of angels
above middle-earth sent to men. (*Bio* 64)

"When I came across that citation," he wrote many years later, "I felt a curious thrill, as if something had stirred in me, half wakened from sleep. There was something very remote and strange and beautiful behind those words, if I could grasp it, far beyond ancient English" (*SD* 236). Although he gave this speech to Alwyn Lowdham, his 1944 time-traveler in 'The Notion Club Papers', the vividness of the description suggests that Tolkien was drawing on personal experience. The key words are "if I could grasp it," for as we will see, he didn't; at least not right away.

He tried first by writing his own Earendel lines, 'The Voyage of Éarendel the Evening Star', in 1914.

Earendel sprang up from the ocean's cup
    In the gloom of the mid-world's rim;
From the door of Night as a ray of light
    Leapt over the twilight brim,
And launching his bark like a silver spark
    From the golden-fading sand
Down the sunlit breath of Day's fiery death
    He sped from Westerland. (*Bio* 71)

The poem has been tagged by Tolkien's biographer Humphrey Carpenter as "the beginning of Tolkien's own mythology" (*Bio* 71) and by John Garth as "the very first beginning of the matter of Middle-earth" (Garth 2014: 33). While this seems obvious in hindsight, it was not so apparent in 1914, even to its author. According to Carpenter, when Tolkien showed "the original Earendel lines" to G.B. Smith, Smith asked him what they were about. Tolkien said he didn't know but would "try to find out" (*Bio* 75). From this, Carpenter concluded that Tolkien saw himself as a "discoverer of legend" rather than as an inventor. But here is where confusion begins. It isn't clear whether by "original Earendel lines" Carpenter was referring to Cynewulf's inspirational couplet – 'original' in that it got the whole thing going – or Tolkien's own 'original' Earendel poem.

The ambiguity complicates both Smith's question and Tolkien's answer. If we don't know which "lines" Smith was asking about, we cannot be sure what Tolkien thought he might "find out." He had already found out from his studies that Earendel's Old Norse name was Aurvandil and his Danish name was Horvendil; that various versions of his story went back to proto-Germanic myth so old it was untraceable; that whatever his name he had a ship called Vingilot in which he voyaged through the skies.[2] Those were answers, but clearly not the one he was hoping to find. Smith's question in all its ambiguity remains: what was it *about*? Tolkien's poem seems to contradict itself. Earendel sprang "up" but sped "down." Where was he going? And how did he get there? Tolkien had still to find out. Thus, out of a name and a question a mythology was born.

The poem's first words, "Earendel sprang up" imply that he is rising, but everything else we know about it suggests that he is not rising, but setting. Tolkien was trying to say without saying that as the Evening Star follows the sun into the west to reappear as the Morning Star ahead of the rising sun in the east, so Earendel's voyage carries him below the western horizon beneath the earth to follow the same trajectory.[3] Tolkien wrote later that "the Anglo-Saxon uses seem plainly to indicate that it was a star presaging the dawn [...] that is what we now call Venus: the morning star as it may be seen shining brilliantly in the dawn, before the actual rising of the Sun" (*Letters* 385). In subsequent versions, he tried to clarify this by showing how Earendel "arose where the shadow flows," while "threading his path o'er the aftermath of the splendour of the sun." But this is a complicated image, difficult to convey poetically and without laborious explanation of orbits and retrograde movement.

Furthermore, celestial mechanics aside, what is the point? What is the reason for this perpetual, repetitive journey? Nothing in the names or the literature behind them answered Smith's question, but Tolkien 'found' his own answer in 'The Shores of Faery', a poem he wrote in 1915 wherein Earendel goes "West of the Moon, East of the Sun/ [...] Beyond Taniquetil /In Valinor" where are "the shores of Faery [...] the Haven of the Star" (*Bio* 76-77).

---

2 For more on this see Hostetter 1991 and, more recently, Honegger (2023: 110-126).
3 See Essay 2, page 26, footnote 12, of this volume.

This is some help, but not much. At least there are placenames to tie the action to, though the reason for the journey is still obscure. One could well ask whether Tolkien's entire *legendarium* might have grown out of his desire to "find out" about Earendel. As readers now know, Tolkien's Earendel – aka Eärendil and other variant spellings – was within the *legendarium* the half-elven son of a human, Tuor of the House of Beor, and an Elf, Idril, daughter of Turgon, Lord of Gondolin. Tolkien made Eärendel thematically important to the story by placing him in Gondolin so that he could escape when the city fell, meet Elwing, receive from her the one remaining Silmaril (the other two being buried in earth and sea), and become its bearer in an endless journey across the skies as a sign of hope to Men.

None of the foregoing was widely known in the days when only *The Lord of the Rings* had been published. Eärendil was a name linked to the starlight Galadriel caught in her Mirror. It was associated with the Silmaril in the story Sam Gamgee suddenly realizes he is part of, sitting on the stairs of Cirith Ungol. Aragorn's prose retelling on Weathertop of the tale of Tinúviel alluded to "Eärendil [...] that sailed his ship out of the mists of the world [...] with the Silmaril upon his brow" (I.I, 11, 206) as did Bilbo's poem at Rivendell (246-49, 250). The few entries under 'Eärendil' in the Index of Volume III (421) informed but did not explain. Not till *The Silmarillion* (1977) was hard information about Eärendil available, after which he seemed to pop up everywhere: in *Unfinished Tales* and *The Book of Lost Tales II* and *The Shaping of Middle-earth* and *Lays of Beleriand* and *The Lost Road*. Like Woody Allen's Zelig, he appears in other characters' stories but never in his own.

It is at this point that Christopher's comment that the tale "was never written" – most notably in *The Book of Lost Tales II* (*LT II* 252; *FG* 241) – invites attention and provokes speculation. Was the fact that the tale was never written the result of inadvertent omission, a sad accident of external circumstances – procrastination, insufficient time, the press of other obligations? Or was it intentional – a planned disruption, a built-in lacuna? A case can be made for the latter. We have Tolkien's own statement that he intended some tales to be "only placed in the scheme, and sketched" (*Letters* 145). It would not be difficult to see the Tale of Eärendel as one such, a tale whose place in the scheme is everywhere sketched but nowhere "drawn in fulness." Examples of such schematic placement are not hard to find. Christopher references a 'Tale of Eärendel' in his 'Prologue' to *The Fall of Gondolin*, citing the original title, *Tuor and the Exiles of Gondolin* as followed by the words: "which bringeth in the Great Tale of Eärendel" (*FG* 23). After which no tale is brought in.

The same bait-and-switch is recorded in *Beren and Lúthien*, where Christopher repeats what amounts to a soundbite from *The Book of Lost Tales II*: "And thus did all the fates of the fairies weave then to one strand, and that strand is the great tale of Eärendel, and to that tale's true beginning are we now come" (*B&L* 246). And the *Lost Tales* version: "Then said Ailos: 'And methinks that is tale enow for this time of telling'" (*LT II* 242). Once again expectations are raised only to be disappointed, as after writing what amounts to a trumpet fanfare, Tolkien inserts an interruption, making sure that the great tale of Eärendel is once again prevented from being told.

These are not the only such instances. Christopher also cites "highly condensed and often contradictory outlines" of such a tale (*LT II* 252). For example, what he calls Scheme B refers to "a mighty tale, and seven times shall folk fare to the Tale-fire ere it be rightly told" (*LT II* 252). This mighty tale was to open with the *Tale of the Nauglafring*, with Eärendel making his entrance in the second part of the outline and continuing in the following numbered segments corresponding to the projected seven visits to the Tale-fire. Christopher comments that if "the six parts following [the *Nauglafring*] [...] were each to be of comparable length, the whole *Tale of Eärendel* would have been somewhere near half the length of all the tales that were in fact written." Nevertheless, he concludes that his father "never afterward returned to [the tale] on any ample scale" (*LT II* 253). The result of this hide-and-seek is an absent presence, never written but written about in the other great tales – which is in itself a circumstance worth noting: Eärendel is there but not there. Now you see him, now you don't. He is the ghost in the photograph.

Tolkien's description of his stratagem (if such it is) has parallels in real-world myth. There is the great lacuna in the *Poetic Edda*, the four leaves torn out of the middle of the *Codex Regius*, creating a hole in the story of Sigurd that must be sketched in from the *Völsunga Saga*. Tolkien himself had a stab at filling in the gap, as Tom Shippey puts it, in his 'New Lay of the Volsungs' published by

Christopher as part of *The Legend of Sigurd and Gudrun*. Another parallel is "the lost *Tale of Wade*," cited by John Garth and R.W Chambers as one of the many fragments of "old Teutonic epic" that haunts Germanic studies (Garth 2003: 86-7, 229). The Tale of Wade *per se* does not exist. It is inferred from Wade's appearances in other peoples' stories. Garth suggests an association between the "lost" tale of Wade and Tolkien's early title for his *legendarium* 'The Book of Lost Tales'. "Wade, like Earendel," says Garth, "crops up all over Germanic legend" (Garth 2003: 86). Wade 'crops up' in Tolkienian legend as well and may in fact have given Tolkien the model for his 'lost' tale of Eärendel.

The Lays of Beleriand devotes Section II to 'Poems Early Abandoned'. The second of these Christopher calls *Fragment of an alliterative Lay of Eärendel* though it has no title, and Eärendel appears nowhere. He dates it to Tolkien's time at Leeds, 1920-25. The opening lines cover the fall of Gondolin, the escape from the city, and the exiles' wandering. The name Eärendel is nowhere found, but at the end of the text is written "several times in different scripts 'Earendel', 'Earendel son of Fengel', 'Earendel Fengelsson'", leading to Christopher's conclusion that the poem was intended to be "a Lay of Eärendel" (*LB* 141). Christopher calls particular attention to line 7: "But Wade of the Helsings wearyhearted," to which is added in the margin "*Tur* [Tuor] *the earthborn was tried in battle.*" He cites Chambers's note on Wade (or Wada) that he "had no story of his own" and notes the resemblance between Wade's boat Guingelot and Eärendel's boat Wingelot. To this should be added Christopher's further comment in *The Peoples of Middle-Earth* that the name Wingalóte [sic] "is connected with the name *Elwing*" the element 'wing' being adopted from her name (*Peoples* 371). Christopher's further comments are worth noting. He argues that the association between Wade and Tuor, was "not casual" (*LB* 143) and that in the suspicious resemblance of the boat-names, "coincidence is ruled out" (*LB* 144). These negations seem to be addressing a question that has not been asked. I will ask it.

Could Tolkien have intended – even in the early stages of his work on the *legendarium* – to build into it instances of apparent loss to attrition and the ravages of time? It would fit his own description of the mythology he envisioned. Could the never-achieved but often alluded to 'Tale of Eärendel' be a Middle-earth version of the lost tale of Wade? Even to the point of explicit association of the one with the other? If the association was not casual, then it was deliberate. If coincidence is ruled out, what is left must be intention. Other evidence supports this view. *Parma Eldalamberon* XV, a journal devoted to Tolkien's invented languages, has a section titled 'Early Runic Documents' which shows on page 97 the following equivalence: "Wade = Earendel."[4] The algebraic economy of this equation leaves no room for doubt.

In this regard it is well to remember that Tolkien's ambition was to fill in gaps in English mythology. One way of doing this would be to find ways of attaching his invented mythos to what was left of the English one. In an early draft of *The Lost Tales*, he inserted Heorrenda, the poet mentioned in the Anglo-Saxon 'Deor's Lament', into his mythos as the son of Eriol and the compiler of the Golden Book of Tavrobel (*LT II* 290-94). Connecting the fictive Tale of Earendel to the historically attested tale of Wade itself – if something nonexistent can have a self – is another example. The popular saying applies: evidence of absence is not absence of evidence; indeed in this case it may in fact be the best testimony in favor. The 'Tale of Eärendel' is the missing tile in the mosaic, the gap in the pattern outlined by the stories that surround it. It is the story we are always trying to find but never do. Tolkien's association of Eärendel with Wade has the effect of making the two figures into one and the two 'lost' tales into variants of one another, thus combining the 'fragments' – one real and Germanic, the other imaginary and Tolkienian – into one single mythology for England.

Another factor can be brought into play here of a decidedly unscholarly kind. That is Tolkien's known propensity for putting one over on unsuspecting victims. His biographer Humphrey Carpenter was the first but certainly not the last to repeat the story of Tolkien handing to "inattentive shopkeepers his false teeth amongst a handful of change" (*Bio* 130). This is not to say that Tolkien confused his false teeth with coin of the realm but that he delighted in practical jokes of a fairly simple kind and particularly in the impact of surprise, the effect of the unexpected in bringing people up short. His biographers agree with his own assessment of himself – that he had "a very simple sense of humor", one which, he ruefully confessed, "even my appreciative critics find tiresome" (*Bio* 130). Examples include his dressing up as a polar bear in a sheepskin and whiteface

4 I am indebted to Andrew Higgins for pointing this out to me.

to attend what was not a costume party or his response to an undergraduate question about the reality of dragons – pulling out of his pocket "a small green shoe, thin and pointed in the toe, made of a leathery substance that felt like reptile skin and declaring it to be a leprechaun's shoe" (Zaleski & Zaleski 370, *C&G* vol. 1, 227, n.845).

If such behavior seems an awkward match with the grandfatherly, pipe-puffing professor of his late photographs, all the more we should pay attention. These episodes were not anomalies but the reverse of the medal, the puckish side of a straight-laced character type. There seems to have been an element of the Trickster mixed in with the archetypal Wise Old Man, an element that would be in harmony with the elaborate stratagems by which he could convince readers of the existence of a tale that never was, identified repeatedly through its absence.

Without explicit documentation the question of whether Tolkien intentionally made the 'Tale of Eärendel' into Middle-earth's lost tale of Wade or just allowed it to become that through inanition, must remain a question we are beholden to Christopher for raising if not answering. It is an unprovable, purely hypothetical conjecture but one that I submit is at least worthy of consideration. Nevertheless – and this is important for what it says about the process of myth-making – at the end of the day, hypothesis is finally of less importance than fact, and the fact is that the hypothesis has now become the fact, defining what the 'Tale of Eärendel' actually is and will be forevermore. That is to say, an 'Untold Tale'. And for that too we are beholden to Christopher.

The Tale of Tinúviel

So much for tales, told or untold. But what of the tellers? *The Book of Lost Tales*, Tolkien's earliest foray into feigned mythology, began with an imagined history "as told to" the mariner Eriol/Ælfwine, who hears the stories in a place variously called the Hall of Play or the Hall of Fire on the island of Tol Eresseä. The storytelling was envisioned as an informal but more or less regular gathering not unlike the Gaelic *ceilidh* but used by Tolkien as the starting-place for the unfolding of the vast pre-English mythology he was bent on dedicating "to England" and for which he made a point of including a variety of storytellers and transmitters – from ancient authorities like Pengoloð to poets like Dírhavel to collectors like Bilbo to scribes like Findegil to translators like Aragorn. The narrative voices, forms, and styles vary from story to story, and the character of the teller affects the tone of the content. At the height of his powers, Tolkien could change and/or interpolate distinct and distinguishable narrative voices – ranging among the intrusive, slightly patronizing narrator of *The Hobbit* to the omniscient narrator of *The Lord of the Rings* to the many interior storytellers within that tale – so seamlessly that the reader is largely unaware of the shift. Merry and Pippin narrate the Entmoot and the Battle of Isengard. Gandalf narrates his fight with the Balrog and the Battle of the Peak. At the Council of Elrond, it takes Aragorn, Legolas, and Gandalf combined to sequentially narrate the story of Gollum's capture, imprisonment, and subsequent escape.

Of the many attempts at the Beren and Lúthien story that Tolkien made over the years, 'The Tale of Tinúviel' is the only one to be what Tolkien described to Milton Waldman as "drawn in fullness," that is, having a consecutive beginning, middle, and end. This arc of completion is just the beginning of the several ways in which it differs from other, more fragmentary versions of the Tale, the other ways being tone, style, and diction. The earliest manuscript, dated by Christopher to 1917, is in ink written over an erased pencil original. Christopher suggests that the ink "*rewriting* [emphasis in original] was considerably later" (*LT I*, 203) and was "one of the latest elements in the composition of the *Lost Tales*" (*LT I*, 204). The exact date of the ink version is not known, but the words "considerably later" allow some leeway. In addition to voice and tone, the ink manuscript has marked differences from the considerably later and more familiar *Silmarillion* version. Here, *Tinúviel* is not an epithet with secondary meaning, but the proper name of the protagonist, while the better-known name *Lúthien* appears nowhere. Here, Tinúviel's father is not called Thingol but Tinwelint, and her mother's name is not Melian but Gwendeling. More importantly, in this version Beren is not a mortal man but a Gnome, a fairy.[5] He thus does not conform to Tolkien's later definition of fairy-stories as

5 Tolkien recognized the anomaly, and when he changed from Vëannë to the unnamed bard of the rhymed 'Lay of Leithian', he also changed Beren's lineage from Elf to human, recasting him as a Man to better conform to his model. But see *The Book of Lost Tales II* page 139, where Christopher cites a marginal note on a rejected passage in 'Turambar and the Fóalokë' suggesting that Beren was even earlier a Man.

not about fairies but about the *aventures* of men in *Faërie*. The word *aventure* does not so much denote 'adventure' (though that meaning is contained within it) as 'chance', 'happening', 'the unexpected'. Since he already inhabits *Faërie*, Beren's *aventure*, then, must be something more than Faërie itself, and indeed it is. It is the unexpected sight of Lúthien dancing. As it should in a fairy tale, this casts a spell, love at first sight, described as a "strange thing" that "befell" (*B&L* 41) – in a word, an *aventure*.

This diction is typical of what Christopher calls this version's "archaisms of word and construction" as well as its "undertone of sardonic humor" and the "extremely individual style" that he finds to be "at times deeply 'elvish mysterious'" (*B&L* 31). In *The Book of Lost Tales II*, he observed that the tone of 'The Tale of Tinúviel' was "altogether lighter and less grave" than the later versions from which it differs (*LT II* 53). Narrative voice is always of importance in Tolkien's work, from the playful, albeit slightly condescending narrator of *The Hobbit* to the scholarly editorial voice of the Prologue to *The Lord of the Rings* to the bardic voice that narrates the Battle of the Pelennor Fields. So, it is important to note that the narrator of 'The Tale of Tinúviel' is not only a rare female among Tolkien's narrators, but a rare child as well, one Vëannë, who sits on Eriol's knee (*LT II* 4) and whose diction and manner of speech manifest the unpolished candor of the very young. Veannë's audience also consists largely of children, and the ages of both narrator and audience are what lead to the shift of tone and style that Christopher has noted.

The naïve voice and the direct address point to a specific influence on Tolkien that as far as I can tell has been hitherto overlooked. This is Marie de France, a 12th-century noblewoman and court poet whose *lais*,[6] drawn from Breton folklore, were notable for their direct address, their sly humor, and their feminine voice. Marie is an unlikely inspiration for the *Beowulf*-loving, Eddic-imitative Tolkien we are more familiar with, and it is unknown exactly when Tolkien might have first encountered her work. An English translation of her *lais* in prose was published by J.M. Dent in 1911,[7] and while it was the sort of book

6 Tolkien himself wrote a *lai* retold from Breton folklore and using its motifs, *The Lay of Aotrou & Itroun*, but its relentless emphasis on evil and transgressive behavior shows it to be a long way from Marie's light-hearted comedies.

7 I am indebted to John Garth for this information.

that would have attracted Tolkien's interest at the time, there is no direct evidence that he read this edition. There is, however, later evidence of an edition he did read: Karl Warnke's *Die Lais der Marie de France* published in 1900, in French with notes in German by Reinhold Köhler.

We may speculate that acquaintance with the Dent translation might have encouraged Tolkien to look for the original. It was listed in the *Catalogue of Books from the Library of J.R.R. Tolkien Held by the English Faculty Library Oxford* issued by the English Faculty Library in Oxford and also in Oronzo Cilli's recent *Tolkien's Library: An Annotated Checklist.*[8] Both the *Catalogue* and Cilli's book describe the Warnke edition as "autographed [by Tolkien] and dated 'Sept. 1920' at first in pencil, later inked in, on the front flyleaf" (*Catalogue* vc 56; Cilli 183, no. 1515). The 1920 date is worth noticing, for it is within the range of what Christopher calls the "considerably later [than 1917]" ink manuscript of 'The Tale of Tinúviel'. Further evidence that Tolkien was familiar with Marie appears among his notes for a lecture on Old Norse poetry, where he wrote, "the gods and heroes go down into their Ragnarök, vanquished, not by the World-girdling serpent or Fenris-wolf [...] but by Marie de France [...] and the small change of French courtesy" (*S&G* 16). It is precisely that "small change" with which Tolkien is so concerned in 'The Tale of Tinúviel'.

Marie is credited with twelve *lais*: 'Guigemar', 'Equitan', 'Le Fresne', 'Bisclavret', 'Lanval', 'Les Deus Amanz', 'Yonec', 'Laüstic', 'Milun', 'Chaitivel', 'Chevrefoil', and 'Eliduc'. They are short, several under 300 lines and only one over 1000. The form is rhymed octosyllabic couplets.[9] Marie's plots often feature a symbolic object or item around which the action revolves. Her plots revolve around thwarted lovers, mistaken identity, disguise, animal characters, and shape-changing. One of her characters, Bisclavret, turns into a werewolf, a possible forerunner of Beren's werewolf disguise in a later version of Beren and Lúthien.[10] Her direct address is written to be read as if spoken aloud, a textual replication of oral tradition. She is also, in a Tolkienian context, what Paul Thomas describes as an 'intrusive' narrator, not quite with the patronizing tone of the narrator of

8 *Catalogue* vc 168-169; Cilli no. 1246 and no. 1247. Cilli's book relies heavily on the *Catalogue* but is easier to access, since the *Catalogue* is currently out of print.

9 Compare Tolkien's 'Lay of Leithian'.

10 See also Honegger 2004.

The Hobbit, but as a participant in an immediate oral situation nonetheless. Here are a few examples from Marie de France's *lais*: *mes tant vos di*, "I'll tell you this much" ('Guigemar' l. 178), *C'est afaire les ore ester*, "But now I'll leave this matter be" ('Bisclavret' l. 14), *Oëz après cument avint!* "now listen to what happened next" ('Bisclavret' l. 185), *Ceo m'est a vis, meïsmes*, "it seems to me" ('Lanval' l. 221).[11]

In his Foreword to an English translation of the *Lais*, John Fowles points out Marie's "surface naivety" (Fowles in Marie de France 1978: xi) that covers hidden depth with an ingenue delivery. Behind Marie's naive storyteller hides an adult author who expects her audience to appreciate the irony inherent in the discrepancy between tone and subject matter. Vëannë's asides to her child audience are very much like Marie's: "Never have I heard," "as thou shalt hear," "they did not blame him and neither do I," "they did more than dance."

In both cases, behind the surface naivety of the narrators hides an adult author who expects the audience to know irony when they meet it. Vëannë's treatment of Tevildo, Prince of Cats, is a case in point. He may be, as Christopher asserts, a precursor of Sauron (he was superseded by Thû who was then replaced by Sauron), but as Vëannë depicts him he is less an avatar than a caricature, a cartoon villain in primary colors. His eyes gleam "both red and green," his whiskers are as sharp as needles, his purr is a drumroll, and when he yells, small birds and beasts fall lifeless at the sound. His ears twitch, catlike, to hear the message he thinks Lúthien brings him. When she announces her name knowing it will be heard by Beren in the kitchen and a crash follows as of someone dropping a loaded tray, Tevildo berates Beren for his clumsiness, but Vëannë's audience is listening on a different level and appreciates the dramatic subtext implied by the sound effects.

Equally cartoonish is Vëannë's treatment of Tevildo's "thanes." Their names, *Umuiyan* and *Oikeroi* and *Miaulë*, meant to replicate the yowling of cats, suggest oral performance. They are in sharp contrast to the word *thanes* with its clannish, warrior connotations. When Lúthien sews Beren into the dead Oikeroi's catskin to disguise him from Melko, we have a mental picture of

11 All quotations of Marie are from the Warnke edition of her *Lais*, the edition that Tolkien bought in 1920. The English translations are from the Dutton edition.

the incongruity and likewise when she shows him how to move like a cat but laments that he can't make the dead eyes gleam. In turn, Beren is angry when she pulls his tail, and he cannot lash it as fiercely as he would like. His inner and outer cats are not in sync. It is hard not to read this as satire, a sendup of the fairy tale genre delivered in the voice of a child. Only in the treatment of Tinúviel's hair is the elvish mysterious quality taken seriously – the gold and silver bowls needed for its washing, the song that makes it grow, and its weaving into a robe of misty black soaked with drowsiness that covers her escape. It also echoes her painstaking descriptions of color and texture, details that make Marie's world so real.

When Vëannë arrives at the moment of Beren's death, she is overcome by tears and declares that she knows no more. An otherwise unknown narrator, one Ausir, makes a cameo appearance to add a happy ending that Beren lived, followed by an unidentified but contradictory voice that closes the story with a brief account of Beren's death and Mandos's judgment. Though Tolkien's text replicates oral performance, Vëannë validates her authority by assuring her listeners that she took it from the "great books"[12] and learned it "by heart" despite, she confesses, not comprehending "all that is set therein" (*B&L* 88). Apparently Vëannë can read beyond her grade level but does not always grasp deeper or wider meanings: "She gives the effect of building with a substance the significance of which she does not completely realise. She may be likened to a child playing with symbols which, in the hand of the enchanter, would be of tremendous import" (Mason in Marie de France 1911: xi). While this could easily be a description of Vëannë, it is in fact a description of Marie from the 'Introduction' to the Everyman edition of her lays (1911). Not again to my knowledge did Tolkien so consciously adopt a particular style or employ such a distinctively naïve voice, such sardonic humor, or elvish mysterious aspect, all of which do so much to distinguish 'The Tale of Tinúviel' from all the other versions of the Beren and Lúthien story.

The two examples I have chosen, one of mythmaking strategy, the other of a narrator persona tried out and discarded, are only part of what Christopher has

12 It is interesting to note that even at this early stage, Tolkien was proposing a manuscript tradition such as Sam envisions in his conversation with Frodo on the stairs of Cirith Ungol in *The Lord of the Rings*.

shown to the world of Tolkien fans and scholars in the years since his father's death. The years since his own death have deepened our appreciation of his work. It has taken two Tolkiens to show to the world the depth and breadth and range of what one Tolkien has created.

Tolkien's Lúthien(s)

The first public appearance of J.R.R. Tolkien's fairy tale heroine Lúthien comes in *The Fellowship of the Ring* in Strider's recitation of her story to the hobbits at Weathertop (where she is called by her nickname Tinúviel). She also appears in a skeletally brief synopsis of the story of Beren and Lúthien and their quest for the Silmaril in Appendix A at the end of Volume Three, *The Return of the King* (*RK* 314). She shows up again in Appendix A's 'The Tale of Aragorn and Arwen', where Aragorn mistakes her descendant Arwen for Lúthien herself (*RK* 339). These fleeting moments are the Tolkienian equivalent of movie trailers, previews advertising a coming attraction. Like Tolkien's other Great Tales, the stories of Húrin or Túrin, the story of Lúthien grew over time in both verse and prose, moving through various versions from a comic fairy tale in the style of Marie de France to a verse romance in rhyming couplets after the practice of the French poet Chrétien de Troyes to the final but never finished prose narrative. Christopher Tolkien gives a full account of Tolkien's development of the character and the story in *Beren and Lúthien*, the third and final volume in his Great Tales series.

My intent here is less sweeping. It is to dig both narrower and deeper into one aspect of her story: the singular way in which Tolkien used, fused, and confused her invented character with that of his real-life wife Edith. "I never called Edith *Lúthien*," he wrote in a letter to his son Christopher, "but she was the source of the story that became [...] the chief part of the *Silmarillion*" (*LettersRev* 590). More explicitly, he stated unequivocally that "she was (and knew she was) my Lúthien" (*LettersRev* 590). To his son Michael, he described Edith as "the Lúthien [...] of my own personal 'romance'" (*LettersRev* 585). But while this carefully distinguishes the personal from the fictional, I hope to show that for him the two areas overlapped and influenced one another.

A caveat here about these very personal quotes: while Edith-as-Lúthien is by now a canonical part of the Tolkien mythos, it is well to remember that at the time Tolkien was writing to his sons (1971-72) this was not a widespread view. The names of Beren and Lúthien were only tangentially familiar to readers through references in *The Lord of the Rings* and its Appendices.[1] The full story would not be published until *The Silmarillion* (1977), itself a composite and heavily edited text, while the more textually authentic *Books of Lost Tales* that followed it would not come out till six years (1983-84) after that. So, to write as Tolkien did that Edith was his Lúthien was not the public declaration that it would be taken for today. It might better be described as a family anecdote, confided to a family audience.

That said, it is a not unusual human reaction to associate a real-life figure with a fictional one. Tolkien's contemporaries Ernest Hemingway and F. Scott Fitzgerald both used real women from their own experience as fictional characters, though neither carried the idea as far as Tolkien, who worked it in both directions. Real sources and fictive characters, while related, are, or should be, distinct categories but to Tolkien Edith was both at once. Not only did she inspire his Lúthien, but he then retro-actively re-imagined her as the real-life version of the Lúthien she had inspired. Such a circular path from life to art and thence to life as art, resulted in the real and invented figures becoming not just similar but reciprocal, the same individual in two different worlds. It is axiomatic that to create fiction out of life takes talent. To re-create the same life in terms of the fiction requires something more – a bi-focal vision such as Tolkien clearly possessed, capable of viewing the same object through two different lenses simultaneously.

Of course, he knew the difference between them – on one level. But on another level, he clearly felt a need to see both the wife and the character as images of one another, as if imagination and reality could share one frame, a double exposure in which each shadowed the other. And there was, of course, a second reciprocity. If Edith was Lúthien, it followed that Tolkien had to be Beren. It was a scenario that sustained him until Edith's death in 1971, when

1 These included Sam's epiphany on the stairs of Cirith Ungol that he and Frodo are in the Beren and Lúthien story (and that it is still going on) and the essentially annalistic material in Appendix A at the end of *The Return of the King* (published 1955).

life overtook fiction and events escaped his control. In his fictional world, love triumphed over death when Lúthien pleaded for Beren's life before Mandos. But in real life, this fairy tale scenario collapsed when Edith (aka Lúthien) died and the survivor, Tolkien/Beren, had no recourse. He wrote to Christopher, "the story has gone crooked & I am left, and *I* cannot plead before the inexorable Mandos" (*LettersRev* 590).

This is a remarkable sentence, not just for the depth of grief it exposes but for the evidence it offers of how deeply the story was rooted in Tolkien's imagination. Three phrases – "gone crooked", "I am left", and "*I* cannot plead" – command attention for the way they toggle between reality and fiction. The story went crooked because the wrong character died – the real-life Lúthien (Edith) instead of the fictive Beren. Another wrong person – the real-life Tolkien instead of the fictional Lúthien – was then left to mourn the death – not of Beren, as in the story – but of Lúthien's real-life personification, that is to say, Edith. If you find this confusing you are in good company. So did Tolkien. His inability to plead before Mandos arose from the very practical circumstance that he was real and Mandos was imaginary. Yet the fact that a real death sent Tolkien to his own fiction to find a context for his grief is evidence of the hold the story had on his mind and his emotions.

That the hold was rooted in his real life can be seen from the story itself. Extracted from the matrix of the surrounding mythology, it consists of the following episodes: 1. Beren's love at first sight of Lúthien dancing; 2. her father King Thingol's hostility to their union and his demand in exchange that Beren bring him a Silmaril from Morgoth's Iron Crown (intended instead to eliminate him); 3. the lovers' successful theft of a Silmaril; 4. Beren's killing by the wolf Carcharoth; 5. Beren's return to life at the pleading of Lúthien before Mandos, Tolkien's imaginary god of judgment; 6. and finally, the lovers' successful reunion and subsequent life together. To a remarkable degree and allowing for translation from life to fantasy, the scenario followed the trajectory of Tolkien's own emotional life, especially with regard to two specific elements. The dancing episode was based on Edith's dancing for Tolkien among hemlocks when they were living at Roos. The unreasonable condition imposed by a father-figure was in real life his, not hers. The villain was Tolkien's guardian, Father Francis

Morgan, who had been his mother's spiritual guide in her conversion to Roman Catholicism and became her sons' as well.

With the best of intentions and clearly concerned that his ward not neglect his Oxford studies, Father Francis extracted a promise from the young Tolkien that he would neither see nor communicate with Edith until he was twenty-one, perhaps hoping, not unlike Thingol with Beren, that the passage of time would discourage his ardor as well as improve his studies. As might have been expected, it had the opposite effect. Tolkien barely passed his exams, and on the day of his 21st birthday wrote to Edith, who had understandably felt neglected during the period of isolation and had in the meantime become engaged to someone else. No whit deterred, he promptly went directly to where she was then living and talked her out of her engagement to the other man and into marriage with him.

The youthful Tolkien viewed this prohibition and ordeal as the quasi-chivalric requirements of a standard medieval romance, albeit grounded in a twentieth-century view of the Middle Ages. However, in later life he appears to have had second thoughts, calling the chivalry an "unreal romantic code" and dismissing the romance as "a boy-and-girl-affair" (*LettersRev* 73). From its earliest conception, then, this story of love at first sight, tested by ordeal and consummated against the odds, was both a deeply interwoven and a conflicted part of the fabric of Tolkien's outer as well as his inner life.

What makes it all the more interesting is the fact that, as if to cement this bifocal identification, Tolkien had the name Lúthien etched in stone directly below Edith's on the latter's grave-marker, sending the message to a world that at that time barely knew the story that the two were one. The message was later ratified by their children, who at Tolkien's death added Beren's name beneath his on the now-shared headstone. But instead of setting the matter straight this had the effect of raising an inevitable question. Edith was Tolkien's Lúthien. Was he her Beren? *He* implied that the answer was yes. But with all due respect, this gives only a one-sided view of a two-sided subject. It tells his story but not hers, which then must be pieced together from the few available sources.

The earliest source, Humphrey Carpenter's 1977 biography of Tolkien, devotes two chapters, "Private lang' – and Edith' (*Bio* 31-43) and 'Reunion' (*Bio* 61-71) to the friendship-cum-courtship of the orphaned John Ronald and the now also orphaned Edith Bratt who had the room below him in Mrs. Faulkner's boarding-house at 37 Duchess Road in Birmingham. Carpenter includes a human-interest anecdote of the two teenagers (he was sixteen, she nineteen) sitting on the balcony of a teashop pelting passers-by with lumps of sugar. He writes with sympathy about their enforced separation by Father Francis. This may have provided a chivalric conclusion to what Tolkien later referred to as a "boy-and-girl-affair" (see above), but real life requires more pragmatic accommodation. Carpenter's biography, while it was considerably shortened at the behest of Christopher Tolkien, who required that some material be excised,[2] does nevertheless observe that while "their letters were full of affection" nevertheless, "when they were together their tempers would often flare" (*Bio* 67). In his companion book *The Inklings*, Carpenter cites the "broken childhoods they had both endured in Birmingham" (Carpenter 1979: 32) and to the "strain" caused by Tolkien's life "with his male friends" (168) which made "the atmosphere in the Tolkien household [...] difficult" (169).

In their exhaustively researched *J.R.R. Tolkien Companion and Guide*, Christina Scull and Wayne Hammond confine their long entry on Edith to reporting facts without comment or interpretation (*C&G* vol. 2, 1304-09). A more recent biography of Edith, Nancy Bunting and Seamus Hamill-Keays's *The Gallant Edith Bratt* is built largely on circumstantial evidence and conjecture. The authors' frequent use of cautionary words such as "probably", "may have", "could have", "it is likely that", undermine their authority and make it risky to draw firm conclusions. These authors speculate about a possible pre-marital sexual relationship between Tolkien and Edith, but their conjecture about how far it might have gone is guarded.

The bare facts are stark. Edith Bratt was the illegitimate daughter of a Birmingham businessman, Alfred Warrilow, through his illicit liaison with a woman named Frances Bratt, his own daughter's governess. That Edith bore her mother's name, that she never spoke to her own children about her father and never "passed [his name] on" to them (*Bio* 38-39) is unspoken testimony of her understandably

2 See Carpenter 1995.

awkward and sensitive feelings around the subject. It is evidence, too, of the Edwardian opprobrium attached to illegitimate birth, a painful circumstance to set beside Carpenter's sugar-lump anecdote, Scull and Hammond's bare facts, and Bunting and Hamill-Keays's unwarranted speculations.

A third story that might qualify as neither his nor hers but theirs is suggested by Tolkien himself in the same passage of the above-quoted letter to Christopher. Here, Tolkien wrote of wanting to share with this son "the dreadful sufferings of our childhoods, from which we rescued one another, but could not wholly heal the wounds that later often proved disabling," and of "the lapses and darknesses which at times marred our lives" (*LettersRev* 590). Loaded words like "dreadful sufferings", "wounds", and "darknesses", and negative terms like "marred", "disabling", "lapses", "could not heal", tend to substantiate Carpenter's cautious allusions to strain and flaring tempers and difficult atmosphere and broken childhoods. Both Tolkien's letter and the biography suggest real human behavior in a real human marriage, one that seems to have had some pretty rocky passages. Tantalizing as these hints are, however, they must remain mere hints. Corroborating details of Edith's life that might have fleshed out the picture are hard to come by and even harder to extract from the few sources available.[3]

To add to that, Tolkien's thought-provoking statement to Christopher that he and Edith rescued one another calls to mind his description in another letter, this time to Michael, of lovers as "companions in shipwreck" (*LettersRev* 68). Like "wounds" and "darknesses", "shipwreck" is a loaded word, evoking images of stress, desperation, desolation, bare survival, and abandonment in lifeboats. The physical situation brought about by a shipwreck inevitably throws its survivors into claustrophobically close quarters, conditions guaranteed to exacerbate differences and ignite conflict even as those same conditions foster dependence one on another. Tolkien's phrase can be confusing, however. Did he mean by 'shipwreck' the relationship itself? Or was he referring to the circumstances in which the relationship occurs? That is to say, the ordinary everyday conditions of human existence, which for a practicing Catholic would be life after the Fall, therefore of necessity a shipwrecked world. I used to subscribe to the latter read-

3 A useful overview of work concerning Edith through 2019 can be found in Nicole duPlessis article of that year.

ing – that he meant life itself is a shipwreck. But a careful reading finds the phrase "the shipwreck of love" on the very next page, where the juxtaposition is clear and the meaning unmistakable.

In either meaning the phrase is a shocker – bleak, bare and unequivocal. It cannot help but recall the opinion expressed by his friend Father Robert Murray that Tolkien was "a very complex and depressed man," whose "imaginative creation" (i.e. *The Silmarillion* of which *The Lord of the Rings* was an integral part) "project[ed] his very depressed view of the universe" as much as his Catholic faith (West 2019: 135). It is difficult to avoid the suspicion that beyond a depressed view of the universe Tolkien may have had his own marriage, described in the letter to Christopher as a mutual rescue from childhood sufferings, in mind when he wrote the phrase. Humphrey Carpenter's description of Tolkien as "a man of antitheses" seems in agreement with such a dichotomy. Throughout Tolkien's life these antitheses – his depression and his religious faith – existed in uneasy tension, a continuously shifting balance that never came to rest either way. The same tension can be found among such disparate word-clusters as "an unreal romantic code", "she was my Lúthien", and "a boy-and-girl affair". The phrases seem at odds with one another, or perhaps their writer was at odds with himself, much as Father Murray described.

What can be learned from such revelations? Could it have been to counterbalance his idea of shipwreck that Tolkien transformed a crucial episode in his life into a fairy-story and re-identified its central characters as real people, only to see the whole construct go crooked when what had been a fictional death was no longer a fiction but an all too real circumstance in his actual life? Tolkien's emotional tie to the figure of Lúthien – to the story he created about her and to the mixed and blended sets of relationships which that story established in his mind – is plain to see. It was the real-life corollary to the many times retold tale of love and death that he made his personal identity-saga and signature-piece.

The Scouring of Frodo

Hi3e sceal þe heardra, heort þe cenre,
mod sceal þe mare, þe ure mæ3en lytlað.

Thought shall be harder, heart the keener,
mood the more, as our strength lessens.

In his scholarly edition of *The Battle of Maldon*, E.V. Gordon cited those lines as "the clearest and fullest expression known in literature of the ancient Germanic heroic code" (Gordon 1937: 26). His colleague J.R.R. Tolkien disagreed. To Tolkien, the heroic code was tainted, made "of gold and an alloy." The gold was the *mod*, the "northern heroic spirit;" the alloy was pride and the desire for reputation (Tolkien 1953: 14). Because of the *mod* of his chieftain Byrhtnoth, Beorhtwold is going to die, and he knows it. Tolkien called this not *mod* but *ofermod*, "overboldness." To illustrate, he wrote an anti-heroic play of his own, *The Homecoming of Beorthnoth*,[1] and backed it up with two essays, 'Ofermod' and 'Beorhtnoth's Death',[2] in which he saw an irony in Beorhtwold's words that Beorhtwold did not see.

1 First published in 1953 in *Essays and Studies* but according to Hammond and Anderson (1993: 303), it was "in existence by 1945. A dramatic dialogue in rhyming verse, clearly a precursor to 'Beorhtnoth', was written circa 1930-3." Evidence for this early fragment of verse clearly from the play is cited in a note by Christopher Tolkien in *The Treason of Isengard* (note 10, 106-7). The earliest reference I have been able to find is a letter to Rayner Unwin written in October 1952, wherein Tolkien mentions "producing" a contribution to that volume (*Letters* 165). The word *producing* could suggest something already written, but that is tenuous evidence on which to base an argument. For a most recent discussion and edition of the relevant texts, see *The Battle of Maldon* together with *The Homecoming of Beorhtnoth*, edited by Peter Grybauskas in 2023.

2 Tolkien's was a powerful voice; nevertheless, some of his contemporaries and a few of his successors expressed reservations about his stance. Mike Drout called Tolkien's position in *The Homecoming* "anomalous" (Drout 2007: 138), that is to say deviating from the norm but commended the two essays for examining "some of the complexities of battle and loss" (Drout 2007: 141). Tom Shippey, the dean of Tolkien scholars, was less forgiving, describing Tolkien's attack on heroism as "an act of parricide" (Shippey 2007: 337), a sacrifice of pagan heroics on the altar of Christianity.

I have called my paper 'The Scouring of Frodo', an obvious riff on 'The Scouring of the Shire', because it is Tolkien's treatment of heroism in that chapter that most clearly contravenes the heroism of Beorhtwold's words.

'The Scouring of the Shire' has always troubled me, not for the scouring itself, but for Frodo's part in it, what I will call his anti-*Battle of Maldon* stance. His refusal to fight is so unheroic, his posture is so much the reverse of either *mod* or *ofermod*, his avoidance of action so extreme that it seems clear Tolkien was making a point, and I propose that the point was the exact opposite of *Maldon*'s "heart the keener, mood the more" sentiment.

This was not the first time Tolkien had challenged academic tradition. His essay on *Beowulf* trashed the critics[3] who saw it as a historical document rather than the work of art he said it was. His essay 'On Fairy-stories' coined two neologisms – *eucatastrophe* and *dyscatastrophe* – to show how much more he knew about fairy tales than the folklorists he was attacking.[4] The same impulse to go against the grain shows up in his revisions to 'The Scouring of the Shire', in which he changed his original ending (and with it the whole ending of the book) of Frodo the conquering hero and replaced him with Frodo the Conscientious Objector.

In *Sauron Defeated*, Christopher Tolkien writes that "in this original version of the story Frodo played a far more aggressive and masterful part in the events than he does in RK" (*SD* 80).

Christopher continues:

> It is very striking that [...] the story when [my father] first wrote it down should have been so different from its final form [...] most of all because Frodo is portrayed here [in the original version] at every stage as an energetic and commanding intelligence, warlike and resolute in action; and the final text of the chapter had been very largely achieved when the changed conception [...] entered. (*SD* 93-94)

3 Some of whose names we know, thanks to Michael D.C. Drout, who in *Beowulf and the Critics* pried them out of their scholarly bedrock. They include W.P Ker, J.J. Jusserand, John Josias Conybeare, R.W. Chambers, N.F.S. Grundtvig, Grimur Thorkelin, and Ritchie Girvan. Heavy hitters, all.

4 At least, those he mentions by name: Max Müller, Andrew Lang (whose Annual Lecture he was giving), and George Dasent, an Honor Roll of Folklore Studies.

Later he notes that in early drafts the chapter's "most notable feature is that Frodo retains his dominance and his resolute captaincy" (*SD* 95). Christopher makes clear that in the original version, a far more capable Frodo had played a far more heroic part than the Frodo of the published book, even to "the slaying of more than one of the ruffians at Bywater, and the slaying of their leader at Bag End" (*SD* 80).

"It was Frodo, not Merry," writes Christopher, "who made the Sheriffs march in front on the journey from Frogmorton" (*SD* 812). It was to Frodo that Tolkien gave an episode omitted from the final text, a stirring fight to the death with Sharkey, who is not yet Saruman at this point but just one of the ruffians.

> He took off his cloak. Suddenly he shone, a small gallant figure clad in mithril [...] Sting was in his hand [...] Sharkey had a sword and he drew it, and in a [fury?] hewed double-handed at Frodo. But Frodo [...] ran in close holding his cloak as a shield and slashed his leg above the knee. And then as with a groan and a curse the orc-man [toppled?] over him he stabbed upwards, and Sting passed clean through his body. (*SD* 92)

This Frodo was a sword-brandisher and ruffian-slayer who vanquished the bad guy in a David-and-Goliath triumph that led to his return as a conquering hero, got him elected Mayor, and established the pattern for him to live (presumably) happily ever after.

It was "[a]t a late stage of work," writes Christopher, that "my father perceived that Frodo's experience had so changed him, so withdrawn him, as to render him incapable of any such rôle in the Scouring of the Shire as had been portrayed" (*SD* 103). Returning to the theme of my paper, I would say that it was at this late stage that, recognizing his own heroic code for the alloy it was, Tolkien scoured from the chapter the heroic figure he had originally envisioned. As Frodo's strength grows less so does his *mod*. Tolkien also scoured Frodo's personality, cleansing him of his pride, his self-confidence, his sense of his place in the world.

So, what made Tolkien suddenly perceive his hero as 'incapable'? We will never know. It could have been a sudden epiphany, the kind of realization that is part of the revision process brought about by the process itself. David Bratman suggests that "it sometimes took [Tolkien's] conscious mind a while to catch on to what his unconscious had been doing" (Bratman 2000: 36). We might infer that Tolkien's anti-heroic unconscious had been directing him before he was aware of it. Whatever triggered the perception, once he arrived at it, he did not hesitate to make the switch.

While Christopher offered no explanation, he was happy to lay out the step-by-step process of the change over three consecutive manuscripts A, B, and C, during the course of which Tolkien radically re-conceived Frodo's role in 'The Scouring'. In the A text he is the instigator and leader. The vehicle for the change was "the complicated second manuscript 'B'" (*SD* 94), in which "the *entirely different* [my emphasis] picture of Frodo's part in the events was brought about by many small alterations (often by doing no more than changing 'Frodo' to 'Merry') and a few brief additions" (*SD* 103). The "complicated [...] manuscript 'B'" changed the direction of Frodo's story from then on and led to the "third, very fine manuscript ('C')" where, according to Christopher, "an important addition was made." He quotes directly from his father's notes: "Frodo had been in the battle, but had not drawn sword, and his chief part had been to prevent the hobbits in their wrath at their losses from slaying those of their enemies who threw down their weapons" (*SD* 104).

This is almost word-for-word the passage as it appears in the published book (*RK* 295-96). In case you still haven't got the point, Tolkien spells it out for you and sets the tone for the rest of the story in which Frodo's behavior is much as we see it in the published *The Lord of the Rings*. He is passive, withdrawn, little regarded in his own hometown, recurrently ill on the anniversary of each of his woundings, devastated and bereft by the loss of the Ring. We have only to compare the Frodo of 'The Scouring' with the Frodo of the barrow to see the difference. As when in a railroad yard the switchman pulls a lever that moves an engine from one set of tracks to another, so here Tolkien has pulled a switch that moves his story onto a whole different set of rails.

So much for Tolkien and heroism and *The Battle of Maldon*.

There are other factors to be considered that also bear on the switch. It has long been acknowledged that the recurrently ill Frodo of the final chapters exhibits classic symptoms of PTSD, Post Traumatic Stress Disorder. Tolkien certainly knew the phenomenon from his time on the Somme, though he would have called it Shell Shock, the term in use in World War I for combat-traumatized soldiers. He also knew it because his second son Michael, during the war in active service as an anti-aircraft gunner, saw combat in the Battle of Britain and was subsequently discharged from the army as "unfit for further military service" (*Letters* 439, n. 74). Tolkien's own description of his son as "a much-damaged soldier" (*Letters* 86) confronts the reality behind the heroic code, a far cry from the last-ditch Beorhtwold of *The Battle of Maldon*. The lesson is that in real life the ordeal of combat may lessen the strength, but it does not necessarily strengthen the will or the heart or mood.

What had not been known until Christopher revealed it was that Frodo's symptoms were also a part of the late-stage modification he sets out in manuscripts A, B, and C. They were the result of Tolkien's radical re-thinking not just of a literary tradition but equally of what trauma does to its victims, as shown in these revisions of the conversation between Frodo and Gandalf during the final ride home:

> [A]t the Fords of Bruinen Frodo halted and was loth to ride through, and from here on to Weathertop he was silent and ill at ease; but Gandalf said nothing.
>
> And when they came to the hill he said 'Let us hasten', and would not look toward it. 'My wound aches,' he said, 'and the memory of darkness is heavy on me. Are there not things, Gandalf, that cannot ever be wholly healed?'
>
> 'Alas, it is so,' said Gandalf. (*SD* 75)

To the fact that his wound aches, Frodo adds: "And my finger too, the one that is gone, but I feel pain in it, and the memory of darkness is heavy on me" (*SD* 76). Notable here is Tolkien's knowledge of the phenomenon of phantom pain in a lost limb or digit, which gives added depth to the concept of Frodo of the Nine Fingers.

The final version in *The Return of the King* distills all the changes:

> 'Are you in pain, Frodo?' said Gandalf quietly as he rode by Frodo's side.
>
> 'Well, yes, I am,' said Frodo. 'It is my shoulder. The wound aches and *the memory of darkness is heavy on me* [my emphasis][5] [...] I am wounded with knife, sting, and tooth, and a long burden. Where shall I find rest?'
>
> Gandalf did not answer. (*RK* 268)

5 I emphasize these words because that is what PTSD is – the memory of darkness.

This passage points directly to the Frodo of 'The Scouring of the Shire', which in turn pivots the story to the bittersweet ending that we know. It gives notice to the reader that a book begun in continuation of a comic fairy-story has turned, not into an Anglo-Saxon hero tale, but an Aristotelian tragedy, tracing the fall of its protagonist, evoking the reader's pity and fear, and effecting a purge of those emotions.

I would argue that this change in Frodo's behavior functions as a scouring on two levels. In a literary sense, it is an editorial clean-up of the kind of conventional heroism Tolkien had found so distasteful in *Maldon*. In a psychological sense it is a scouring of Frodo's personality, scrubbing away his pride, his self-confidence, his sense of his place in the world. This goes hand in hand with the equally dramatic change in attitude that moves him from the parochial hobbit of *The Fellowship* who thought big people were stupid and found the idea of Gollum as a hobbit loathsome, to the magnanimous Frodo who can offer sanctuary to Wormtongue and show mercy toward Saruman. Like the light of Galadriel's phial, the change in Frodo becomes the light in his own darkness, albeit a light that comes at a high price.

There have always been two faces to Tolkien's fiction, one light and one dark. The schoolboy humor of *Farmer Giles of Ham* is balanced by the bitter tang of *The Story of Kullervo*; the faërian beauty of *Smith of Wootton Major* is offset by the grim irony of *The Lay of Autrou and Itroun*. The up-beat allegory of *Leaf by Niggle* is the exception that proves the rule. Contrasting perspectives have been characteristic of Tolkien's work from its very beginning. C.S. Lewis pegged it when he wrote in 'On Stories' about *The Hobbit*'s "very curious shift of tone. As the humor and homeliness of the early chapters, the sheer 'Hobbitry', dies away we pass insensibly into the world of epic. It is as if the battle of Toad Hall [in *The Wind in the Willows*] had become a serious *heimsókn* [roughly 'attack on a home'] and Badger had begun to talk like Njal" (Lewis 1947: 104).

This shift is manifest not just in the published text but as the story developed over time in Tolkien's drafts. John Rateliff's masterly unpacking of the manuscripts in *The History of The Hobbit* shows clearly how through successive visions and revisions that story become darker and darker, moving from the comic incursion of the Dwarves into Bilbo's uneventful life through the quasi-mythic quest for the dragon's hoard, Bilbo's moral lapse in taking the Arkenstone, the deadly conflict of the Battle of Five Armies, and finally the death of Thorin Oakenshield. That Thorin's death scene, the most moving episode in the book, was not part of the original story, is typical of Tolkien's tendency to go from fantasy to realism. He begins to write a fairy story, and then he thinks 'real life is not like that', and he stops writing fairy story and writes real life. Such movement informs so much of Tolkien's work that we may call it a hallmark of his fiction.

'The Scouring of the Shire' was originally titled 'The Mending of the Shire' (*SD* 94). The change from *mending* to *scouring* is notable and follows the same downward trajectory as Tolkien's change for Frodo. The historical context for the A, B, and C drafts cited above is that they were probably written in late 1948, after but in the shadow of World War II that was the book's most insistent background. The war was now over, but it is not difficult to imagine that its effects might still have shadowed Tolkien's will and heart and mood. And his writing. There is not much to choose between the official description of Michael Tolkien as "unfit" and Tolkien's description of Frodo as "incapable."

The switch of Frodo from conquering hero to conscientious objector switched Tolkien's story from extended fairy-tale to full-blown tragedy. Often read as providing the escape and consolation of a fairy tale, *The Lord of the Rings* now performed instead the task of a mythology, which is to account for the world as it is, not as it should be, to portray things as they are rather than as we wish they were. The path of the story turns downward, things go wrong, mistakes are made that bring on never-ending consequences. And people must live with them. That is the recognition, the epiphany that powered Tolkien's last-minute correction. It was this recognition, ushered in by the circumstances I have just described that switched his story from comedy to tragedy and its genre from fairy tale to myth, that took Frodo from conquering hero to much-damaged soldier unfit for further service. Here, I suggest, is where Tolkien's conscious mind caught up with his unconscious.

This is signaled in Frodo's speech to Sam: "I tried to save the Shire, and it has been saved; but not for me. It must often be so, Sam, when things are in danger; someone has to lose them, give them up so that others may keep them"

(*RK* 309). That's pretty bleak. It is also true to life. Readerly reaction to this *dyscatastrophe* is profound and overwhelming, a grief so piercing that it brings tears. More even than that, it produces what Aristotle tells us is the instinctive response to tragedy – pity and fear. It stirs our pity for the protagonist's fall and awakens our fear for our own, the dreadful suspicion that our destinies may follow the same path.

The tears of Merry and Pippin on the quayside at the Havens, the ship's dwindling departure down the long firth, all these had their beginning in 1948-50 in manuscript B. But Tolkien did not stop there. With writerly thrift, he kept Escape, Recovery, and Consolation; There and Back Again; the homecoming welcome and the Happy Ending. He gave them to Sam, whose "Well, I'm back" at once warms the heart and underscores the poignance of Frodo's departure. The story is now both *eucatastrophic* and *dyscatastrophic* as it moves toward the two endings – one conventionally happy and one unbearably sad. Comedy and tragedy riff off each other like ritual cantio and response. Happy ending and tragic outcome are linked in perpetual dialogue and debate with one another, as they are across the breadth of Tolkien's work.

Less important than *how* is *what*. What is the result of this change of direction? I suggest there are several. First, the turn from comedy to tragedy ennobles the story and its protagonist, giving both more weight in the literary scales. Comedy is entertaining. Tragedy is gripping. The turn from one to the other catches the viewer by surprise, and the effect is unsettling, destabilizing, and ultimately moving. It was Tolkien's genius that took the tragic destiny the Greeks reserved for their great men – for Oedipus and Achilles and Agamemnon – and gave it to a 'little' man in both the physical and the socio-political sense of that word.

Second and by the same token, tragedy arouses a more profound emotion than does fairy-story, which according to Tolkien offers escape and consolation. Frodo as the happy-ever-after Mayor of Hobbiton would satisfy our sense of justice. It is a fitting reward after all he has been through. It is what ought to happen. Knowing this, we can turn out the light and go to sleep. But Frodo broken by his ordeal, Frodo damaged beyond repair, Frodo as a stranger in his own hometown, that is not right, that ought not to happen. Not after all he has done. Such an outcome is perturbing and anxiety-producing. It is the reverse of consolation. It offers no escape from the kind of thing that in real life actually does happen. Bad things happen to good people. It is a deeply disturbing vision that haunts our dreams and interrupts our sleep. We can escape into fairy tales and enjoy the Consolation of the Happy Ending they give us, but the experience of tragedy takes us to a deeper place in the human psyche, a dark place that for all its danger is one we all must visit sooner or later.

Third, there is the value of contrast. Tolkien's paired endings, the light and the dark, play off one another to the greater effect of both. Our hearts are warmed for Sam and at the same time broken for Frodo. Each response highlights and shadows the other. And this is as it should be. The ordinary processes of daily life do not cordon off comedy and tragedy into separate compartments, as in a theatre, but switch from one to another without notice and without barrier. It is a fact worth contemplating that for most of our time on earth we simply do not know what will come next. And that, I suggest, is what makes life in all its unexpectedness worth living. That is what gets people up in the morning, sends them out the door on any given day. It also sends them to Tarot cards and crystal balls and fortune-tellers in search of answers. It sends people to great books in search of a different kind of answer, for books can arrange for us to meet in fiction what we would shrink from in real life.

Nobody does it better than Tolkien. The *dyscatastrophic/eucatastrophic* scene at Mt. Doom in *The Lord of the Rings* is as shattering on the 20th reading as it was on the first, yet we return to it again and again. Frodo's sacrifice is as wrenching, his losses as unfair and bitter as Sam's Happy Ending is appropriate, satisfying, and consoling. It is exactly this tension in opposition, this tug-of-war between the poles that has kept the book and its author in their high place in the pantheon and library of modern fantasy for nigh on a century. I venture to guess that with a little help from their friends, both the book and its author will be good for another century or so.[6]

---

6 I believed this when I wrote it, which was before the advent of the present Amazon franchise, *The Rings of Power* series. Now I'm not so sure. Amazon's dilution and debasement of Tolkien's world and its story may increase the damage done by the Peter Jackson films, further changing Tolkien's complex psychological study into a big, noisy action cycle and eliding as un-commercial the very qualities I've just been praising.

It would be perfectly possible, I am well aware, to argue for the very opposite of what I have just been saying, to propose that Frodo's moral courage has been hardened and his will strengthened by his ordeal. But that would be another paper.

The Dragon and the Railway Station

J.R.R. Tolkien's essay 'On Fairy-stories' is an *omnium gatherum* of his knowledge of and opinions about fairy-stories, primitive societies, children, tale telling, the origin of language, King Arthur, Charlemagne's mother, and banana-skins. An odd collection, but perhaps the oddest of all are his subsequent comments on dragons, motor cars, clouds, railway stations, and rainbows. For example, his statement that "[t]he notion that motor-cars are more 'alive' than [...] dragons is curious" (*MC* 149), seems equally as curious as the original notion itself. Likewise, his admission further down the same page that he cannot convince himself "that the roof of Bletchley[1] Station is any more 'real' than the clouds" (*MC* 149). The implied analogy is that dragons are to motor cars as clouds are

Bletchley Station as Tolkien knew it before renovation in 1965-66.
<https://www.mkheritage.org.uk/archive/jt/railway/railway.html#chapter5>

1 From Fr. *Blechelai*, 'Blecca's Leah'. One of those colorful English place-names, like Tooting or Nether Wallop that through the accident of modern spelling (and in this case because of its association with the dialectal word *bletch* 'dirt', 'smear', 'smudge'), communicates a meaning entirely divorced from its municipal identity.

to station roofs. But the central issue in both sets is the relative nature of reality. Moreover, the second comparison is flawed in its component parts. Bletchley Station is not a generic category like motor cars; it is a single item, a locality with a specific address – quite a solid bricks-and-mortar building in comparison to a cloud, as the photograph shows.[2]

The bricks and mortar, of course, are the very reasons why Tolkien picked a railway station. It may have been that the busy to and fro of ordinary travel provided just the humdrum everyday contrast with the celestial tranquility of a cloud that he needed to make his point. And the railway station also offered scope for more elaborate comparison, allowing him to go inside the building, to declare that "[t]he Bridge to Platform 4 is to me less interesting than Bifrost [the rainbow bridge between heaven and earth of Norse mythology] guarded by Heimdall with the Gjallarhorn" (*MC* 149).

Cloud > station, Rainbow Bridge > Platform bridge. So far, so good. But why Bletchley in particular? The question gains interest when we learn that not only was the railway bridge less interesting than the rainbow bridge, Bletchley Station itself wasn't Tolkien's first choice as an example of reality.[3] A previous (1939) draft of the essay cited the better-known Paddington Station (*TOFS* 238) and didn't replace it with Bletchley until 1947, nearly a decade later. The post-war shift from a London hub to a regional branch – and the added detail of the platform bridge – invites speculation that the new example might have been more germane to Tolkien's own travel history than was the old. Moreover, the bridge to Platform 4 is not a neutral example like the motor car but one with as much symbolic meaning as the dragon. Platform 4 is the arrival and departure point for travel between Tolkien's Oxford and Bletchley Park, a mansion near Milton Keynes in Buckinghamshire established in 1938 as a secret center of Allied code-breaking operations, later known as the Government Code & Cypher School and later still as GCHQ.

The intrusion of Platform 4 introduces an ultra-railway association into what has up to this point been a mere citation of comparative realities. It changes

2 For more information on Bletchley Station, see the excellent article on Bletchley's Railway Heritage on <https://www.mkheritage.org.uk/archive/jt/railway/railway.html#chapter5>.

3 Pointed out by Christina Scull and Wayne Hammond in their comprehensive three-volume *J.R.R. Tolkien Companion and Guide* (*C&G* vol. I, 206, 705).

the equation, and the nature of the change may reveal the process of Tolkien's associative thinking. At this point in the essay Bletchley Station can be seen as more than a railway terminus; it is the port of entry to a specialized venue whose focus is the manipulation of words to disguise reality. What is more, the Platform bridge, like the Norse rainbow bridge, connects the traveler to a destination whose meaning transcends its locality. The proximity in the essay of the dragon to the railway station and via Platform 4 to Bletchley Park suggests that these items came together in Tolkien's mind as he wrote. The same proximity also raises the vexed question of Tolkien's connection with code-breaking at the time of World War II. Just before the outbreak of the War, Bletchley Park ran courses for hand-picked individuals who might join the organization in the event of war. One of them was Tolkien, at the time a professor at Pembroke College Oxford, who was enrolled in just such a course, as this list shows.

	March 27th	March 28th	March 29th	March 30th
D.J.Allan	Commercial	Commercial		
Dr. Beeston	Near East	Near East	Near East	Near East
Professor A.H.Campbell	Air	Air	Military	Military
J.M.Dawkins	Near East	Near East	Near East	Near East
L.Forster	Naval	Naval	Naval	Naval
Professor Fraser	Mr. Turner	Mr. Turner	Mr. Turner	Mr. Turner
E.Lobel	Research	Research	Research	Research
Professor Norman	Military	Military	Air	Air
Dr. E.G.C.Poole	Research	Research	Research	Research
F.A.Taylor	French	French		
Professor Tolkien	Scandinavian	Scandinavian		
Professor Waterhouse	Naval	Naval	Naval	Naval
Professor Willoughby	Naval	Naval	Naval	Naval

<https://www.gchq.gov.uk/information/jrr-tolkien-was-keen-become-cryptanalyst>

Enrollment would not have been unusual at a time when experts in language and communication were being recruited as part of the national war effort by MI5, the British domestic counter-intelligence service. The roster names are listed alphabetically and next to each is the relevant area of specialization, which for Tolkien included "Scandinavian" (he was fluent in Old Norse) and "Spanish," a language he would have heard from Father Francis Morgan, the half-Spanish, half-Welsh Catholic priest who became his guardian after his mother died. Some names on the list have hand-jotted annotations in pen or pencil beside them. One scribble says "good," another notes "Naval intell." Next to Tolkien's name is written the word "keen," which might be a comment on his enthusiasm but could easily be a directive on how to pronounce the last syllable of his name.

Tolkien's possible/probable connection to the railway platform and the code-breaking center to which it leads seems real enough for argument. His relationship to dragons is even more demonstrable, for in life, as in art, dragons seem never to have been far from his mind. On 1 January 1938, he gave a lecture on dragons to children in the University Museum, Oxford, a talk which offered a kind of literary taxonomy of the dragon in myth and legend complete with illustrations (*C&G* vol. I, 310.). Of coincidental interest in the context of the present discussion linking dragons with railway stations is the closing paragraph of the Museum talk in which Tolkien compares an express train with its puffing engine to "a smoking dragon" (Tolkien 2018b: 62). Dragons also come in for discussion in both of Tolkien's two great essays, 'On Fairy-stories' (discussed above) and '*Beowulf*: The Monsters and the Critics'. In addition to the already-mentioned dragons no less real than motor cars, the fairy-story essay extols "the prince of all dragons" (*MC* 135), Fáfnir, the mesmerizing wyrm of the Volsung story who beguiles Sigurd the Volsung with his human speech. The *Beowulf* essay devotes considerable space to Beowulf's dragon, which though it is not sufficiently "plain, pure fairy-story dragon" for Tolkien, and does not speak, is nevertheless described as the "personification of malice, greed [...] a foe more evil than any human enemy of house or realm" (*MC* 17). And in Tolkien's own fiction, there are dragons aplenty: Farmer Giles's wily Chrysophylax, Bilbo's chatty Smaug, and Túrin's taunting Glaurung, all dragons with a mythological pedigree attached to a modern spin on how and to whom they talk.

A talking dragon is a mythic embodiment of the power of words, usually to persuade, confuse, deceive, spin, or distort reality. I want to suggest that this is not unlike encoding, whose purpose is essentially the same, and that Tolkien's train of thought in the fairy-story essay may have taken a wandering route by way of a dragon to a motor car, from there to the clouds and Bletchley Station analogy and thence to codes and code-breaking activities at Bletchley Park against a "foe more evil" than any dragon. If so, this says something worth pondering about the relationship of his own fairy-story to the real world. Far-fetched as it may seem, I propose a connection in Tolkien's mind between the word-spinning Glaurung and his role in the lives of the children of Húrin and the more general idea of coding/code breaking as a feature of war at Bletchley Park, a connection not so much in content as in idea, which is in both cases the distortion of reality. Glaurung's destructive word-spinnings in his encounters with Túrin – his lies and half-truths, his distortions of fact and re-inflections of meaning, revealing truth when it will carry the most shock and withholding information when it would do the most good – are very like a code in that both are efforts at linguistic misdirection.

Glaurung's litany after the fall of Nargothrond, his recital of Túrin's sins both of omission and commission – his description of Túrin as: "thankless fosterling [of Thingol)] outlaw [with Mim and the dwarves], slayer of your friend [Beleg], thief of love [Finduilas and Gwindor], usurper of Nargothrond [from Orodreth], captain foolhardy [in building the bridge], and deserter of your ki" [Morwen and Nienor]" (*Children* 179, S 213-14) – all this infects Túrin with guilt and distorts his self-awareness so that he sees himself "as in a mirror misshapen by malice" (*S* 213-14, *Children* 179). Every word of what the dragon says is true, but the slant he puts on his accusations ignores all mitigating circumstances. Only his persona as a dragon marks as fantasy what in real life would simply be called spin – selective presentation of facts to emphasize a partial truth. Both methods of treating fact – the imaginary and the real – are designed to misdirect the uninformed; both are instruments of data manipulation; both are hostile activities designed to bemuse and bewilder a target audience. Finally, and most contextually similar, both are parts of a particular war effort.

To sum up my argument: the close proximity in Tolkien's essay of the fantastic dragons of myth and legend to the concrete realities of Bletchley Station and

Platform 4 seems to me a coincidence more causal than casual. The point I wish to make is that encoding and word-spinning are related manipulations of language in that both deploy symbol-using systems to obfuscate, disguise, and/or conceal meanings. It seems to me obvious that breaking a code involves the same process as devising one but in reverse. The road goes in both directions. Tolkien's dragon fulfills the same function in Middle-earth as Bletchley Park in Buckinghamshire. To posit a direct connection between Glaurung's speech in Nargothrond and Tolkien's awareness of activities at Bletchley Park may seem like a bridge too far, though as we have seen, a number of factors contribute to the connection. Dragons are no less real for Tolkien than motor cars, and the roof of Bletchley station is not more real that the clouds. Art and life imitate one another, as Tolkien was well-aware. "Mythology is language," he sweepingly declared in that early draft of the fairy-story essay, "and language is mythology" (*TOFS* 181).

How right he was.

Part II
Myths

Whose Myth is it?

The 'Athrabeth Finrod ah Andreth' (*Morgoth* 301-366) or 'Debate of Finrod and Andreth' is a late and for many readers problematic addendum to Tolkien's *legendarium*. It is a conversation between an Elf, Finrod, and Andreth, a mortal woman, between whom the major difference is that one is doomed to die and the other to endure immortality. The subject of their conversation is mortality.

The dialogue opens with Finrod's expressed condolence at the death of Andreth's grandfather Boron. Like Tolkien's readers up to now, Finrod assumes that the death of Men is part of Eru's plan and is therefore not just necessary but right. To Finrod's surprise, Andreth contends that death has not always been in the plan and is consequently neither necessary nor right. What began as a conversation slides into a heated argument in which both characters reveal hidden emotions and entrenched preconceptions. Andreth is angry. Finrod is condescending. She is resentful. He is shocked.

The apparently philosophical tone of the argument masks the emotional subtext that is the real reason for Andreth's bitterness – a broken love affair. The differing life spans of Elves and Men has divided her fate from that of her only love, Finrod's brother Aegnor. She will wither and grow old. He will remain in his youthful prime. She will die. He will not. This turns debate into tragedy, and the inherent drama would be enough for most authors. It is just the beginning for Tolkien. Underlying the dialogue is Tolkien's real purpose, to interrogate the function of death in his sub-created world. Christopher Tolkien characterizes the 'Athrabeth' as "the record of a prolonged interior debate" (*Morgoth* 369) of the author with himself. The dialogue runs for many pages and ends with the question still unanswered.

Sooner or later every mythology worth its salt has to address the presence of death in its particular world, and Tolkien's was no exception. Indeed, his made the issue more immediate than most. In a world where some people die and others do not, those who do are going to wonder why. Calling death the "gift of Ilúvatar" (e.g. *Morgoth* 37) is an explanation but not a justification. Let us give Tolkien the credit he deserves for having the authorial honesty to interrogate the assumptions of his invented world and courage to make that interrogation an integral part of the very world it questions.

To establish that credit I will consider three questions that the 'Athrabeth' raises – who, why, and how. My argument will be circular, or rather spiral, for the *why* and the *how* will lead around in a widening and ascending arc to the *who.*

First, *who*? Whose myth is it? Who owns the story? Second, *why*? What impelled Tolkien to write the dialogue? Why did he externalize the "interior debate"? Last – and most important for what is after all art and not history – *how*; by what mechanism did he do it?

I'll begin as I intend to finish, with who. Whose myth is it? This is a question to which even Tolkien came to no clear answer, as the following statements will show.

1. In the letter to Milton Waldman in 1951 he wrote, "the point of view of the whole cycle is the Elvish" (*Letters* 147).

2. At some time during composition of the prose Túrin saga (for which there is no definite date), he scribbled a note saying "the cosmogonic myths are Númenórean, blending Elven-lore with human myth and imagination" (*Morgoth* 374).

3. In or about 1958 "or later" according to Christopher, Tolkien wrote that: "the Mythology must actually be a 'Mannish' affair [...] what we have in the *Silmarillion* etc. are traditions [...] handed on by *Men* in Númenor and later in Middle-earth (Arnor and Gondor); but already far back – from the first association of the Dúnedan and Elf-friends with the Eldar in Beleriand – blended and confused with their own Mannish myths and cosmic ideas" (*Morgoth* 370).

There you have the question. Just whose myth is it? Is it Elvish? Is it Mannish? Is it a blend? The 'Athrabeth' raises all these questions and then refuses any final answers. Its dialogue is driven by contending points of view. Far from "traditions [...] blended and confused", we have traditions unblended and competing, and it is the reader who is confused. Finrod and Andreth each stake a claim to their own interpretation of the myth, and the inherent trap for the reader is to read the text in light of one or the other debater's position: that if either side is right the other must be wrong.

Tolkien's own statements provide a way out. Listen to these words from the quote just cited: 'lore', 'imagination', 'point of view', 'traditions', 'ideas', 'blended', 'confused'. Here are clear indications of his developing awareness that as truths are partial, all stories depend on and derive from a human, therefore fallible, source.

I suggest that the key to the puzzle lies in one of the phrases just cited: "point of view." The 'Athrabeth' is not a final statement; it is a debate between contending points of view, those of Elves and Men. As Tolkien himself said, it is "an example of the kind of thing that enquiring minds on either side, the Elvish or the Human, must have said to one another" (*Morgoth* 329). The seeming contradictions are parts of a process, not a final pronouncement. Each of the debaters has a point of view shaped by identity, background, and history.

At this point the question of whose myth it is would seem to have its answer; it belongs to whoever is speaking whenever they are speaking. Putting aside the obvious fact that it is Tolkien's myth, and he can make it whatever he wants it to be, it would be well to remember that it has been presented all along not as gospel truth (Christopher's *The Silmarillion* volume bears responsibility for this misreading) but as tales told by various and intentionally disparate tellers. Tolkien has used multiple voices from different times and different Middle-earth cultures – Eriol/Ælfwine, Rúmil, Pengoloð, Daeron, the Minstrel, Edwin Lowdham, not to mention Bilbo and Frodo Baggins and Samwise Gamgee. In this patchwork company, the voices of Finrod and Andreth and Adanel are only three in a long line.

They are among the most important, however, for their disagreement about the death-fate of Men leads to my second question – *why*? Readers were content with Middle-earth the way it was or appeared to be, and the assumption was that on the whole Tolkien also was satisfied with it. The account of his growing dissatisfaction came as a revelation. One of the tenets of his sub-creative process was that the imaginary world had to have "inner consistency" (*TOFS* 60). This didn't just mean geographically or phenomenologically but also philosophically. Its inhabitants had to understand the circumstances underlying mortality and death.

Through the debate between Finrod and Andreth Tolkien was now introducing doubt where heretofore there had been only the unquestioned word of Eru. Doubt is not what Tolkien's readers expected or wanted. They were used to certainty, the assurance that his sub-created world would stand still, that it would always be as it was when they first met it. In altering the rules of the game, Tolkien was putting at risk everything he had already written about it, gambling on his readers' intelligence and ability to accept change. This is a big chance for any author to take, especially one whose invented world has become so real to so many readers that they assume its proper names and wear its costumes. Thus, a major problem lies not just in the debate – whether within its author or in the voices of Finrod and Andreth and Adanel – but also in its effect on readers accustomed to a fixed picture. This is the essence of the *why* question. Why play fast and loose with a mythology not only already established but much beloved by its legions of readers? My answer is that Tolkien had no choice. He was too honest a writer, too honest a thinker to fudge so critical an issue. He came to see that he could not avoid the problem, and so he wrote the 'Athrabeth'.

Which brings me to my last question – *how*? How did Tolkien handle what was patently an ethically difficult and theologically risky problem for his invented world? He used three strategies:

Strategy number one: he avoided answering once and for all my first question – whose myth is it? Instead he allowed the competing voices to speak for themselves, each to make its own case. There is precedent for this. Recall the two competing versions of creation in the biblical Genesis, the conflicting portrayals of the Norse gods by the contemporaries Snorri Sturluson and Saxo Grammaticus, the marked difference between the gods of Æschylus and those of Euripides. In such primary sources, it is a given that any and all versions of a myth are interpretations derived from particular voices, particular times, and particular stages of development. Tolkien simply sped up the process by putting the competing voices in touch with one another and at the same time.

Strategy number two: he made sure that none of his competing voices spoke with final authority. When Andreth remarks sarcastically: "All ye Elves deem that we die [...] by our true kind" (*Morgoth* 308), Finrod replies that the Elves speak "out of knowledge, not out of mere Elvish lore" (*Morgoth* 308). Andreth counters by citing "the Wise" among her people, who say that Men were not made for death, although, she admits, they do not have the "sure knowledge" of which Finrod boasts, only the aforementioned "'lore', from which truth must be winnowed" (*Morgoth* 309). Backed by *The Silmarillion* as published plus the earliest versions of the myth in *The History of Middle-earth*, most readers will probably prefer Finrod's knowledge to Andreth's lore, which sounds at best circumstantial, at worst unreliable.

Tolkien will not allow us to accept so easy an answer. In his 'Commentary' on the 'Athrabeth' he wrote that "it must be understood that [Finrod] starts with certain basic beliefs, which he would have said were derived from one or more of these sources: his created nature; angelic instruction; thought; and experience" (*Morgoth* 330). What Finrod calls "knowledge", Tolkien calls "beliefs", a scarcely more reliable source than Andreth's lore. In addition, it is worth noting that he casts Finrod's position in the conditional mode; they are "beliefs which Finrod would have said were derived" from the sources he cites. This is a probability not a certainty and leaves Finrod with no more authority than Andreth. Both speakers talk in terms of their own beliefs, hopes, fears. Andreth declares that her people say Men were not made for death, for Men to die is the work of Morgoth. "[If] your tale is true," Finrod tells Andreth, "then all in Arda is vain," but he adds "I do not believe your tale" (*Morgoth* 313). The debate has moved from certainty to belief.

So far so good. Tolkien has successfully negotiated the *fact* of death as an element of his world. But he has not yet come up with any *reason* for death. To a Christian and Catholic like Tolkien, human mortality derives directly from the Fall. In the letter to Waldman, however, he said that in this invented world "mortality is not explained mythically; it is a mystery," and so the "first fall of Man [...] nowhere appears" (*Letters* 147). But he also said, and in the same letter: "There cannot be any story without a fall – all stories are ultimately about the fall – at least not for human minds as we know them and have them" (*Letters* 147). He has thereby put himself in a cleft stick. If he stood by either statement, the other would be invalid. He decided in favor of the second statement. Once he gave his mortals permission to question their mortality, he felt obliged to let them devise and answer. The Fall of Man had to appear.

The necessary (as he felt) introduction of The Fall, or a fall, while it solved one problem led to an even greater problem. A note in a very early draft makes it clear that Tolkien was aware of the hazard:

> Query: Is it not right to make Andreth refuse to discuss any traditions or legends of the 'Fall'? Already it is (if inevitably) too like a parody of Christianity. Any legend of the Fall would make it completely so? (*Morgoth* 354)

At this point my original question, 'Whose myth is it?', takes a left turn out of the secondary world into the primary one. No longer umpiring a fictive contest between fictive voices, Tolkien is now asking a real question about the relationship of his mythology to a real-world mythos – Christianity. It was a question Tolkien saw coming (recall his word "inevitably" in the note just quoted). In the letter to Milton Waldman, he had faulted Arthurian legend for being "involved in and explicitly contain[ing] the Christian religion" (*Letters* 144), and now he saw his own legend teetering on the brink of the same trap. Indeed, Christopher Tolkien cites this as his father's primary reason for his original insistence that the Fall of Man must happen offstage (*Morgoth* 354).

Tolkien might also have had in mind C.S. Lewis's explicit re-use of Christianity in *The Lion, the Witch, and the Wardrobe*, published in 1950. When in that story Aslan gives up his life in place of Edmund, when time begins to run backward, the stone table breaks and Aslan is resurrected, the story does become a parody (deliberately so in Lewis's case) of Christianity. It no longer has its own life. Nevertheless, although Tolkien was acutely aware of this threat to his story's autonomy, he did not surrender to his own warning doubts. Although the 'Athrabeth' was already potentially too like a parody of Christianity which any legend of the fall would make ... completely so, he went ahead to add to it a legend of a fall, the 'Tale of Adanel' (*Morgoth* 345-49). Which leads me to strategy number three.

The 'Athrabeth' itself is not about the Fall; it is about death. There is no mention in the dialogue of any fall, only veiled suggestions by Andreth that something, she does not specify what, must have happened to doom Men to death. Late in the argument, Tolkien has Finrod pin her down.

> 'Therefore I say to you, Andreth, what did ye do, ye Men, long ago in the dark? How did ye anger Eru? For otherwise all your tales are but dark dreams devised in a Dark Mind. Will you say what you know or have heard?'
> 'I will not,' answers Andreth. 'We do not speak of this to those of other race.'
> Finrod persists. 'Are there no tales of your days before death, though ye will not tell them to strangers?' (*Morgoth* 313)

If Men had committed some misdeed whereby they had angered Eru, there would surely, in this world of tale-tellers be tales about it. If there was such a tale, and if Andreth knew it or knew of it, Finrod's question would be the obvious cue for its introduction into the dialogue. Concerned with good reason that to introduce such a tale would turn his myth into a parody of Christianity, Tolkien's strategy was not to include it in the 'Athrabeth' proper but to subordinate it as an appendix to his commentary on the debate.

Even there, he made sure to present it as lore, not knowledge or even belief. The 'Tale of Adanel' adds not just one more voice but several, all of them, like Finrod's and Andreth's, to some degree unreliable. Where Christopher's *Silmarillion* (1977) begins with the declarative "There was Eru" (*S* 15), Adanel opens her tale in conventional story-telling style with the indeterminate "Some say" (*Morgoth* 345). What we are given is hearsay and third hand at that, from the unnamed "some" to Adanel, from Adanel to Andreth, from Andreth to Finrod. Indeed, Tolkien explicitly said that "Nothing is hereby asserted concerning its [the story's] 'truth', historical or otherwise" (*Morgoth* 344). We are a long way from authority.

And finally, Tolkien replaces a Fall, which is by definition swift and precipitous, with a Decline, which is by its nature gradual and gentle. Instead of a watershed moment in which all is lost, he substitutes a continuing process played out over an indeterminate period. At a time "before any had yet died" says Andreth, quoting Adanel, quoting "some", Men ceased to listen to the (undefined) Voice and turned instead to worship of the enemy. At the end of this period, the Voice spoke to humanity one last time, saying: “Ye have abjured Me, but ye remain Mine. I gave you life. Now it shall be shortened, and each of you in a little while shall come to Me” (*Morgoth* 347). Note the language! It is not “Ye shall surely die” (*King James Bible*) or “Ye shall die the death” (*Douai Bible*) but “Ye shall come to me” with its biblical echo neatly avoided. Moreover, it would seem that even then death did not come to everyone. Adanel says only that “some began to die.” In sum, through a strategy whereby one speaker answers another by quoting a third who quotes an indeterminate fourth who cites an unnamed and unattested Voice, Tolkien managed to introduce the question and simultaneously distance himself as author, his multiple fictive speakers, and his real-world audience from any final answer.

The ‘Tale of Adanel’ is Andreth’s third-hand answer to Finrod’s question, “How did ye anger Eru?” (*Morgoth* 313) and “Are there no tales of your days before death?” (*Morgoth* 313). But it is only a tale and only one tale among several. Does it therefore qualify as Tolkien’s definitive Fall of Man? And if it does, does it make this part of Tolkien’s *legendarium* a parody of Christianity? Or are his mythos and that of Christianity simply trying to do the same thing – to answer with whatever means are at hand the same cosmic questions, to find a way to find meaning in the terrible and beautiful Middle-earth in which we live?

To these questions we must find our own answers, but as I hope I have shown, in exploring *how* and *why*, we have come to *who* and my initial question ‘Whose myth is it?’ My answer is that it is not Finrod’s nor Andreth’s nor Adanel’s. It does not belong to Elves or to Men. Or to Christianity. It cannot and will not speak with one voice. We must give Tolkien credit not just for the courage of his convictions and beliefs but also for his doubts. Such honesty in a writer should be matched by an equal honesty on the part of his readers. Only if we can accept multiple voices, conflicting and competing interpretations, and contending points of view, only if we can be as honest and as doubtful and as hopeful as Tolkien was, only if we can answer the question ‘Whose myth is it?’ by acknowledging that it is in all its indeterminacy and irresolution Tolkien’s, only then can we truly say also that it is ours.

"A Fearful Weapon"

The words of my title are quoted from the 'Myths Transformed' section of *Morgoth's Ring*, volume 10 of Christopher Tolkien's *History of Middle-Earth*. They vividly convey Christopher's opinion of his father's late and drastic revisions to Tolkien's *legendarium*. "It seems to me," he wrote, "that he was devising – from within it – a fearful weapon against his own creation" (*Morgoth* 371).

When I first read these words (*Morgoth's Ring* was published in 1993), I had an immediate sense of *déjà vu*, for I had heard something very like them before, in a farmhouse kitchen in Provence where Christopher, pacing up and down in pajamas and bathrobe, breakfast mug of Nescafé in hand, talked about the havoc such revision wrought in his father's mythology and worried out loud about what they would do. He was right to be concerned, for the changes were sweeping, and their publication would inflict bodily harm on a major element of Tolkien's creation myth, the role of the Two Trees in bringing light to Middle-earth. For Christopher this was an imminent, not a hypothetical problem, as he was then approaching the stage in his editing of his father's manuscripts when these revisions would be up next.

In the end, he did publish them in 1993. The result was *Morgoth's Ring*, volume 10 of *The History of Middle-earth*. But the problem remains, and the damage it caused is the subject of the present enquiry. Was Christopher's assumption correct? Have Tolkien's revisions been in fact a weapon against the supremely beautiful story he originally conceived? Certainly, their dogged realism is a 180° turn for the man who once declared unequivocally that "Fantasy remains a human right" (*TOFS* 66). His 1932/33 poem 'Mythopoeia', addressed to C.S. Lewis, had asserted much the same but more romantically:

> Though all the crannies of the world we filled
> with elves and goblins, though we dared to build
> gods and their houses out of dark and light,
> and sowed the seeds of dragons, 'twas our right
> (used or misused). (*T&L* 87)

I call attention to the word 'right', used twice to defend what Tolkien called "sub-creation" (*TOFS* 42 et al.), the making of an imaginative Secondary World. But the concept of sub-creation was not just a nose-thumb at stuffy academia, it was a firm tenet of his belief as well. "We make in our measure and in our derivative mode because we are made," he wrote in his essay 'On Fairy-stories', "and not only made, but made in the image and likeness of a Maker" (*TOFS* 66). The late revisions that so worried Christopher now threatened to revoke that right on the grounds that it had indeed been 'misused' by the very man who claimed it.

This was in specific reference to what he now deemed his *legendarium's* "astronomically absurd business of the making of the Sun and Moon" from a flower and a fruit of the Two Trees (*Morgoth* 371). Tolkien was saying: "You cannot do this anymore" (*Morgoth* 371). And the five words of the sentence – at once a judgment and a renunciation – are addressed to their author. The man who introduced the term 'sub-creation' to a generation of readers was now abjuring its use, saying that "the art of the 'Sub-creator' cannot, or should not attempt to, extend the 'mythical' revelation of a conception of the shape of the Earth and the origin of the lights of heaven that runs counter to the known physical truths of his own days" (*Morgoth* 371). To be sure, Tolkien had made many revisions to his *legendarium* over the years but none so literally world-shaking as this, which on its publication immediately generated readerly pushback. The changes introduced in 'Myths Transformed' (Morgoth 369-431) were not well received. Readers accustomed to the old version of Tolkien's legendarium did not welcome the readjustment and resisted its arbitrary re-arrangement of their familiar fantasy world. One reader, Kaj André Apeland, compared it to Heraclitus's dictum that you cannot step in the same river twice, averring that Tolkien had left the river and was now observing it from the bank (Apeland 1998: 46).

The word 'anymore', with its implicit goodbye to a Middle-earth left behind, is wistful in its melancholy, carrying a feeling of regret for a paradise not so much lost as renounced. Tolkien was not just saying goodbye to his invention; he was saying farewell to his art, for it is worth noting that in the years following that renunciation, he produced only one new story that in fact illustrated the pain of the renunciation he performed. This was *Smith of Wootton Major*, in 1967. *Smith* is a brief and bittersweet fantasy in which the hero, a blacksmith given a magic star that admits him to Fairyland, learns that he must give up both his visits and the star that enables them to return to the everyday world. The known circumstances of Tolkien's life make it impossible not to read this story as deeply autobiographical. Facing imminent retirement, Tolkien himself had called it "an old man's story, filled with the presage of bereavement" and "written with deep emotion" (*Bio* 243). We must agree, for as 'Myths Transformed' makes clear, Tolkien's own late exchange of fable for fact was hauntingly like Smith's farewell to Faery, a reluctant giving-up of an imaginative vision he could no longer rationally justify. But the seed of renunciation had been planted years before.

As early as 1958, we find him writing: "It is now clear to me that in any case the Mythology must actually be a 'Mannish' affair. [...] What we have in the *Silmarillion* etc. are traditions [...] handed on by *Men* [...] [These traditions have been] blended and confused with their own Mannish myths and cosmic ideas" (*Morgoth* 370). This was sub-creation one step down, no longer a God-given right but an authorial strategy that de-throned the original vision. The change that divided the *legendarium* into Mannish versus Elvish traditions widened the story by introducing the notion of point of view. But it also narrowed each approach to the point of view being held. This undermined the authority of the original myth by making it one version instead of a mythological truth. Here is where Christopher's dictum comes into play and the fearful weapon is unleashed. 'Myths Transformed' is the record of a "prolonged interior debate" over the revision process. It chronicles Tolkien's "intellectual and imaginative stress in the face of such a dismantling and reconstitution, believed to be an inescapable necessity, but never to be achieved" (*Morgoth* 369). The key phrases – 'intellectual and imaginative stress', 'inescapable necessity', and 'never achieved' – capture Christopher's concern for his father's struggle over his own past work.

This creates a kind of Grand Canyon stratification of literary layers frozen in time, each from a different era and all on view all at once – Christopher's present thinking about his father's past thinking about Tolkien's even farther past thinking about his work. The middle layer is the most revealing, for that is where the geographical and astronomical cataclysm – the struggle that created the fearful weapon – is recorded. That struggle was innate, for Tolkien's imagination has always been matched by his capacity for logical and analytic thinking. The one led him to the creativity of mythmaking, the other to the science of linguistics, and from early days he oscillated between the two. In his all-important letter to Milton Waldman, Tolkien protested (but who was he arguing with?) that myth and language were not "divergent interests [...] but integrally related" (*Letters* 144). Yet, in the same letter, he referred to linguistics as "the other pole" (*Letters* 145), which suggests exactly the opposite. It is the paradox of his nature that both statements were true. His invented languages followed strict linguistic rules, while the fantasy world they generated followed his imagination.

He was like the man in Rudyard Kipling's 'The Two-Sided Man'[1] a paean to seeing both sides, who said of himself:

> Much I owe to the Lands that grew
> More to the Lives that fed
> But most to Allah Who gave me two
> Separate sides to my head.

There have always been two sides to Tolkien's head. His first biographer, Humphrey Carpenter, called him "a man of antitheses" (*Bio* 95), by nature "cheerful almost irrepressible" but also "capable of bouts of profound despair" (*Bio* 31), and this two-sidedness persisted throughout his life. In terms of Christopher's dictum, it is a pity that it was the logical and not the imaginative side that got the last word and made the final decision; that became in effect a weapon against his own creation.

How and *when* and most importantly *why* did this momentous change take place? Christopher has done a meticulous job of laying out the how of Tolkien's process insofar as that can be divined from the physical evidence, collating

1 See <https://www.poetryloverspage.com/poets/kipling/two_sided_man.html>.

and setting in approximate order the bewildering sequence of rewrites that led to Tolkien's brave new world. If *The Silmarillion* as originally published can be conjecturally called 'A', the text Christopher designates as 'B' was the "fine pre-*Lord of the Rings* manuscript" which "became the vehicle of massive rewriting many years later" (*Morgoth* 3). This revision was carried out "on the blank verso pages" of 'B', thus creating two distinct texts on the same physical manuscript and one nightmare for the editor. Christopher calls the second text 'C' but goes on immediately to a typescript "also directly based on *Ainulindalë* B" and containing what he saw as "a much more radical – one might say a devastating change in the cosmology," the sun as already pre-existent in Arda (*Morgoth* 3). This typescript he calls 'C*'.

The changes and variations among B, C, and C* are dizzying, and I won't attempt to sort them out; my purpose is to call attention to their existence, for such overlapping and piggy-backing of version on version on version gives a vivid picture of the mental gymnastics Tolkien must have gone through as he transferred his *legendarium* (I suspect painfully) from the rich, artistically coherent worldview he had developed over decades to the mythologically barren, meaning-impoverished skyscape that reflected his own world. So complex a process cannot have happened all in an instant and was much more likely to have taken shape over time. *When* is the most difficult question to answer for the scholar trying to chart a straight course, for unlike actual revision, which is demonstrable, inspiration is ephemeral and hard to pin down. Scull and Hammond point to a time "in the mid-1940s when he had considered whether to make Arda a round world from the beginning, but rejected the idea, at least temporarily" (*S&H* vol. I, 569).

Christopher has taken an educated guess. "I believe," he writes, "that virtually all of [the changes] came from [...] the late 1950s, in the aftermath of the publication of *The Lord of the Rings*" (*Morgoth* 369). Christopher's *when* may help to answer the final and to my mind most important question of *why*. Why did Tolkien decide to disassemble his own creation? What happened that impelled him to replace the beautiful concept of the light from the Trees with our contemporary-oriented but story-impoverished Solar System? My answer is *The Lord of the Rings*. In this case, the post hoc fallacy may not be as fallacious as usual. The overwhelming success of *The Lord of the Rings* may actually have retrospectively affected its precursor, the Silmarillion. A look at Tolkien's published letters from 1955 (when *The Return of the King* was published) onward shows that many were in response to readers who had written with questions about this or that aspect of Middle-earth, from its geographic relationship to the real world to genetic aspects of the cross-breeding of Elves and Men to free will and the nature of evil.

The phenomenon is not unlike the crossover into the real world of the fictive Sherlock Holmes, whose imaginary apartment at 221b Baker Street came to be seen as a real address, with the added corollary that it has now become one, a real building on a real street with its own blue plaque marking it as a historic site. Nevertheless, there is a distinct difference. A defining circumstance is that Holmes's London was contemporary with that of his readers, while Tolkien's Middle-earth is a never-land calqued on the real one, a fictive overlay of a Secondary World on a distant and ill-defined past of the Primary one. As it did with Holmes (whose creator, Sir Arthur Conan Doyle, was forced at the insistence of his voracious fans to resurrect the hero he had killed off) I suggest that the realism of Tolkien's phenomenal world also worked against itself. The concrete details of his Middle-earth piqued his readers' curiosity about their practical operation – laws of time and place, mortality and deathlessness (as in Elves) – and their eagerness for evidence of its reality invited him to take their queries seriously and ultimately to reconceive his mythology in response to their expectations.

His painstaking and sometimes lengthy explanations of how things were supposed to have worked in his once-upon-a-time fictive world forced him to look with a critical eye at the relationship of that world to the real one and eventually caused the real one to assume dominance. This was not revision but re-envision, a complete restructuring of some of the most visible aspects of his imaginary world. The geographic shift from a flat earth to a round one inevitably changed the orientation of the sky and everything in it – sun and moon, stars, night and day – and of time itself. This was a seismic change and according to Christopher, not one for the better. "Why is the myth of the Two Trees," he wrote, "more acceptable than that of the creation of the Sun and Moon from the last fruit and flower of the Trees as they died? Or indeed, if this is true, how can it be acceptable that the Evening Star is the Silmaril cut by Beren from Morgoth's crown" (*Morgoth* 371). Good questions, both. But if the Silmaril is not the Evening Star, then how does its light – first in Galadriel's mirror and then in her phial – function as the salvation of Frodo and Sam in Shelob's tunnel? As each question arises, one can see the dominos begin to topple – one against another against another until the original integrated and consistent sequence of events falls of its own weight.

The questions, and Tolkien's answers, were almost certainly instrumental in nudging him toward another debate arising out of the same dilemma of myth versus logic. The 'Athrabeth Finrod ah Andreth', which Christopher included in *Morgoth's Ring*, is the debate between Finrod (an Elf) and Andreth (a human woman) – with occasional help from her ancestress Adanel – about the necessity for death, hitherto provided as the 'gift of Eru/Ilúvatar' to his race of Men. But unlike Tolkien's earlier debate with himself, this was a dialogue played out in the theatre of his imagination, using as mouthpieces an Elf and a human who argue about their perceptions and misconceptions regarding the designs of their creator. Of all of Tolkien's late writings, the 'Athrabeth' is the most perplexing to understand and the most problematic from which to draw any conclusions, predicated as it is on an unresolved argument and dependent for its power entirely on opposing points of view – the Mannish as over against the Elvish version. If this sounds familiar, there's a good reason. Christopher conjecturally dates its composition to 1959 and nestles it among the late 1950s writings that included 'Myths Transformed' (*Morgoth* 304, 369), together with which it is paired in the volume.

For those looking for a message in Tolkien's work, the 'Athrabeth' has something for everyone, for here we see Tolkien arguing all sides at once, playing a kind of writerly hide-and-seek, dodging in and out among conflicting opinions, teasing his reader with unsubtle allusions to Christianity in one breath and questioning them in the next. Using circumstantial evidence – it was written on a new typewriter and preserved folded in newspapers of January 1960 (*Morgoth* 304) – Christopher conjecturally dates its writing to 1959, the epicenter of Tolkien's revisionist period and its most extreme representation. It can be seen as something like Tolkien's *Rashomon*, an exercise in point of view wherein the object is not to arrive at 'truth' but, by showing how differing perceptions may color the same phenomena, to undermine the notion that a single truth can be arrived at. In this case, the phenomenon is death, and it is clear that in spite of his subdivision of species into Men and Elves, and his statements in the *Letters* about death and deathlessness, Tolkien had not entirely resolved to his own satisfaction the ultimate human question – *why* do we die? As an Elf, Finrod is certain that death is Iluvatar's gift not to be questioned. The human woman Andreth thinks it is that same god-figure's punishment for which she is angry and resentful. To the 'wise-woman' Adanel it is a mystery, a 'voice out of the dark', which is the ultimate cop-out and the only answer that covers all the bases. Having had Finrod ask the final question: "What did ye do, ye Men [to anger Eru]?" (*Morgoth* 313), Tolkien threw in the towel and finally admitted that the 'Athrabeth' was "too like a parody of Christianity" (*Morgoth* 354).

A final question to be answered loops back to the phrase that provides my title and to the attendant decision that was Christopher's in deciding to publish what his father had not. Have Tolkien's revisions, radical as they are, been "a fearful weapon" against his own creation? And if they have, how has the perception of that creation changed since the publication of *Morgoth's Ring* in 1993? Has Tolkien's weapon destroyed his imaginary world? My answer would have to be a qualified 'yes'. 'Yes' because we cannot pretend the changes do not exist. Middle-earth can no longer claim to be the actual Old World of this planet without acknowledgment of the changes Tolkien implemented to actually make it so, changes which validated the science even as they ruined the Faërie. 'Qualified' because readers can still make a choice, still choose the old over the new and ignore the reversal of *Morgoth's Ring* as an aberration. We can still re-visit *The Lord of the Rings* with something of the same old pleasure (though the Jackson films have skewed its values, still more the Amazon series), but its presumed background in the parent myth of *The Silmarillion* has been at the least tarnished, at the worst called into question, while textual references to the earlier stories may no longer have the same power to illuminate. The mythological ground has shifted, and the arc of the story has literally come down to earth – or to geology – where we land with a thud at an uneasy destination to which we hadn't planned to arrive, looking around us for a road we can follow that will still go ever on.

'The Lost Road' and 'The Notion Club Papers': Myth, History, and Time-travel

Although they are usually regarded as secondary works, lesser addenda to his *legendarium* and therefore relatively little studied, J.R.R. Tolkien's two unfinished time-travel stories, 'The Notion Club Papers' and its precursor, 'The Lost Road', occupy a unique and important place in his canon. This is not just because they are science fiction rather than the fantasy for which he is known but also because they cross boundaries of time and space, their action taking place half in the present and half in the past, half in the 'real' and half in the fantasy world. While 'The Notion Club Papers' is so drastic a revision of 'The Lost Road' as to be in effect a completely new story; nevertheless, the two are in some ways interdependent, expressing the same ideas and following in intention if not in execution the same concepts of serial identity and inherited memory. Both stories, together with their accompanying notes and outlines, have been edited and published by Christopher Tolkien in his *History of Middle-earth* series, 'The Lost Road' in 1987 in volume 5 (*The Lost Road*) and 'The Notion Club Papers' in 1992 in volume 9 (*Sauron Defeated*).

The stories are important for several interrelated reasons. First, they mark the introduction into his *legendarium* of the downfall of the island nation of Númenor, Tolkien's Atlantis.[1] The drowning of Númenor altered the geology, politics, and history of Tolkien's imaginary world, changing its shape from flat to round and giving its history a line of kings culminating in Aragorn, son of

1 While Atlantis is the best known, it is far from the only mythic account of the drowning of a land mass Tolkien might have encountered. The country of Lyonesse, a locale of some of the Arthurian Tristan material, was said to have sunk beneath the sea near what are now the Scilly Isles. The Kingdom of Ys in Brittany, ruled over by King Gradlon, was submerged under the sea when the King's daughter, Dahut, stole the key to the city and gave it to the devil. A violent storm sent waves over the city, entirely submerging it. Ireland, too, has its tradition of a great wave, the *tonn*, which periodically sweeps over the shore and far inland. The latter portions of Part Two of 'The Notion Club Papers' have Lowdham and Jeremy in Ireland, where they hear stories of a ghostly black wave that swept over the land on the night of the Oxford storm, reaching as far inland as Clonfert, the traditional home of St. Brendan.

Arathorn, Isildur's son, heir of Elendil. A second point of importance about the stories is that they connect Tolkien's mythology for England to aspects of his personal life. Third, but no less important, between the two of them, the stories supply an elaborate, highly structured framing mechanism to account for the transmission of his storied history from the deep past of his *legendarium* to his own time and place. And fourth, they offer in the King Sheave episode the first hard evidence that Tolkien meant to attach actual myths/legends to his invented one. That other such evidence has now come to light reinforces the place of these stories in the Tolkien canon. The web of relationships among these elements is complex, and over the years, as he worked on his so-called mythology for England, the strands crossed and recrossed in often confusing ways as Tolkien's ideas developed and proliferated.

Númenor: The Missing Link

The whole enterprise began with a friendly yet challenging bargain between two old friends and colleagues. As recounted by Tolkien (*Letters* 209, 342, 347, 378), the genesis of the time-travel idea was a coin-toss between himself and C.S. Lewis, conjecturally dated by Christopher Tolkien to circa 1936-1937 (*LR* 7-8). Agreeing that there was not enough of their favorite kind of reading (fantasy and science fiction), Tolkien and Lewis decided to write more themselves and did a heads-or-tails to see which should take space-travel and which time-travel. Lewis got space travel, promptly packed his hero into a spaceship and sent him off to Mars, and a scant two years after the bargain, published his story as *Out of the Silent Planet*, the first book of his so-called Space Trilogy.

Tolkien got time-travel and found a more psychological and credible way to take his protagonists from one time to another. He wrote four chapters in which a present-day English father and son called Alboin and Audoin Errol dreamed their way back through time from modern-day Cornwall to his newly invented prehistoric Númenor, where they reappeared as Elendil and Herendil. Tolkien intended Númenor to be the "missing link" between the Elder Days of his mythology and the Age of Men (*Letters* 232). He described it as his "personal alteration of the Atlantis myth and/or tradition, and accommodation of it to my general mythology" (*Letters* 361). The idea was by a regression through receding time of ever-earlier dreams to bridge the gap between the England of Tolkien's own time and the Middle-earth of his imaginary past.

Simple enough in synopsis, the idea was complex in its concept and would have been (had Tolkien ever finished it) equally complex in execution. As he described 'The Lost Road' in 1964:

> The thread was to be the occurrence time and again in human families [...] of a father and son called by names that could be interpreted as Bliss-friend and Elf-friend [...] It started with a father-son affinity between Edwin and Elwin of the present, and was supposed to go back into legendary time by way of an Eädwine and Ælfwine of circa A.D. 918, and Audoin and Alboin of Lombardic legend, and so to the traditions of the North Sea concerning the coming of corn and culture heroes [...] In my tale we were to come at last to Amandil and Elendil leaders of the loyal party in Númenor, [...]. (*Letters* 347)

While the notion of a sequence of dreams seems to have been Tolkien's own, his use of dream as a vehicle for time-travel was in a literary tradition popular in the late nineteenth and early twentieth centuries. Salient examples are Charles Dickens's *A Christmas Carol* (1843), Edward Bellamy's *Looking Backward* (1887), William Morris's *A Dream of John Ball* (1888) and his *News From Nowhere* (1890), and Mark Twain's *A Connecticut Yankee at King Arthur's Court* (1889). In 1891, the year before Tolkien was born, George Du Maurier's *Peter Ibbetson* told a story of lovers separated in real life who travel together through time in their dreams.

In 1935, the year just preceding the coin-toss, Tolkien had read with interest J.W. Dunne's *An Experiment With Time*, a nonfiction work which proposed time as a field-like space where an observer in a dream state can move in any direction. Dunne's ideas influenced a generation of English writers from J.B. Priestley to Rumer Godden to Tolkien.

The elaborateness of Tolkien's 'thread' concept may be one reason the story was abandoned, but another reason must surely have been the looming publication of *The Hobbit*, followed almost immediately by Tolkien's start on the 'new

Hobbit' that turned into the time-consuming *The Lord of the Rings*. Whatever his reasons for breaking off work on the project, it lay fallow for another eight years. Tolkien picked it up again in late 1944, writing to his publisher that he had "in a fortnight of comparative leisure round about last Christmas written three parts of another book, taking up in an entirely different frame and setting what little had any value in the inchoate *Lost Road*" (*Letters* 118). Thus, the time-travel idea got a new lease on life as 'The Notion Club Papers' with the same purpose of bridging the gap between Tolkien's imaginary past and his own time. But after a promising start, it too was abandoned, probably because as Tolkien wrote to his publisher, he was "putting *The Lord of the Rings* [...] before all else" (*SD* 145).

The plots of both stories (in so far as they are written) seem simple enough. In each, a pair of modern-day Englishmen, deeply interested in both myth and travel through time, experience increasingly intense flashes of extra-personal memory connected to their long-ago Middle-earth avatars and ancestors. These flashes of memory contain scattered bits of information, scraps of unknown languages, incomplete accounts of some great disaster. Narrative style differs from story to story. 'The Lost Road' is related through a straightforward third-person narrative. 'The Notion Club Papers' are couched as the minutes of Notion Club meetings reported in the first person by the Club's recorder and thereby acquire an immediacy which 'The Lost Road' lacks. The fact that both stories break off just as the main action, the time-journey, gets underway makes it difficult to imagine just how Tolkien might have planned to bring either story to a satisfactory close.

While the dream mechanism is less overt in 'The Notion Club Papers' than in 'The Lost Road', modern Englishmen were to enter Tolkien's imaginary world in both stories. As Tolkien handles it, the time-travel device moves characters and readers, often violently, between his twentieth-century England and the fictional prehistoric world of his mythology with no advance notice and with no perceptible transition. His use of serial memory to achieve this seems more psychological or even psychic than science fictional.

The opening two chapters of 'The Lost Road' take place in an unspecified present, which is clearly Tolkien's own time, and a specific place, Cornwall, which is unabashedly Tolkien's own Britain. There live Oswin and Alboin Errol, a father and son with a strong interest in history, languages, and the history of languages. Opportunity for confusion arises here, as, having introduced one father and son pair, Tolkien then passes the torch to the following generation. Oswin dies, and the new father-son pair, Alboin Errol and his son Audoin, take over, as in Tolkien's description cited above. As both Alboin and Audoin fall asleep, the story jumps from the Errols in modern Cornwall to Elendil and Herendil (not Amandil as in Tolkien's description) in Tolkien's Númenor.

There are hints that the times overlap. We are told that, since childhood, Alboin has had the desire "to go back. To walk in Timc, pcrhaps, as mcn walk on long roads" (*LR* 45). But the connection between past and present seems narratively remote. Alboin has dream conversations with a shadowy figure who reminds him of his father but who announces himself as Elendil and who tells him he may have his desire "to go back" (*LR* 48). The closest the story gets to what is clearly intended as the denouement, the Downfall of Númenor, is when Alboin falls asleep saying "There is storm over Númenor" (*LR* 51) and the closest to actual time-travel when he says later "We start when the summons comes" (*LR* 53).

Although 'The Lost Road' must be credited with getting Tolkien started on time-travel, he later apologized to his publisher for sending him a draft, noting, "I hope it is forgotten" (*SD* 145). He was probably right in that the playing out of the thread would have resulted in an overlong series of flashbacks, a cumbersome, step-by-step transition such as is handled more efficiently in films by dissolve. In the 'The Notion Club Papers', Tolkien went further, making his real-world events take place in his own Oxford but at two specific periods in the future of his own time, 1980-1990 and 2012.

Nevertheless, 'The Lost Road' is important for contributing to the concept of the 'The Notion Club Papers' (Englishmen traveling into a fictive past) and mechanism (dream as a vehicle). Tolkien's interim writing experience – he was "'on the last chapters' of *The Lord of the Rings*" (*SD* 13) – materially improved his craft so that 'The Notion Club Papers' is a more skillful piece of work than its predecessor. While the 'The Lost Road' father-son thread is not wholly abandoned in 'The Notion Club Papers', it is relegated to the back-story, and the reclusive, philologically inclined Errols in Cornwall are replaced by a larger, more variegated cast of characters. The Notion Club members are friends and colleagues who drink, joke, argue, carouse (occasionally breaking furniture), and give no quarter in debate. They are voluble, opinionated, analytical, passionate, fond of wordplay, and given to outrageous puns. In their own scholarly way, they are a rowdy bunch. Their dialogue, caught on the hoof as it were, has the immediacy, the energetic give-and-take, the bite of actual speech.

While they are presented as contemporary Englishmen, the major characters are, like those of 'The Lost Road', avatars of their Númenórean forebears as well. But more so than in 'The Lost Road', the balance between the periods is uneven. The energy of the story and the force of the narrative lie far more in the modern characters and their interactions than in their Númenórean avatars. This is partly because the Númenórean episodes are barely sketched, hardly more than intrusions into the present-day narrative but also because the modern Englishmen are livelier and more interesting than their Middle-earth counterparts.

As in 'The Lost Road', the island nation of Númenor is the terminus of the time-travel. Its drowning in a geological catastrophe is the event which was to change the direction of Tolkien's mythology, reshape his world from flat to round, alter its relationship to its god-figures the Valar, and provide the quasi-theological concept of the Straight Road to Valinor, best known as the path taken by Frodo's ship as it sails down the Firth of Lune. Coincident with each time travel story is a separately written account of this catastrophe. For 'The Lost Road', it is 'The Fall of Númenor'; for the 'The Notion Club Papers', it is 'The Drowning of Anadûnë'. Both stand in a similar relationship to the better known 'Akallabêth', published in *Unfinished Tales*. 'The Drowning of

Anadûnë' also introduced a new language, Adûnaic,[2] which apparently entered the *legendarium* with Part Two of 'The Notion Club Papers' comparatively late in the development of the mythology.

Strongly Biographical Elements

Christopher Tolkien has noted the presence of "strongly biographical" elements in 'The Lost Road', which were "closely modelled" on his father's own life (*LR* 53). These include the academic career and linguistic interests of one of the characters, Alboin. There are also biographical elements in 'The Notion Club Papers', but the references are on two different planes, one social and one psychological. The Notion Club is modeled on Tolkien's own informal Oxford club of the Inklings (Inkling = Notion). Early drafts of 'The Notion Club Papers' show Tolkien assigning (and reassigning) specific Inkling identities to specific Notion Club characters. C.S. Lewis was first 'Ramer' and then 'Frankley'. Tolkien also was 'Ramer' at one point, but he too was changed, in this case to 'Latimer', before finally emerging as 'Guildford', who not by accident is the Club's recorder and thus the author of the minutes of the meetings which make up 'The Notion Club Papers'.

Hugo Dyson seems consistently to have been the model for 'Lowdham', and Humphrey Havard was 'Dolbear'. But this preliminary casting was almost certainly modified and ultimately receded as the fictional characters developed

2 Adûnaic, from all accounts the last of Tolkien's invented languages to be developed, is part of the strongly linguistic course of thought which runs through Part Two of 'The Notion Club Papers', and which is almost entirely missing from 'The Lost Road'. The concept of memory of unknown language is derived from Tolkien's idea of native language, by which he means language inherited through birth, as opposed to cradle tongue, by which he means language learned in infancy. In Part One of 'The Notion Club Papers', Ramer voices this theory, explaining to the Club that everyone has a native language (*SD* 201). Tolkien returned to the idea in his 1962 O'Donnell Lecture 'English and Welsh' (published in 1963), where he maintained that "We each have [...] a native language. But that is not the language that we speak, our cradle-tongue." He went on to emphasize, in words very like Ramer's, "the difference between the first-learned language, the language of custom, and an individual's native language, his inherent linguistic predilection" (*MC* 190). This is the premise behind Alboin Errol's dreams of what he calls Eresseän or Elf-Latin (the few quoted words of which are Quenya and Sindarin). In similar fashion, Lowdham in 'The Notion Club Papers' first dreams of individual words and then gets fragments of a text in two languages and makes copies which he shares with the Club shouting, "More than mere words. Verbs! Syntax at last" (*SD* 246). These fragments he identifies as Avallonian (Quenya) and Adûnaic, which he speculates are "passages out of some book" (*SD* 248). For further information on Adûnaic, see "Lowdham's report on the Adûnaic Language" and Christopher's following note (*SD* 413-40).

a life of their own. In any case, in the earliest draft, what Christopher Tolkien calls manuscript A, Tolkien addressed a 'Preface to the Inklings' in which he both acknowledged and disclaimed intended resemblances to real persons, for "the mirror is cracked", and the countenances "distorted", with "noses and other features" distributed without attribution (*SD* 148-49). And it may be that what Tolkien was drawing on was as much a dynamic of speech and social interaction as of specific character per se.

It is through the concept of the destruction of Númenor that more autobiographical reference enters the story. Unsurprisingly for Tolkien, this is conveyed through names and the meanings of names. It begins in 'The Lost Road', whose father and son pairings – Alboin (Ælfwine, 'Elf-friend') and Audoin (Eädwine, 'Bliss-friend') – include grandfather Oswin (Anglo-Saxon for 'God-friend'). The 'friend' component is the chief autobiographical clue, for it is echoed in the names in Tolkien's own family. Tolkien's father, Arthur, Tolkien himself, and all four of his children have as a middle name Reuel, a Hebrew name which means 'friend' or 'God-friend'. The parallel between Tolkien's fictive grandfather-father-son thread with names containing the 'friend' element – God-friend, Elf-friend, Bliss-friend – and a similar 'friend' name passed from grandfather to father to son in his own family is too striking to be accidental.

The destruction of Númenor also carries an autobiographical reference, this one more deeply personal and psychological, perhaps even psychic. In several of his letters, Tolkien describes a recurrent dream, which he called his "Atlantis complex", or "Atlantis-haunting", and which he characterized as a "dim memory of some ancient history" (*Letters* 347). This was of being inundated by a Great Wave, which swept over him and threatened to drown him and from which he awoke "gasping, out of deep water" (*Letters* 347). It was the inspiration for his island nation of Númenor, which exists (apparently) only so it can be destroyed in an oceanic cataclysm that changes the shape of the world. The dream was "Possibly inherited," he wrote to W.H. Auden, "though my parents died too young to transfer such things by words. Inherited from me (I suppose) by only one of my children [his second son, Michael, *Letters* 445 n.163], though I did not know that about my son until recently, and he did not know it about me" (*Letters* 213).

In a draft of a letter to a Mr. Thompson, he repeated the story: "That vision and dream has been ever with me – and has been inherited (as I only discovered recently) by one of my children" (*Letters* 232).

Possibly inherited by Tolkien from his parents. Inherited from him by one of his children. Two instances for certain and a conjectural third of inherited memory in one family, memory across (perhaps) three generations of an event that none of the dreamers, apparently, had experienced in real life. It is no great stretch to imagine that Tolkien might have wanted to believe not only that he had inherited as well as passed on the dream but that it was in fact "the dim memory of some ancient history," an actual event. If this were indeed the case, it would underpin his structural concept of the familial father-son thread by which he proposed to bring his prehistoric mythology into his modern-day England. In any event, he seems to have got it out of his mind by writing it into his fiction, releasing, as he wrote in a letter, "some hidden 'complex'" (*Letters* 232), "now exorcised by writing about it" (*Letters* 347). "I don't think I have had it [the dream]," he wrote to Auden in 1944, "since I wrote the 'Downfall of Númenor' as the last of the legends of the First and Second Age" (*Letters* 213).

While this is persuasive evidence for the link between life and art, it is circumstantial evidence and raises questions about just how to connect the dots. The letters in which Tolkien talks about the dream are obviously later than the time of the discovery itself, but how much later is unknown, and 'recently' is too vague a term on which to posit a coherent sequence. Tolkien's discovery that his son had the same dream may have come before or after he introduced Atlantis and the dreaming fathers and sons into the story. There is no way to know. His speculation that he may have inherited it from his father is just that, which may be why the first-generation figures in both stories, Oswin in 'The Lost Road' and Edwin in 'The Notion Club Papers', have little or no role in the actual time-travel.

Autobiographical reference does not stop here. 'The Lost Road' grandfather, Oswin, is replaced in 'The Notion Club Papers' by father Edwin (Eädwine, Audoin), who is Alwyn (Ælfwine, Elendil) Lowdham's father. (The pattern of proliferating and overlapping names is part of what makes Tolkien's underlying concept so difficult to sort out). Edwin Lowdham, a voyager who disappears at sea and who has no role in the action, is the apparent source for a mysterious page in "Númenorean script" dropped by Lowdham at the end of one meeting. It turns out to be a translation of the Adûnaic account of the Fall of Númenor. To compound the autobiographical references, the translation is identified by "old Professor Rashbold at Pembroke" as "Old English of a strongly Mercian (West Midland) colour" (*SD* 256). Now Rashbold, as Tolkien trivia experts know, was Tolkien's translation of the German form of his own surname, *toll* 'rash, foolhardy' and *kühn* 'keen, eager, bold', while his first faculty position at Oxford, Rawlinson and Bosworth Professor of Anglo-Saxon, was attached to Pembroke College. He has allowed himself a cameo appearance in his own fiction, no doubt thoroughly enjoying the inside joke.

The Frame is Part of the Picture

Part One of 'The Notion Club Papers', subtitled 'The Ramblings of Ramer', is a largely theoretical discussion of framing devices for space-travel, a topic of lively debate. How you get to the unknown planet must be of a piece with the rest of the story and indeed an integral part of the story. H.G. Wells's time-machine and gravitation-insulator, David Lindsay's 'back-rays', and C.S. Lewis's crystal torpedo are all roundly criticized as being poorly integrated, unbelievable contraptions, ill-fitting frames for the story they contain. Guildford actually says at one point in the argument that in "normal probability" the only means for landing on a new planet is "by being born" (*SD* 170). In view of the transmission of the 'Great Wave' memory from generation to generation already discussed, it does not take a great leap of imagination to suppose that Tolkien might have thought "being born" would work just as well for landing in a new time.

In addition to drawing on actual characters to provide verisimilitude, Tolkien gave the story an elaborate, multi-frame design to impart a sense of reality to what is, in fact, fantasy. The central and most fantastic episode, the actual travel backward in time, is nested within the minutes, kept by Nicholas Guildford, of the fictive but realistic Notion Club. These minutes, in turn, are framed as a bundle of papers discovered in the basement of the Oxford Examination Schools by a Mr. Howard Green and edited by him. The whole is then presented as published in a 'Second Edition' with history, notes, and editorial commentary by J.R. Titmass, a historian, W.W. Wormald, a "Bibliopolist", and D.N. Borrow, a linguist. 'The Notion Club Papers' thus belong to the found manuscript genre of fantasy and science fiction, a tradition that stretches from H. Rider Haggard's *She* to Margaret Atwood's *The Handmaid's Tale.* The fact that 'The Notion Club Papers' are the minutes of fictitious meetings and thus spread over a sequence of numbered nights, gives Tolkien some leeway. He has less to develop a plot than to chart the progress of an argument.

As edited by Christopher Tolkien, the narrative falls into two parts. Part One is dominated by Michael Ramer, Part Two by Arundel Lowdham and Wilfred Jeremy. All three are well-realized personalities, psychologically and psychically complex, with hidden and largely unsuspected depths. There are supporting characters Philip Frankley and Rufus Dolbear, plus a cast of minor club members, bit players who complicate discussion but do not affect the action. The narrative opens with a discussion of Ramer's just-read (but not included) story. This provokes a discussion of 'frame', the device by which a story is carried from one place or time to another, specifically in this context, how science fiction (their word is 'scientifiction', a term introduced in 1926 by Hugo Gernsback, publisher of *Amazing Stories, The Magazine of Scientifiction*) manages travel from one planet to another. Forced by the club to defend himself, Ramer acknowledges the clumsiness of his framing device. It is this that brings on the discussion of vehicles for both time- and space-travel and results in the Club's criticism of Wells's time machine. Commanded by Dolbear to 'come clean', Ramer reveals that the story is an account of his actual, self-induced and controlled dream wanderings to other, apparently extra-terrestrial worlds.

This sets the stage for Part Two of 'The Notion Club Papers', subtitled 'The Strange Case of Arundel Lowdham'. Here, Tolkien gets down to business, and the conversation turns from space-travel to time-travel. Time-travel leads to history and history leads to myth and the point where they intersect. Lowdham has increasingly intense flashbacks to what appears to be Númenor, in which he curses 'Zigūr' (the Adûnaic name for Sauron). He also has dreams of Númenor, and more particularly of strange languages, which he calls A and B, or Avallonian (Quenya) and Adûnaic. While Adûnaic appears to be a name of Tolkien's own invention, Avallonian cannot but recall to lovers of myth the Avalon of Arthurian legend. Tolkien's connection of Avalon with Númenor suggests a deliberate linking of the invented myth with the actual one, about which more anon.

In the course of one night's discussion, Jeremy raises the question: "If you went back [in time] would you find myth dissolving into history or history into myth? [...] Perhaps," he suggests, "the Atlantis catastrophe was the dividing line?" (*SD* 249). 'The Notion Club Papers' suggest that Tolkien's answer is 'yes'. With the 'Atlantis catastrophe', his dream of the great wave as an inherited dim memory enters the story, and his fictive mythology joins his personal, therefore his contemporary, history. Lowdham and Jeremy are gradually revealed (first to the reader and then to themselves) as avatars, direct descendants, and psychic and psychological reincarnations of Númenórean figures in Tolkien's own mythology. In the course of one night's discussion, they are overtaken and engulfed by a sudden, unexpected storm of terrifying proportions, and we are to understand that it is happening simultaneously in Oxford and Númenor and that it is, in fact, the Drowning of Anadûnë. They are possessed by their Númenórean identities of Nimruzīr (the Adûnaic form of Anglo-Saxon Ælfwine) and Abrazān (the Adûnaic form of Anglo-Saxon Tréowine).

It is this night's discussion, storm, and crisis of identity that precipitate the actual time travel. Interestingly, however, Tolkien inverts the process, and instead of the characters moving into past time, a past event (the destruction of Númenor) erupts into their present lives, and their past identities take charge of their present selves. In a sort of waking dream, the two men go on an extended search for more information, relying for guidance on their dreams. When they return, Lowdham narrates one such dream experience to the Club, a first-person account in his atavistic persona of Ælfwine, of the mythic story of King Sheave.

So powerful is the spell Tolkien casts that when Lowdham ends the story with the words "And with that, I think I must end for tonight," and returns to his Oxford self (*SD* 276), the reader is startled by the abrupt transition, pulled suddenly out of the world of myth into the everyday. Unfortunately, it is here that all too soon and all too frustratingly, the narrative breaks off, forcing the reader to make another abrupt transition from the world of the Notion Club to the realization that this too is a story.

The introduction of King Sheave attaches tradition to invention and links a pre-historic, English culture hero to Tolkien's own mythos. With Christopher Tolkien's publication of Tolkien's unfinished *The Fall of Arthur* (2013), new material has come to light suggesting that this is not the only such attempt and reinforcing the concept.

An Arthurian Ending

Christopher Tolkien's edition of *The Fall of Arthur* includes his father's outline for the end of the poem, which among other things, sends Arthur into a West that strongly recalls Tolkien's own mythos. It is not hard to see a parallel between the 'undying land' of Valinor and the Isle of Avalon, where legend has it Arthur was taken to be healed of his wounds. Tolkien himself described the departure of Bilbo and the wounded Frodo from Middle-earth to Valinor as "an Arthurian ending" (*SD* 132). *The Fall of Arthur* outline extends that ending farther by having Lancelot follow Arthur into the West, as some "hastily penciled notes" (*FA* 136) show. The key passage is as follows: "Lancelot parts from Guinevere and sets sail for Benwick but turns west and follows after Arthur. And never returns from the sea. Whether he found him in Avalon and will return no one knows" (*FA* 137).

This is not just a departure from the traditional story but the co-option of an existing legend into an invented one. Arthur's and Lancelot's departure becomes part of the westward trajectory of Tolkien's own mythology. Among what Christopher describes as "tantalizing notes" are the isolated words "Eärendel passage" identified by Christopher as the "separate sheet of alliterative verse in typescript" (*FA* 136) which accompanies the notes. He gives it in full:

> The moon mounted the mists of the sea,
> and quivering in the cold the keen starlight
> that wavered in the waiting East
> failed and faded; the foam upon the shore
> was glimmering ghostly on the grey shingle,
> and the roaring of the sea rose in darkness
> to the watchers on the wall.

O! wondrous night
when shining like the moon, with shrouds of pearl,
with sails of samite, and the silver stars
on her blue banner embroidered white
in glittering gems, that galleon was thrust
on the shadowy seas under shades of night!
Eärendel goeth on eager quest
to magic islands beyond the miles of the sea,
past the hills of Avalon and the halls of the moon,
the dragon's portals and the dark mountains
of the Bay of Faery on the borders of the world. (*FA* 137-38)

"In these lines," writes Christopher, "my father was expressly introducing elements of the mythical geography of the First Age of the World as originally described in *The Book of Lost Tales*, but which largely survived into much later texts of 'The Silmarillion'" (*FA* 157). Christopher goes on to acknowledge his father's "deliberate and substantial evocation of a cardinal myth of his own 'world', the great voyage of Eärendel to Valinor, in relation to Sir Lancelot of Arthurian legend" (*FA* 160). He writes further that "it seems at least very probable that 'Avalon' here bears the meaning 'Tol Eressëa', [...]. If this is so, then where my father wrote in a 'Silmarillion' context that *Tol Eressëa* was renamed *Avallon*, he also wrote *Avalon* for *Tol Eressëa* in an Arthurian context" (*FA* 161). Christopher concludes:

> It seems then, that the Arthurian *Avalon*, the Fortunate Isle, *Insula Pomorum*, the dominion of Morgan la Fée, had now been in some mysterious sense identified with Tol Eressëa, the Lonely Isle. But the name *Avallon* entered, as a name of Tol Eressëa, at the time when the Fall of Númenor and the Change of the World entered also [...], with the conception of the Straight Path out of the Round World that still led to Tol Eressëa and Valinor, a road that was denied to mortals, and yet found, in a mystery, by Ælfwine of England. (*FA* 162-63)

In both his Arthur and his King Sheave treatments, Tolkien challenges the hegemony of powerful predecessors – the *Beowulf* poet, whose opening lines about Scyld Scefing invoke the Sheave figure and the preeminent Arthurian Sir Thomas Malory, whose Arthur sails to Avalon to be healed. As with the King Sheave episode in 'The Notion Club Papers', Tolkien's Arthur notes leave us hanging, unsure of where the story is going or what is meant to happen. But we may with some confidence rely on Christopher's own statement from

The Lost Road that at this stage in his father's development of his mythos, he intended it to absorb, or at least conjoin with, some elements of existing legend:

> With the entry at this time [the 1936 'Lost Road'] of the cardinal ideas of the Downfall of Númenor, the World Made Round, and the Straight Road, into the conception of 'Middle-earth', and the thought of a 'time-travel' story in which the very significant figure of the Anglo-Saxon Ælfwine would be both 'extended' into the future, into the twentieth century, and 'extended' also into a many-layered past, my father was envisaging a massive and explicit linking of his own legends with those of many other places and times: all concerned with the stories and dreams of peoples who dwelt by the coasts of the great Western Sea. All this was set aside during the period of the writing of *The Lord of the Rings*, but not abandoned: for in 1945, before indeed *The Lord of the Rings* was completed, he returned to these themes in the unfinished *Notion Club Papers*. (*LR* 98)

In assessing how or even whether Tolkien might have gone on to assimilate Arthurian legend directly into his own *legendarium*, we should keep in mind that the notes and ancillary verses are the fallout, not the final vision. Christopher's word for them is 'tantalizing'. Unlike the King Sheave episode in 'The Notion Club Papers', the Arthurian references are hints, not direct treatment. To be sure, there are Arthurian echoes in 'The Notion Club Papers': Frankley makes explicit references to Camelot, and one of Lowdham's dream-languages is Avallonian, an unmistakable gesture to Arthur's Avalon as it appears in Geoffrey and Malory. But that is as far as Tolkien went, for both 'The Notion Club Papers' and *The Fall of Arthur* are unfinished. The Arthurian ending was finally given to Frodo in *The Lord of the Rings*.

Two projected continuations (carried over and fleshed out from 'The Lost Road') of the King Sheave episode close the last recorded meeting of the Notion Club. Lowdham/Ælfwine and Jeremy/Tréowine set out to sea and sail West. Both continuations bring the voyagers to the Straight Road, but their ship is driven back by a storm. The sketches break off there, with an outline following:

> Tréowine [Jeremy] sees the straight Road and the world plunging down. Ælfwine's [Lowdham's] vessel seems to be taking the straight Road and falls [sic] in a swoon of fear and exhaustion.
>
> > Ælfwine gets view of the Book of Stories; and writes down what he can remember.
> > Later fleeting visions.
> > Beleriand tale.
> > Sojourn in Númenor before and during the fall ends with *Elendil*

> [Lowdham] and *Voronwë* [Jeremy] fleeing on a hill of water into the dark with Eagles and lightning pursuing them. Elendil has a book which he has written.
> His descendants get glimpses of it.
> Ælfwine has one. (*SD* 279)

Also among Tolkien's notes is a single enigmatic scrap of paper which reads simply: "Do the Atlantis story and abandon Eriol-Saga, with Loudham, Jeremy, Guildford and Ramer taking part" (*SD* 281). Cryptic though it is, the note may be the best clue to what at this point Tolkien intended – not just for 'The Notion Club Papers', which is clearly "the Atlantis story" in which "Loudham, Jeremy, Guildford and Ramer" are principal characters – but for the shape of his entire mythology. The "Eriol-Saga" was the 'Silmarillion' mythology "for England," a work in progress from 1917 until *The Hobbit* interrupted it in the mid-1930s and then *The Lord of the Rings* in the late 1930s and 1940s. Tolkien's mythology was framed as tales told by the Elves (at first called 'Fairies') to a voyager (compare Edwin Lowdham) named Eriol or Ælfwine, who carries them from Valinor back to what will become England. Christopher Tolkien has proposed that "the Eriol-Saga had been, up to this time, what my father had in mind for the further course of the meetings of the Notion Club, but was now rejecting in favour of 'Atlantis'" (*SD* 282).

Another possibility is that Tolkien was not rejecting the Eriol-Saga outright but was considering attaching one frame story to another, joining the Eriol-Saga to the Atlantis story (the drowning of Númenor) by way of 'The Notion Club Papers', much as Jeremy suggested that myth might blend into history with Atlantis as the dividing line. There is no way to know just how Tolkien might have planned for Lowdham, Jeremy, Guildford, and Ramer to take part, though we may speculate that he intended some sort of time-travel for all of them. Nevertheless, in the context of this note, the outline cited above, the "Book of Stories", Elendil's book, and the fact that "Ælfwine has" a copy of it, must be seen not just as Tolkien's description of an imaginative concept, but as his envisioning of the prototype credibility device for the whole mythological conceit. All this makes 'The Notion Club Papers' a bridge by which his imagined prehistoric mythology, connected by time-travel to the Notion Club, would be brought forward in time by the discovery and publication of its minutes by Mr. Howard Green.

A Mythology for England

Dreaming fathers and sons, inherited memory, Atlantis turned into Númenor, a story passed down through time, echoes of Avalon – all this does much to explain Tolkien's otherwise seemingly arbitrary choice of Atlantis-Númenor. He was basing this part of his mythology directly on his own experience. And although the execution may be over-complex, the basic idea is clear enough. Thus, these time-travel stories, first 'The Lost Road' and second, and more significantly, 'The Notion Club Papers', have a formative role in Tolkien's mythology and are crucial to our understanding of it. Tolkien's proposal to "do the Atlantis story" would not just bring his mythology into the present; it would, in effect, start it off there.

The contemporary time-travel stories, written in a style closer to that of a modern novel than mythic history, were to be the frame for his whole mythology for England, which would then be English because its modern English protagonists were connected by inherited memory to their Númenórean ancestors. It would cross the "dividing line" (*SD* 249) between myth and history by means of the "book" of which Elendil's "descendants get glimpses" (*SD* 279) and of which Ælfwine has a copy and which, if the conceit of transmission via time-travel had been carried through to its conclusion, would have become part of 'The Notion Club Papers', which the modern reader would then have in hand. The page of West Mercian Anglo-Saxon transcribed (from Elendil's book?) in Númenórean script and narrating the drowning of Númenor would be evidence of the transition from myth to history.

It is clear, therefore, that although they stand a little to one side, as it were, of Tolkien's major mythological works, *The Silmarillion* and *The Lord of the Rings*, nonetheless, 'The Lost Road' and 'The Notion Club Papers' deserve serious attention as significant elements in Tolkien's Middle-earth canon. They changed the shape of his world, and without them there would be no Elendil, no Isildur, and no Aragorn as we know him. The notes and outlines of 'The Lost Road' give us the clearest view of Tolkien's overall vision, while 'The Notion Club Papers' contain some of Tolkien's most vigorous writing as well as some of his most deeply felt insights into the workings of the human psyche. That both stories, but most especially 'The Notion Club Papers', stopped short of final resolution may turn out to be one of the greater losses, not just to the reader pulled so unexpectedly out of "King Sheave", but also to Tolkien's whole vision. Had 'The Notion Club Papers' been completed, it would have provided a rounding out and summing up that might have successfully brought up to date the mythology for England he began in 1917.

This was not to be. After *The Lord of the Rings*, the overarching concept of stories told, heard, written down, and carried forward was transferred to the 'Red Book' and its attendant volumes of Elvish lore. These were then conceived as a compendium of the 'Silmarillion' tales, *The Hobbit*, and *The Lord of the Rings* as collected by Bilbo, completed by Sam and Frodo, passed from Brandybuck father to son, carried to Gondor, transcribed by "Findegil, King's Writer", stored in Minas Tirith (*FR*, 'Prologue' 19-20), and finally – as the Cirth and Tengwar running header and footer to the titlepage of *The Lord of the Rings* tell us – translated into English by J.R.R. Tolkien. His identification of himself with Guildford as recorder in the early draft of 'The Notion Club Papers' is replaced by his identification of himself in his own persona, not in the text but hidden in plain sight in the runes and script of his invented writing systems.

Gone are all the Elf-friends and Bliss-friends, the Ælfwines and Tréowines and Alboins and Audoins. Gone too are Guildford, Lowdham, old Rashbold of Pembroke, and Mr. Howard Green, all replaced by J.R.R. Tolkien in his own identity. It may well have been the elaborate framing superstructure of 'The Notion Club Papers' that caused the whole edifice to collapse under its own weight. Christopher Tolkien has commented that "the whole conception [had] now developed a disturbing complexity" (*SD* 280), one "so intricate that one need perhaps look no further for an answer to the question, why were *The Notion Club Papers* abandoned?" (*SD* 282). He may be right. It is difficult to imagine how such an intertangled pattern could have been sorted out and its complexities made plain. This notwithstanding, the existence of 'The Notion Club Papers' and the insight the story gives into the workings of Tolkien's mind are valuable in their own right. 'The Notion Club Papers' may be a failed or at least an abortive attempt, but they are valuable as much for what they suggest as for what they do or do not accomplish. It is Tolkien's reach, not his grasp that serious students of his work should pay attention to here.

Defying and Defining Darkness

> "Look at how a single candle can both defy and define the darkness."
> Anne Frank, *Diary*

The dual assignment of defying and defining Darkness, is both an inspiration and a challenge. It is an inspiration because defying darkness is what humans have tried to do ever since Prometheus brought us fire, and we're still trying. It is a challenge because what it proposes – defying and defining – assumes that you know what you're up against or at least what you're talking about, which in the case of darkness is not as easy as you might suppose. Inspired, challenged, but also in need of help, I turn to the dictionary.

The *American Heritage Dictionary* tells me that 'defy' means, "to confront or stand up to," with a second meaning, "to resist successfully, withstand," and a third, "to challenge." The same dictionary defines 'define' as "state the precise meaning of." So far, so good. I know what I'm talking about.

Rounding out the set, the dictionary defines 'darkness' with elegant simplicity as "total or almost total absence of light." It is here that I run into trouble. Elegance is all very well, mathematically speaking, but simplicity turns out to be, in this case, the reverse of precise meaning. Not only is it not precise, it isn't even close. This is the reverse of a definition, a retreat to what something isn't rather than an explanation of what it is. When I'd closed the dictionary, I thought of what Frodo says to Gildor in *The Lord of the Rings*: "Go not to the Elves for counsel, for they will say both no and yes" (*FR* 93).

With the dictionary saying both no and yes, I went for counsel to J.R.R. Tolkien instead, hoping to get from the wordsmith of modern fantasy a little more certainty. But searching his work for instances of defining or defying darkness, I found instead that like his own Elves – and the dictionary – Tolkien also says both no and yes. I only found one instance (which I will get to in due time) where he states a precise meaning for darkness. Otherwise, rather than defining it, he has it play hide-and-seek, or tag-you're-it, or catch-me-if-you-can. Most of the time, he gives his readers a powerful sense and feel of darkness without necessarily naming it as such, and sometimes he names it something else and lets readers figure out the meaning for themselves. In similar mode, sometimes he defies darkness and sometimes he doesn't.

So, in this essay I'd like to try out some instances of what I see as Tolkien saying both no and yes on the subject of darkness, not so much to argue a case as to begin a conversation on this important aspect of fantasy in general and the work of J.R.R. Tolkien in particular. Let me make one thing clear: I am not talking about evil in Tolkien's work, a much larger and more complex – albeit related – subject. I am talking about how he treats darkness. From the myriad examples in his fiction I've selected a few to analyze how an element which may – or may not be – defined as darkness either is – or is not, or is only partially – defied.

External Darkness

My first example is from *The Hobbit*, the early scene in Chapter One with the dwarves in Bilbo's parlor. When the dwarves begin their music and Bilbo is "swept away" the narrator tells us that the "dark came into the room from the little window" (*H* 21). It's a wonderful sentence and deliberately designed not to define darkness but to create it as a presence. The reader is invited to imagine a physical entry. Burglars come in through the windows. Kids sneaking home after curfew come in through windows. So, in telling us that darkness came in from the window, Tolkien is investing it with individuality and substance, if not necessarily form. This is sub-creation. Darkness has become a character in the story. It comes in the room as obviously and physically as the dwarves do – almost as a guest at the party. This is neither defiance nor definition. It is not absence. It is presence.

And when Tolkien tells us that dark "filled all the room," he is inviting us (I would almost say 'daring us') to *see* darkness. And when Bilbo says, "What about a little light?" and the dwarves answer that they "like the dark [...] dark for dark business!" (*H* 23), we have gone in one leap from personification to metaphor. The dwarves' 'dark business' will be their greed for gold, felt by Bilbo as the desire at the hearts of dwarves, which will play an important role as the story develops. Which, of course, is the point of the whole exercise. We can see how cleverly Tolkien has snuck up on us when we were not looking. In this first encounter in *The Hobbit*, while darkness is vividly pictured, it is neither defied nor defined. It is, however, memorably introduced in ways that will pay off later in the story.

Internal Darkness

Granted, this is all on the level of children's story, and the tone is more than halfway tongue-in-cheek. The story and the tone and the treatment get progressively more serious as the narrative develops, and we get real darkness in Smaug's cave inside the mountain and psychological darkness with Bilbo's theft of the Arkenstone.

Bilbo makes three trips inside the Mountain, but for brevity I will lump them together as representing the crux of the Hero Journey, the descent to the underworld taken by Aeneas, Orpheus, Beowulf, and Bilbo. This is the hero's initiation, the ordeal that leads to change and return. In Jungian psychology, it is the journey inward that leads to confrontation with the self. Bilbo goes "down, down, down into the dark" (*H* 183) – into the heart of the Mountain. And what he finds there is light – the glow of Smaug. This switcheroo of dark and light upends all notions of defining, and while Bilbo does defy the dragon (who glows), he eventually gives in to the 'dark business' of the dwarves (which we first saw coming in through the window in Chapter 1) and gives in to his inner darkness by stealing the Arkenstone. "'Now I am a burglar indeed!' thought [Bilbo]" (*H* 201). See again how cleverly Tolkien has moved darkness from stage setting to psychology to action. Bilbo loses the battle, though he will eventually win the war.

The Lord of the Rings

These are foreshadowings of things to come in *The Lord of the Rings*, where dark seems to come out of the woodwork and attack from all sides. Take for example, the chapter called 'Fog on the Barrow-downs', where Tolkien treats darkness in much the same way, escalating it from atmospheric to psychological to metaphorical.

Separated from his companions and fallen off his pony, Frodo, like Bilbo before him but more dramatically, is overtaken by darkness in a landscape far darker than Bilbo's parlor. The Barrow-downs are "dreaded hills" (*FR* 142) with their own dark reputation, and in them, Frodo is benighted in every sense of that word. The darkness is part time of day (nightfall), part weather (the fog), and part state of mind (Frodo is lost, confused, and frightened). The fog is actual and so is the time of day, but the "darkness [that seems] to fall" (*FR* 150) around Frodo is at first as much psychological as real. But as it develops, it becomes increasingly actual. Stars appear, and "clinging night" (*FR* 150) closes about Frodo. I call your attention to the word 'clinging'. Again, Tolkien is giving darkness agency, as if it were an active force. The darkness that clings to Frodo matches and reflects his mental state. This is T.S. Eliot's 'objective correlative', the outside world mirroring the inner one. But again, this is not a definition – it is an evocation.

Is darkness defied? Like the elves and the dictionary, Tolkien says both no and yes. Disoriented and scared, Frodo tries to call to the other hobbits but gets an answer from another source.

> 'Where are you?' he cried [...] both angry and afraid.
> 'Here,' said a voice, deep and cold, that seemed to come out of the ground. 'I am waiting for you!'
> 'No!' said Frodo, but he did not run away. (*FR* 150-51).

Frodo then looks up to see "a tall dark figure" with eyes "lit with a pale light." He feels a grip "stronger and colder than iron" that seizes him and he passes out (*FR* 151).

Both the emphatic 'No!' and the fact that he does not run away fit the dictionary's definition of 'defy' as 'stand up to', which Frodo certainly does. What he stands up to – the voice – is not described as dark but "deep and cold." Inside the barrow, Frodo wakes in darkness that fades to "a pale greenish light" as a chant begins in which "night [is] railing against the morning" and "cold [is] cursing the warmth" (*FR* 152). Again, let's look at the words Tolkien uses: 'deep', 'cold', 'iron', 'pale light', 'greenish light'. He is creating emotional and psychological darkness without ever naming it as such. It is presented, but it is not defined.

Nor is it defied. Far from resisting, Frodo thinks of flight:

> [A] wild thought of escape came to him [...] He wondered if he put on the Ring, whether the Barrow-wight would miss him [...] He thought of himself [...] free and alive [...] Gandalf would admit that there had been nothing else he could do. (*FR* 152)

The narrative tells us explicitly that "he wavered, groping in his pocket" but adds that he "then fought with himself again" (*FR* 152). This certainly qualifies as defiance. But what makes this example worth attention is that the defier and the thing defied are one and the same. The battle is internal, and the darkness is within Frodo, what Tolkien called "the real battle between the soul and its adversaries" (*MC* 22). Thus, it is implicit but not defined. Things become more overt when Frodo wins the battle with himself and takes physical action, seizing the sword and severing the crawling hand, whereupon the *light goes out* in a paradoxical conjunction of metaphorical darkness and psychological illumination.

In this complex episode, 'defy' increases exponentially from Frodo's instinctive 'No!' to his moral victory over himself to decisive action, each a successively greater act of defiance. But as we have seen, darkness is not so much described or defined as evoked. This is what I mean by hide-and-seek and catch-me-if-you-can. Darkness is there but not there, just around the corner, ready to jump out at any minute. We sense it rather than see it. But with Frodo's victory over the hand, the moment where any fairy tale worthy of the name would have given the hero the princess and left them happy ever after, Tolkien is just getting started on darkness.

My next example is Weathertop, where we get characters described as so dark they look like holes against the dark night. They are Black Riders, and the name clearly evokes darkness. But it is darkness without substance. The Riders are wraiths, ghosts. Apart from their white faces and burning eyes and haggard hands, there's nothing inside those cloaks. They are insubstantial; they are precisely the presence of an absence that the dictionary called for. It is notable that in this struggle against this absence, Frodo gives in and puts on the Ring. The obvious question is: what exactly is Frodo giving in to? The power of the Ring? The pressure of the Riders? His own inner darkness, as in the barrow? Probably – but implicitly all three. But he does not give way entirely, striking at his enemy and with a last gesture, takes off the Ring. Darkness is enacted rather than defined.

Both Frodo and Tolkien do a little better at the Ford, where Frodo confronts this same darkness, these same Black Riders:

> Frodo sat up and brandished his sword.
> 'Go back!' he cried. 'Go back to the Land of Mordor and follow me no more!' […] His enemies laughed […] 'Come back! Come back!' they called. 'To Mordor we will take you!'
> 'Go back!' he whispered.
> […]
> 'By Elbereth and Lúthien the Fair […] you shall have neither the Ring nor me!'
> […] Frodo was stricken dumb. He felt his tongue cleave to his mouth and his heart labouring. His sword broke and fell out of his shaking hand.
> […]
> […] Then Frodo felt himself falling, […]. He heard and saw no more. (*FR* 226-27)

Here is defiance, loud and clear, heart-stirring. With better (though still partial) success this time, Frodo does stand (or sit) up against and challenge the Riders. Indeed, he is the only one until the great scene with Éowyn and Merry, who ever does so. But his defiance is ultimately ineffective. It is Elrond, aided by Gandalf, who defeats the Riders and their darkness, not with light, but with water.

I am aware that these examples are selective. I could pick other representatives of darkness, like Old Man Willow, or get into real psychology with characters like Boromir and Denethor and Gollum, but I think I am being fair both in presenting the problems and in tracing a continuum of increasing intensity. I will give you now one of the clearest examples of defying darkness in *The Lord of the Rings*, explicit and unequivocal. This is the heart-stopping moment at the end of Book IV when Frodo holds aloft the star-glass and walks down the tunnel to confront Shelob. The scene is written as a set-piece; you can almost hear the trumpets and drums as sword in hand and holding the phial aloft: "Frodo, hobbit of the Shire [walks] steadily down to meet the eyes [of Shelob]" (*TT* 330). For the reader it creates – and was clearly intended to create – what Tolkien called the "catch of breath," the "beat and lifting of the heart" that he says a fairy-story can produce.

How dark is Shelob? Tolkien surrounds her with words like 'shadow' and 'night'. Her eyes reflect the light of the star-glass, and behind them "a pale deadly fire glows within, a flame kindled in some deep pit of evil thought" (*TT* 329). Again, we find that odd confusion of light and dark. To really understand her, we must leave *The Lord of the Rings* and turn to *The Silmarillion* and Shelob's ancestress Ungoliant, whose name means 'dark spider', related to ungol, defined as 'unlight', and we are right back where we started with 'absence of light'. Ungoliant sucks the light from the Two Trees and belches forth "black vapours [...] a darkness that seemed not lack but a thing with being of its own" (*S* 76). Tolkien gives us not just one concrete image, but two. Both light and dark are reified, light as a liquid, dark as a gaseous residue. It is with this image of darkness made out of light that Tolkien comes closest to a definition, a precise meaning in dictionary terms. Here, he has created a presence not an absence. Here, there is no hesitation such as we saw with Frodo at the barrow, no internal struggle, no objective correlative.

Nevertheless, the rhythm of *The Lord of the Rings* seems to require that every victory and every defeat be followed by their opposite, every up by a down, every down by a compensatory lift, an oscillation between light and dark that might be the hallmark of Tolkien's story-telling style. So, Frodo's defiance of Shelob is not the end of the story, or even the end of the episode, as the reader quickly discovers, for Tolkien provides a down by having Shelob capture and disable Frodo. The scene where Sam thinks Frodo dead is one of the darkest moments in the book. But the darkness is metaphoric, a far cry from the vomit of Ungoliant or Shelob. In a further oscillation, it is followed almost immediately by Sam's discovery that Frodo is alive, and this discovery is followed by a further defiance of the dark when, unable to locate Frodo in the Tower, Sam begins to sing and is answered by Frodo. *The Lord of the Rings* is full of such alternations large and small.

The subsequent scene where Sam finds Frodo alive at the top of the tower shows this oscillation at its most compressed. Sam has found Frodo alive only to provoke his predictable, terrible response when Sam tells him he has the Ring. "You can't have it!" "No you won't, you thief!" The narrative tells us that, "Sam had changed before his eyes into an orc again, leering and pawing at his treasure, a foul little creature with greedy eyes and slobbering mouth." Frodo's remorse is poignant: "O Sam [...] What have I said? What have I done? Forgive me!" (*RK* 188). Frodo's anger is followed by his remorse, just as his fear in the barrow was followed by his courage, and his ordeals at Weathertop and the Ford followed by recovery in Rivendell.

I want to bring another term into play here, a word of Tolkien's own coinage directly related to the light-dark back-and-forth I've been talking about. The word is 'eucatastrophe', from his essay 'On Fairy-stories'. Eucatastrophe, as you probably know, means 'good catastrophe' and describes the 'turn' in a fairy-story when last-minute rescue reverses the downward trajectory, turns the story from tragedy to comedy and provides the Happy Ending. This brings us directly to the Cracks of Doom, the darkest moment in a story full of dark moments, when Frodo defies his own mandate by refusing to do what he came to do. "I will not do this deed. The Ring is mine" (*RK* 223).

How are we to parse this stupefying moment? It must stand as the most stunning reversal in twentieth-century literature, and it fulfills everything we have been told about the Ring from Chapter 2 onward. And I venture to say that it creates darkness in the reader as well as in the story. I know it did for me the first time I read it. But again, we get oscillation. At the Cracks of Doom, Tolkien goes from dark to light to dark to light and racks up more changes on his own concept of eucatastrophe than even Gandalf could contrive. Catastrophe and eucatastrophe braid themselves around one another and follow so hard on one another's heels that the reader is hard put to keep up with the pace or tell one element from the other.

The catastrophe for Middle-earth that is Frodo's claiming of the Ring is followed by a eucatastrophe for Gollum who recovers the Ring by biting it off Frodo's hand, but his Happy Ending when he re-possesses his treasure is followed immediately by his dyscatastrophe when he and the Ring fall into the fire. Frodo's catastrophe in coming wholly under the Ring's power is followed by a second catastrophe, losing it, which is paradoxically also his first eucatastrophe since it forces him to give it up, which he would not otherwise have done. The Ring's eucatastrophe in conquering first Frodo and then Gollum causes its own catastrophe when Gollum, holding it aloft, falls into the fire, which becomes Frodo's second eucatastrophe in freeing him of its power and returning him to sanity, robbed, maimed but master of himself.

Even for a book whose pace is based on alternation, as noted above, the dizzying rapidity of the switch-backs in this scene is beyond the skill of any magician less than Tolkien. Yet, even in its mind-blowing alternation, the scene manages to keep an equilibrium that is not static but dynamic. For all its shifts and changes, it elevates balance over position, favors suspense over stillness, and prefers tension to immobility. It is, in short, as close to real life as Tolkien can bring it, as realistic as fantasy can be.

That realism has its roots in a section of Tolkien's fairy-story essay that has something to offer beyond eucatastrophe, something he feels is as essential to fantasy as the Happy Ending. He calls it "hard recognition." For Fantasy, he says,

> is founded upon the hard recognition that things are so in the world as it appears under the sun; on a recognition of fact [...] So upon logic was founded the nonsense [...] in the tales and rhymes of Lewis Carroll. If men really could not distinguish between frogs and men, fairy-stories about frog-kings would not have arisen. (*MC* 144)

Without this recognition of the world as it is, fantasy could not do riffs on how it might be. No matter how high you fly, you have to push off from the ground under your feet. However far out your fantasy, it must be founded on the hard recognition that "things are so" in the real world, that pain exists, that life leads to death, that there's no guarantee.

Thus, the destruction of the Ring is both eucatastrophe and catastrophe for Frodo, who is freed from its power by losing what has become his dearest possession. And while his own inner darkness is defined – both for him and for the reader – that does not mean it can be defied, for the hard recognition is that it is a part of Frodo. The battle that he won against himself in the barrow becomes the much greater battle he loses at Mt. Doom, the knowledge of which he has to live with. About Frodo, Tolkien commented in a letter that "one must face the fact [that] the power of evil in the world is *not* finally resistible by incarnate creatures, however 'good'" (*Letters* 252). Frodo, says his creator, was "tempted to regret [the Ring's] destruction, and still to desire it" (*Letters* 328).

In this respect, *The Lord of the Rings* is not a fantasy. The recognition is too hard, the situation too realistic to be fantastic. It is a tragedy. It may not conform 100% to Aristotle's requirements, for it is the fall not of a great man but a little one and in this respect more modern than its detractors are willing to allow. But it brings self-knowledge, the hard recognition that things are so in the world, and ranges Frodo not just beside Oedipus but Lear and Macbeth. Tolkien's notes and letters make it clear that the scene at the Cracks of Doom was envisioned from the very beginning, that Tolkien deliberately set up a situation in which his protagonist could not win but must inevitably, like Oedipus, lose the struggle. Thus his stretching out of that struggle over six books and over 900 pages must stand as the longest tease in literary history, the most cynical exercise of authorial power, and the most candid acknowledgment that, as he stated in the essay is *Beowulf*, "within Time the monsters would win" because "the monsters do not depart, whether the gods go or come" (*MC* 22).

It would be dishonest of me to leave the subject there, with the deck so stacked that there is no hope of debate, so I have one more example to offer, and I present it because it is in every way the opposite of all the episodes I have just been talking about, proof of Tolkien's biographer Humphrey Carpenter's characterization of him as a man of antitheses and evidence of either his tendency to contradict himself or his capacity for paradox, the ability to hold oppositions in tension. This is the splendid episode on the Pelennor Field when Éowyn and Merry between them defy the darkness of the Nazgûl Lord and together bring about his death – Éowyn with her triumphant revelation that she is a woman (take that, Tolkien misogynists!) and Merry with the blade of Westernesse from the barrow.

This is perhaps the most completely realized moment of victory in the whole book, brought about by the two least likely agents, both of whom were forbidden to be there in the first place. To this day, I cannot read this passage out loud without my eyes pricking and my voice quavering not from sadness but the kind of joy that comes when against all the odds the thing that ought to happen actually does. I cannot resist pointing out that this moment is immediately followed by Merry "blinded by tears" and Éowyn at the point of death. Nevertheless, it is eucatastrophe on a grand scale and clear evidence that Tolkien can defy darkness when he wants to. What I find interesting is that he so often seems not to want to.

And that leads me to my final point. I have been talking as if these were real people. They are not. They are realistic, but that is a different thing. We need to remind ourselves that what we are talking about today is fiction. There is no Frodo, no Gollum, no Éowyn or Merry or Witch-King, in fact, no Ring. There is only Tolkien. And we should pay attention to that fact. If Merry and Éowyn succeed it is because Tolkien writes their success into the world he has invented. If Frodo fails, it is because Tolkien designed his failure. Tolkien wrote this book, and although he may say and, in some sense, believe that he is not the Author, nevertheless he is controlling the story. His many revisions (he rewrote the first chapter six times), his notes and rough drafts give evidence of extensive rethinking, backtracking, giving up and starting over, casting and recasting the words he puts in his characters' mouths, the actions he has them perform, and the ends to which he conducts them. *The Lord of the Rings* may be, as Tolkien says of the lines of *Beowulf*, "wrought to a high finish" (*MC* 14), but the operative word is 'wrought', past participle of 'work', that is to say 'made', 'crafted'.

The Lord of the Rings has been called an epic, a romance, a fairy tale, a fantasy, and a war novel. And in truth, a case can be made that it is each – indeed all – of these genres. But in all of them, the overriding theme is not so much light and dark – that's just the backdrop. The overriding theme is loss. Théoden asks Gandalf at Helm's Deep, "May it not so end that much that was fair and wonderful shall pass forever out of Middle-earth?" Gandalf's answer is, "It may. The evil of Sauron cannot be wholly cured, nor made as if it had not been" (*TT* 155). Both Théoden and Gandalf speak here for Tolkien, whose longing for a lost and irretrievable past led him to make one up that suffuses his work. And Tolkien speaks for Frodo, who loses the Ring, his health, his innocence, his home. So do we all.

At this point, you might well be thinking that Professor Tolkien cannot make up his mind or that I am thinking he cannot make up his mind. You would be wrong on both counts. He can, and I have no doubt that he can. But I also think that the makeup of his mind reflects the paradox of the human condition – the terrible circumstance that to be human is to be faced with a perpetual oscillation between hope and despair, between the promise of a happy ending – or at least some resolution – and the ineluctable fact of what Tolkien called 'the long defeat' that is human history in a fallen world.

For Tolkien, the scales are weighted more toward doom than consolation, in this world at least. And while his story encompasses both, it is based as much on the 'hard recognition' that the world is the way it is as on eucatastrophe and the Happy Ending. For Frodo, it is the hard recognition that at the crucial moment he failed the test. To switch briefly from 'On Fairy-stories' to the *Beowulf* essay, Tolkien's story recognizes, as does *Beowulf*, that *eal scæceð, leoht and lif somod* (*MC* 19), 'all perishes, light and life together'. For, said Tolkien, "the monsters do not depart, whether the gods go or come" and "within time the monsters [will] win" (*MC* 22). To make sure you get the point, Tolkien goes on to characterize the theme of *Beowulf* as, "man, each man and all men and all their works shall die," a theme, he said, that "no Christian need despise" (*MC* 23) and one, he declared, that will "ever call with a profound appeal – until the dragon comes" (*MC* 34).

So, at the end of the day, where do we stand on Tolkien defying and defining darkness? More importantly, where does Tolkien stand? My reading of *The Lord of the Rings*, his masterpiece and centerpiece, the work by which all the others are judged, is that he says both 'no' and 'yes', but that he says 'no' more often than he says 'yes'.

Unlike some of his contemporaries and successors, Tolkien didn't just set up straw men and knock them over. He saw and acknowledged the power of the dark. He lived in a dark world dominated by two terrible wars that did as much to shape his fiction as they did that of Ernest Hemingway, or James Jones, or Erich Maria Remarque – none of whom are identified as writers of fantasy. Nor, I venture to suggest, should Tolkien be so identified. At least not exclusively, for at the end of the day, it is the realism even more than the fantasy that makes his work stand out from the others in that genre. It is its darkness as much as its light that has earned *The Lord of the Rings* its deservedly high place in the world's literature. It is Tolkien's recognition that the dark is a necessary aspect of the search for light that has drawn readers to his work generation after generation for over sixty years and counting.

What we are left with is neither 'no' nor 'yes', neither a consistent defiance of darkness nor its clear definition but something stronger and more resilient than either of those. What Tolkien gives us is a vision of a world in which darkness is recognizable if not necessarily definable, a world that balances eucatastrophe and the Happy Ending with the hard recognition that 'things are so' and cannot always be defied. I hope the evidence I have offered today shows that Tolkien recognized darkness as a real force, not just an absence but also a presence, not always easy to define and more often than not hard to defy, but a thing in itself, always to be reckoned with – the dragon that waits for us. Especially hard to define and even harder to defy when, as so often happens, the dragon is us.

Listening to the Music

On February 24, 1950, J.R.R. Tolkien wrote to his publisher Stanley Unwin concerning his long-overdue but by then completed manuscript of *The Lord of the Rings*: "my work has escaped from my control," he cautioned Unwin, "and I have produced a monster: an immensely long, complex, rather bitter, and very terrifying romance, quite unfit for children [...] and it is not really a sequel to *The Hobbit*, but to *The Silmarillion*" (*Letters* 136). His work had not, in fact, escaped from his control, but he seemed concerned that it might have escaped from Unwin's. *The Silmarillion* Tolkien referred to was a vast, as-yet-unpublished mythology he intended to "dedicate [...] to England" (*Letters* 144). He had labored over it – in what time he could spare from academic duties – for a good twenty years and now wanted very much to see in print. At the time he was writing to Unwin, he was in concurrent (but unmentioned) discussions with Milton Waldman, then an editor at the London publishing firm of Collins, about publishing *The Silmarillion* and the "monster" together as "one long Saga of the Jewels and the Ring" (*Letters* 139). In the end, we can be grateful that this did not happen, for it was only the separate and prior appearance of *The Lord of the Rings* that created a readership for *The Silmarillion* and thus prepared the way for its publication. Tolkien's Feb. 24 letter seems to have been part of a strategy to dissuade Unwin from accepting *The Lord of the Rings* as a sequel to *The Hobbit* so that Collins could publish it as sequel to *The Silmarillion*.

The Monster

In point of fact, it was a sequel to both, and that hybrid origin (for the two source-works are poles apart in tone and treatment and audience) has complicated its reception and confused its genre since the day it was published. How you approached *The Lord of the Rings* depended to a great extent on which context you placed it in and what prior knowledge you brought to it. Begun as a follow-up to *The Hobbit*, it rapidly grew beyond that book to be 'captured', as Tolkien described it to Unwin (*Letters* 136), by the older but continuously evolving *legendarium* that was his life's work. It was thus an amalgam – "as indivisible as I could make it," Tolkien wrote in another letter to Unwin (*Letters* 138) – of narrative types ranging from Grimmsian fairy tale to Edwardian children's story to medieval epic. It went beyond any of these, however, to achieve something unlike anything that had gone before. The only word available was fantasy, a genre at that time confined largely to pulp magazines and the by-then out of favor stories of William Morris and Lord Dunsany, to which it bore only a superficial resemblance. Aside from the Frankenstein allusion and the 'unfit for children' comment (disproved by over six decades of children who've found it quite fit), Tolkien's own description of his masterpiece was, and is, spot on.

It is long. At over a thousand pages and half a million words, *The Lord of the Rings* is not just "immensely long," it is enormous. It is complex both structurally and psychologically. Its six interlaced books, with their overlapping time schemes and storylines that are narrated in a number of voices and multiple shifts in point of view. It is terrifying. The sniffing, un-bodied Black Riders, shadow-men on real horses, the cold chant of the Barrow-wight whose groping arm walks through the tomb on its fingers, the half-world of the Ring that engulfs Frodo, are the stuff of nightmares. Most of all, it is bitter. Written between two world wars, its message that every win is temporary and what is lost is gone forever is a great deal more than just "rather bitter."

"I am a Christian," Tolkien wrote in response to a reader, Amy Ronald, in December 1956, "and indeed a Roman Catholic, so that I do not expect 'history' to be anything but a 'long defeat' – though it contains (and in a legend may contain more clearly and movingly) some samples or glimpses of final victory" (*Letters* 255). While *The Lord of the Rings* offers both "samples or glimpses" of victory and also the "long defeat" of history, readers have on the whole tended to prefer and to emphasize the victory over the defeat. Not so Tolkien, for whom the long defeat met his expectations, and the victory was only a glimpse, a fleeting, partial vision.

Four years after the letter to Unwin and following considerable back-and-forth between Tolkien and the two publishers, volume I of the monster was finally published in July 1954 – by Unwin, and without the *Silmarillion* – as *The Fellowship of the Ring*. Volume II, *The Two Towers*, followed later that same year and volume III, *The Return of the King*, in 1955. The book was generally well-received, though it was inevitably and misleadingly read by the light of *The Hobbit*. Critical opinion ran the gamut from glowingly positive ("lightning from a clear sky," "beauties that pierce like swords or burn like cold iron," "a book that will break your heart") to condescension ("boys masquerading as adult heroes") to outright calumny ("juvenile trash"). There was in addition some perplexity about exactly what species of animal it was – science fiction? modern novel? adventure story? all of the above? But despite the attempts at classification, no reviewer I am aware of found *The Lord of the Rings* to be "bitter." In that respect, I submit, they missed Tolkien's point.

Two years later, however, in 1957, Douglass Parker, a professor of classics at UC Riverside, wrote an article in *The Hudson Review* that came close. Though Parker was off the mark in some regards – he called the book a trilogy, dismissed the hobbit names as "ridiculous," assumed there was a Shire in *The Hobbit*, and left out Merry and Pippin – nevertheless, he correctly pegged the book as fantasy, calling it, "probably the most original and varied creation ever seen in the genre, and certainly the most self-consistent" (Parker 1957: 602). Himself the designer and teacher of a course in 'para-geography', the study of imaginary worlds, Parker was well qualified to judge the self-consistency of Tolkien's invented world against that of others. Moreover, he said, *The Lord of the Rings* exemplifies what an imaginary world can do better than a realistic one, which is to distance reality from itself, as a looking-glass at an angle can make the familiar look strange. The fantastic elements of Tolkien's world, he argued, its Elves, Dwarves, and Hobbits, reflect reality in an angled mirror that lets us see ourselves in skewed perspective as strangers in a strange land.

It was in his summation that Parker came closest to Tolkien's judgment. "Tolkien's whole marvelous, intricate structure," he wrote, "has been reared to be destroyed, that we may regret it" (Parker 1957: 609). Parker didn't explicitly call it 'bitter', but his description was not far off the mark. 'Regret', after all, carries the notion of rue, remorse for something not done that should have been, or for something done that should not have been. If Tolkien got ahead of himself saying his monster was unfit for children, Parker was ahead of most critics in recognizing that beneath the fantasy elements – and even more effective in contrast to their enchantment – there lies a deep stratum of pain, of sorrow for loss. Though it has comedic elements and happy moments, some bordering on what Tolkien called "Joy beyond the walls of the world" (*MC* 153), *The Lord of the Rings* is not at bottom a happy book. It is more than anything a lament, a cry of grief for a lost and unrecoverable world, re-created only so that it may be lost again and lost so that it can be mourned. It is to Parker's credit that he perceived the long defeat in Tolkien's story before he or anyone had knowledge of its larger framework.

Christopher Tolkien's serial publication from 1977 to 2018 of his father's entire mythology has given us that larger framework. We now have the history of Tolkien's fictive world from its lofty creation in celestial music to Sam Gamgee's homely return to Bag End at the end of the Third Age. Christopher has re-positioned the looking-glass, thereby putting *The Lord of the Rings* in longer perspective to show it as something more than just itself. It is the culmination of a multivalent narrative that Tolkien himself called an "evil-aroused story" (*Letters* 246). Taken in its entirety, it is, like *The Lord of the Rings*, not a happy story. To be sure, there are in the complete *legendarium*, as in *The Lord of the Rings* by itself, "some samples or glimpses of final victory", but they remain glimpses only, potential but not actual. Tolkien's mythology did not withhold the possibility of hope from his readers, but he was too honest to guarantee it.

With the whole of Tolkien's mythological world now displayed, a myriad components of the fabric of Middle-earth, not just Lórien and Moria and the Entwives and the trees along Bagshot Row but those far in the past of the *legendarium* (Númenor and Gondolin and Nargothrond and Doriath), all provide context for one another as "reared to be destroyed" so that we may feel their loss. More than seventy years after Tolkien's caveat to Unwin and sixty years after Parker's melancholy summing-up, we can see how *The Silmarillion* supports and underscores both Tolkien's and Parker's key words, 'bitter' and 'regret'. *The Lord of the Rings* is the culmination, narrative end-point and realization of a long, terrifying, bitter saga. But fully to understand this end-point, we must go back to the starting-point of the whole long story.

The Beginnings

Tolkien's *legendarium*, conceived when he was still at school, had many starts and stops before it settled down (to the extent that it ever did!), and its compositional history is intertangled, complex, and confusing. There have been many efforts (some of them Tolkien's own after-the-fact attempts at dating) to pinpoint the earliest burgeoning of his myth-making impulse. The beginning of an idea can be hard to locate, especially in retrospect after the notion has already taken shape. There are paintings, poems, references in letters, all evidentiary, none conclusive. Tolkien's invention of languages, begun with his earliest stories, is also a major factor in his mythmaking. He felt that a culture's language encodes its myths just as the myths invigorate the languages; they are co-temporaneous and coeval.

In the exterior, real-world chronology of his writing life, his earliest serious attempts at mythology seem to have been two poems, the 1914 'Voyage of Eärendel' and the 1915 'Shores of Faery'. Written before his 1916 military service in France, the poems are in spirit and essence largely Edwardian and thus to some degree retrogressive to the nineteenth-century prettification of faërie that Tolkien later deplored and abjured. Not till his military service had ended with trench fever and sick-leave in England, and at the suggestion of his friend Christopher Wiseman that he "ought to start the epic,"[1] did Tolkien begin in 1916 or 1917 his first serious attempt to write a story in which both Middle-earth and Valinor were taking shape in his mind. By that time, his invented world was neither Edwardian nor pretty. It was contemporary and realistic.

'Tuor and the Exiles of Gondolin', later renamed 'The Fall of Gondolin', was the story of the betrayal and overthrow of a great city and the subsequent wanderings of its refugees. For all its mythological elements and tone, its content derived from Tolkien's war experience and anticipated the graphic war portrayals of such fellow veterans as Wilfred Owen and Siegfried Sassoon. It was fantasy doing what Parker said it does best, reflecting reality at an angle, its metal dragons and belching flame re-imagining and intensifying the tanks and flame-throwers of Tolkien's World War I experience on the Somme. "I shall

1 See <https://www.tolkienguide.com/modules/newbb/viewtopic.php?post_id=60533>.

never write any ordered biography," Tolkien once wrote to Christopher, "it is against my nature, which expresses itself about things deepest felt in tales and myths" (*Bio* 97). Like his real world, Tolkien's post-war invented world reflected his experience in its "tales and myths." Other stories from that world followed over the next twenty or so years in a start-and-stop progression as he changed jobs, raised a family, moved from city to city and house to house.

The story of Tuor and Gondolin was the first of his mythology's three Great Tales, the other two being the bitter, tragic story of Túrin Turambar and the bittersweet love story of Beren and Lúthien. Written and re-written again and again, sometimes in prose and sometimes in verse, they form, together with the story of the Silmarils, the backbone of Tolkien's extended story. They are not happy stories. The Túrin story ends in a double suicide. 'The Fall of Gondolin' is just that, the overthrow and sack of a city and the wanderings of its refugees. Only the Beren and Lúthien story has what might be called a happy ending, and even that ends in death.

But Tolkien's world also had its own interior timeline, one that began with the creation. Christopher assigns the earliest version of the creation story, the 'Ainulindalë', to the period of Tolkien's work on the *Oxford English Dictionary* (at that time called *The New English Dictionary*, shortened to *NED*), between the years 1918 and 1920, that is to say, *after* but not long after 'The Fall of Gondolin', suggesting that Tolkien may have had the arc of the story already sketched out. Since he was an observant Catholic, it is noteworthy that his creation story omits the Fall of Man. It has no prohibition, no temptation, no disobedience, no punishment; none of the elements that make up the foundation story of Judeo-Christianity. This is a hugely significant change, removing Original Sin (therefore guilt) and replacing it with cosmic disharmony that misshapes the world before humanity comes on the scene. The 'Ainulindalë', or 'Music of the Ainur', tells how the godhead Eru gives to his offspring the Ainur a musical theme and invites them to develop it together. Their harmony is interrupted when the chief among them, Melkor, intrudes a competing theme of his own, causing some of the Ainur to abandon Eru's theme and join his instead.

The result is a musical war in heaven as the two themes contend. The consequent discord prompts Eru to call a halt and begin again with a second theme, which gets the same treatment. In a final attempt, Eru incorporates Melkor's disharmony into yet a third theme, this one described as "wide and beautiful but slow and blended with an immeasurable sorrow" that weaves the rebellious theme "into its own solemn pattern" (*S* 16-17). It is with and through this third theme that the created world comes into being, a history at once divinely inspired and "evil-aroused," flawed in its inception through the Music that plays out both its beauty and its evil, the theme and variations of the long defeat. It is well to remember that Tolkien was neither writing religious apologetics nor creating an allegory. Rather, he was telling a history of the world as he imagined it might once have been but also as he experienced it, as a long defeat.

However, this invented world underwent a shift of direction in the nineteen-thirties with the intrusion of *The Hobbit.* Starting as a playful story Tolkien first told to his children and then as it grew longer read aloud to them, this was not a mythology *per se* but a children's book that strayed from its genre into the older mythology. Its popularity commissioned a sequel, *The Lord of the Rings*, which in turn took *The Hobbit* with it as it attached itself to the *Silmarillion.* The huge physical and mental endeavor of pushing *The Lord of the Rings* to completion, towing *The Hobbit* in its wake, took Tolkien twelve years. It was his final great effort, and he succeeded in bringing it to a close, but the interruption broke the rhythm of the *Silmarillion*, and he was never able to satisfactorily go back and finish the parent mythology. The result is that for all practical purposes *The Lord of the Rings* stands as that mythology's zenith, narrative climax and *de facto* ending.

The Endings

That ending comes about not with its protagonist Frodo, who is sent offstage before it happens, but with Sam Gamgee, to whom Tolkien gave the story's dual finale in which the exterior and interior chronologies come together. The exterior chronology of Tolkien's composition, the arc that sprang up in 1916-17 from Gondolin's defeat and the exile of its inhabitants, may be said to come to earth with the interior story that ends with Sam's homecoming and his famous "Well, I'm back" (*RK* 311), for it was here that Tolkien brought his story to a close. Yet, the later-initiated but earlier-positioned arc of interior history that began with creation can also be said to end a few lines earlier in significant words describing Sam at the Havens. After Frodo's ship has gone beyond his sight, Sam stays "far into the night, hearing only the sigh and murmur of the waves on the shores of Middle-earth, and the sound of them sank deep into his heart" (*RK* 311). Although this appears in Draft A of 'The Grey Havens', Tolkien saw fit to say it again several pages later and in almost the same language in his discarded 'Epilogue' (which Christopher describes as a continuation of the same draft). Directly after Sam's reunion with Rosie, they "went in and shut the door, but even as he did so Sam heard suddenly the sigh and murmur of the sea on the shores of Middle-earth" (*SD* 119). It seems clear that Tolkien saw the sigh and murmur as essential to his vision of the ending.

Now more than ever it seems clear that Tolkien's decision to omit the 'Epilogue' with which he first tidied up the loose ends was a wise one. News of Sam and Rosie's growing family, of Gimli and Legolas, and the King's Letter is informative but anticlimactic. Tolkien came to this conclusion reluctantly, writing to Katherine Farrer in October of 1955, shortly after the publication of *The Return of the King*: "I still feel the picture incomplete without something on Samwise and Elanor, but I could not devise anything that would not have destroyed the ending" (*Letters* 227).

It was not until 1977, when Christopher Tolkien published *The Silmarillion* and we read the 'Ainulindalë' that we learned the significance of those waves and found out what was encoded in their restless, never-ending sigh and murmur. Only then could we know what Sam was actually doing, or why. He was listening to the Music. Thanks to Christopher, we now have the information that "in water there lives yet the echo of the Music of the Ainur" (*S* 19). Sam was listening because "many of the Children of Ilúvatar" – of whom Sam is one – "hearken still unsated to the voices of the sea, and yet know not for what they listen" (S 19). This is a moment packed with meaning for Tolkien's world. The Children of Ilúvatar, Elves and Men, come only with Eru's third theme and with its message – which Sam is hearing – that the world is inherently imperfect, flawed in its inception, therefore flawed in its realization.

We are not told whether Sam knows what it is he is hearing, only that the sound "sank deep into his heart," but we do know – thanks to Christopher – that

Tolkien was not just creating atmosphere; he had something quite specific in his mind for which the key word is 'echo'. The waves Tolkien has chosen as the vehicle for his message are themselves recurrent and endless, telling and retelling the tragedy of Creation, the story of a world that began with harmony and wound up in discord. Sam hears repetition, reverberation, the re-statement (as in a musical theme) and playing out of the Music of creation. In thus reconnecting his world to its intentionally flawed beginning, Tolkien was using fantasy to do what Parker says it does best, to show his readers their actual world reflected in his invented one as a place where things repeatedly go wrong, a world in which even the most promising start will be affected by the founding flaw.

Readers in 1956, however, had no access to that knowledge. Back then, the scene with Sam was unexplained; his mood at the Havens was left for readers to fill in the blank – grief? longing? Douglass's key word 'regret'? – and it's a safe bet that many readers wouldn't have known which of these to choose. Yet, even then it was clear that something was going on to which readers were meant to respond to even though the actual meaning was beyond their knowledge. By thus referencing hidden information, Tolkien was taking a page from his own scholarship and blending it with invention. In his landmark 1936 lecture '*Beowulf*: The Monsters and the Critics', he talked about "the mood of the author, the essential cast of his imaginative apprehension of the world" as essential to understanding of that poem, particularly what he called its fusion of Christian and pagan elements (*MC* 20). Pondering the fragments of pagan mythology still remaining in *Beowulf*, Tolkien twice lamented the present lack of information about it. "Of English pre-Christian mythology," he said in his lecture, "we know practically nothing" (*MC* 21). He returned to the subject a few pages later, reiterating that, "we may regret that we do not know more about pre-Christian English mythology" (*MC* 24).

In the immediate context of un-glossed allusions in *Beowulf* to English mythology this fits his essay's argument. But a second context makes it equally apposite to *The Lord of the Rings*. That is the fact that at the time Tolkien was regretting the loss of an English mythology he had been for twenty years engaged in inventing just such a mythology expressly designed to fill in the blank. Nor was this the only such instance. Read in this light the word 'regret', used in similar contexts by both Tolkien and Parker, packs a triple whammy. It describes (1)

Tolkien's attitude toward the missing mythic knowledge in *Beowulf*; (2) his attitude toward the storied past of his own work, and (3) the profound emotion Parker says *The Lord of the Rings* is meant to arouse.

The scene with Sam at the Havens then takes on a new meaning, with the unmentioned *Silmarillion* as the lost history of which at the time readers knew "practically nothing." The important thing is that its author knew and built that "nothing" into the emotional subtext of his narrative. And now we know everything. We now have Tolkien's *Silmarillion* in its entirety to illuminate what then was unclear. With the whole corpus now available for survey, we can see that Tolkien wanted to make sure the two narratives made "one long Saga."

He used this wordless scene with Sam and the Music to connect the two, to loop the story back to its distant origin in Eru's third theme, "wide and beautiful but slow and blended with an immeasurable sorrow" (*S* 16) and bring it forward again to make Frodo's departure also part of that third theme. But that was not the finale. Tolkien added a coda, a few last words to his there-and-back-again story which he also bestowed on Sam – quite literally, not just because Sam is in it but because it is Sam who utters the words. This is the simple and moving account of Sam's return to Rosie after his farewell at the Havens:

> Sam turned to Bywater, and so came back up the Hill, as day was ending once more. And he went on, and there was yellow light, and a fire within, and the evening meal was ready, and he was expected. And Rose drew him in, and set him in his chair, and put little Elanor upon his lap.
>
> He drew a deep breath. 'Well, I'm back,' he said. (*RK* 311)

These are the last words in the narrative proper. The rest of the page is blank. The dramatic shift from the melancholy vigil at the Havens with the sigh and murmur of the waves to the cozy domesticity of the homecoming – the yellow light, the fire, the evening meal, the reunited family – is both heartwarming and reassuring. Sam has come back, and life goes on. Everything is all right. The paratactic sentence structure with its succession of 'ands' (there are seven over the course of a sentence and a half) is emblematic of continuity. The *legendarium* that began with refugees fleeing a fallen city ends with Sam's return to a restored and revitalized Shire, a happy ending if ever there was one. At first glance his understated "Well, I'm back," seems to reinforce this.

A second glance suggests another possibility. The announcement is so bare, its message so unnecessary as to imply hidden depths, simplicity cloaking profundity, a world in a grain of sand. We know Sam is back, we have just been told that. We don't need to be told again. Nor does Rosie. Tolkien must have had a purpose beyond the obvious in telling us what we already know. He had. "Well, I'm back" is there both to evoke Bilbo's return at the end of *The Hobbit* and to invoke the *There and Back Again* (to give the full title) motif that rounded that book. But in the context of the larger *legendarium*, in the context of the Music that Sam has just been hearing with its reverberation of the long defeat, above all in the context of Frodo's departure, his final words are not just about there and back again. They can also be, like Tolkien's regret for the lost pre-Christian mythology, a reminder of all that is lost – of all those who are not back, most especially those unlike Sam who cannot come back, who will never come back – not just Frodo but also the anonymous Man of Harad whose death far from home so distressed Sam at the battle of Ithilien; or the heroes dead on the Pelennor Fields whose names are preserved in the song of the Mounds of Mundburg: Harding and Guthláf and doughty Grimbold and Hirluin the fair and Forlong the old, all those who fought and "fell [...] in a far country" and now lie "under mould [...] under grass in Gondor by the Great River" and never to their own country "returned in triumph" (*TT* 125); or the other exiles and outcasts of Tolkien's imaginary and all too real world – Húrin and Túrin and Morwen and Nienor and Fili and Kili and Thorin Oakenshield.

Sam's "Well, I'm back" stands in contrast to all of these. His last words bring to a close both *The Lord of the Rings* and the larger myth to which the Music re-connects him. These words – which are also Tolkien's – are not the "rather bitter" ones of their author's description to Unwin, but in the context of all that has gone before and of all that is lost and will never come back, they are at best bittersweet. They make a fitting finish to this long, complex, and rather bitter story, a marvelous, intricate structure reared expressly to be destroyed that we may regret its loss.

These two scenes with Sam illustrate how knowledge of Tolkien's background can change our reading of the foreground. Effective in themselves, one for its melancholy, the other for its cheerfulness, both episodes are also tied into a web of implicit meaning that reaches beyond their immediate placement to put them in the context of and relevant to the larger mythology. They bring to a close *The Lord of the Rings*, but they also mark the *de facto* ending of the whole *legendarium* that surrounds it. For though Tolkien wrote and re-wrote till almost the end of his life, he never succeeded in carrying his mythology to its projected but never fleshed out conclusion. In terms of the whole story, then, the scenes we have looked at must stand not just as Sam's farewell but in a practical sense also Tolkien's. Freighted with implications that we can now fully grasp, they are emblematic of both Tolkien's and Parker's words for the story, words that give deeper insight into a book and a world we thought we already knew.

Now that we have it all, we can begin to evaluate the breadth and depth as well as the height of an extended history within which *The Lord of the Rings* still stands out as the masterpiece and enduring monument to Tolkien's genius. The *legendarium* was Tolkien's for the sixty or so years during which it grew under his hands in ways not even he could have anticipated. *The Silmarillion* has been Christopher's for the last forty-some years during which he undertook the enormous task of editing and making the whole corpus available – his life's work. His contribution to his father's vision and to the field of Tolkien studies is incalculable.

The publication in 2018 of *The Fall of Gondolin*, which Christopher announced as his last, both closes and re-opens the book of Tolkien's *legendarium*. With it, Christopher says, he has laid down his pen. He has in a sense said to the many fans, critics, lovers, and scholars of his father's life's work, those who have had the benefit of his own life's work, 'over to you'. He has made it is ours. We are in his debt.

Part III
Words

Words, Words, Words

"Mythology is language and language is mythology."
J.R.R. Tolkien, 'On Fairy-stories' MS A (*TOFS* 181)

"But how powerful, how stimulating to the very faculty that produced it, was the invention of the adjective: no spell or incantation in Faërie is more potent."
J.R.R. Tolkien, 'On Fairy-stories' (*TOFS* 41)

Romanticism is most frequently understood as an artistic movement involving music and literature and the plastic arts. But it also manifests a pronounced political aspect in which the arts become the expressions of and advocates for cultural change. The particular aspect of Romanticism I want to connect to Tolkien is romantic nationalism, an advocate for change whereby a nation-state finds its identity not with some exterior hegemony but from the internal ethnos of its language, culture, and mythology. This was a movement that swept western Europe in the 19th and 20th centuries and led to unrest in the political and literary landscape that is still going on today. The epigraphs above, taken from one of Tolkien's most important essays, derive from and reflect this movement, and though they were written seventy-odd years ago they are still relevant today.

They express two related and highly romantic ideas. The first connects language and myth as interdependent, the second idea identifies the power of words to create what they describe. Both concepts express the essence of Tolkien's attitude toward and feelings about language – and both inform his work and can be tied directly to romantic nationalism. The first epigraph states unequivocally that a culture's belief system is encoded in its language, while the second champions the idea that words create what they communicate. That Tolkien made these statements in an essay about fairy-stories is neither surprising nor insignificant. They are evidence, if any is needed, of his lifelong engagement with the world of imagination he called Faërie, a world called into being, so his fairy-story essay maintains, through words. Moreover, Tolkien is on record as saying that his own so-called "mythology for England"[1] was "primarily linguistic in inspiration and was begun in order to provide the necessary background of 'history' for Elvish tongues" ('Foreword', *FR* 5).

The Myth-Language Connection

The first of the two epigraphs is about as simple a construction as grammar can provide. It consists of two independent clauses that mirror each other and are linked by 'and'. Each clause is a simple three-word declarative: noun+verb+noun, a subject followed by a predicate followed by an object. Tucked into that deceptive simplicity, however, is a complex message of interdependence and reciprocity. The first clause, saying that mythology is language, pretty much explains itself: myths are the stories of a culture's origin and history, and the stories that arise from a culture are perforce told in the words of its language. The second clause is harder to unpack, though its grammar is equally simple, for it makes a leap from words to metaphysics. To say that language is mythology is to say in essence that encoded *in the words* and indivisible *from the words* are the beliefs and assumptions of the culture, the national soul that undergirds the stories.

To try to divide a culture from its traditional language is to rob that culture of its history, its worldview, and its identity. It is to destroy its individual nature and its sense of selfhood. Real-world examples abound: One is what Tolkien described in his essay 'English and Welsh' as the "legal oppression" of spoken Welsh by the Tudor decree that all legal proceedings in Wales must be in English (*MC* 165), another is the 19th and early 20th centurys' Anglo-American practice of sending Native American children to English-only boarding schools. These culture-bending practices had their imaginary parallel in Tolkien's own

---

1 The phrase "a mythology *for England*," introduced in Humphrey Carpenter's biography of Tolkien (*Bio* 89), was one the man himself may never have used, at least not in writing. But it has become current and remains in popular usage. I use it here to refer to the combined work of his *The Silmarillion*, *The Lord of the Rings* and its 'Appendices', and, to a lesser extent, *The Hobbit*.

Silmarillion, where Thingol, King of the Sindar Elves, forbade his kin, the Noldor, the use of their language, Quenya, throughout his realm.

The first epigraph could easily have been the slogan for the romantic nationalism of Europe and the British Isles in the 19th and early 20th centuries, when the realization of the deep connection between myth and language became a movement for ethnic and cultural independence. Newly formed or self-realized nations discovered in their indigenous folk and fairy tales evidence of the ancestral 'folk' who told those tales, the presumed regional and cultural forebears whose existence would validate a resurgent nationhood. This evidence was assumed to be encoded in archaic vocabulary, words as relicts, the leftovers of a once-shared mythology and worldview now fossils embedded in the matrix of the stories. This climate of thought led by a winding and comparative route to the so-called Indo-European theory of the origins of language families, a theory that dominated language studies in the 19th and early 20th centuries and had considerable influence on both the art and the scholarship of J.R.R. Tolkien, the pre-eminent and most influential fantasy writer of the 20th century.

Tolkien was familiar with the scholarship that fueled that theory: books such as Jacob Grimm's *Deutsche Mythologie*, Alois Walde and Julius Pokorny's *Indogermanisches etymologisches Wörterbuch*, Max Müller's five-volume *Chips from a German Workshop*, and Andrew Lang's *Custom and Myth*. He knew as well the great collections of orally transmitted folktale and folk-poetry that both preceded and followed them: Jacob and Wilhelm Grimm's *Kinder- und Hausmärchen* (first published 1812), Elias Lönnrot's Finnish *Kalevala* (first published in 1835), Hersart de la Villemarqué's Breton *Barzaz-Breiz* (first published in 1839). They all were published and read as evidence of ancestral culture and, more importantly, used to promote newly-formed national identity.[2] Lönnrot's collection of Finnish folk-songs (*runos*) in particular was credited with contributing materially to the growing nationalist movement in Finland (in previous centuries under the political domination of either Sweden or Russia) and was a direct inspiration for Tolkien's invented mythology. In the same vein, the early 20th century Celtic revival encouraged the rediscovery and re-telling of the tales

2 The catalogue of Tolkien's books on philology, etymology, folklore and mythology now held by the English Faculty Library in Oxford runs to 90 folio-sized pages and 277 card entries.

of Irish and Welsh mythology[3] by William Butler Yeats and Lady Guest and Lady Gregory. Like their Germanic and Finnish and Breton counterparts, the Celtic stories were grounded in the Irish language and ethnic worldview and, in the case of Ireland especially, in the revived ethnic and national consciousness that led to the Easter rebellion of 1916.

The second epigraph, lengthier in content but simpler in concept, was equally important both to Tolkien's art and to his scholarship. It declares unequivocally that words influence the very faculty that uses them – that is to say, the human mind. Words create the phenomenon they purport to describe. They shape the thought and perception of the very culture they express. This is the essence of Romanticism as well as nationalism, the elevation of cultural as well as personal selfhood to a position of supreme importance, a mythic history encoded in the words that both preserve and create it. The well-worn phrases that grounded Romanticism in personal experience – Wordsworth's "spontaneous overflow of powerful feelings," and "emotion recollected in tranquility" – have been graven on the minds and in the copybooks of generations of post-Victorian schoolchildren as the very definitions of romantic poetry. It is this elevation of the value of experience, *emotion*, *feelings*, that impelled Wordsworth to seek out ruined abbeys, that kept Keats loitering on the cold hillside, that led Coleridge to Xanadu.

A Mythology for England

It will come as no surprise to readers of *The Lord of the Rings* that J.R.R. Tolkien, the 20th century's pre-eminent mythmaking author, had his own highly personal version of romantic nationalism. This was his realization, as he described in a letter to a publisher, that England had no mythology of its own, which sparked his consequent ambition to create a mythology he could "dedicate" to England (*Letters* 144). The idea began when as a schoolboy at King Edward's School in Birmingham he read the Finnish *Kalevala* "in Kirby's poor translation"

3 For Ireland this was the Fenian and Ulster cycles featuring the deeds of the heroes Finn MacCool and Cuchulainn; for Wales it was the *Mabinogion*.

(*Letters* 214) and burgeoned a year or so later when, as an undergraduate at Exeter College, Oxford, he checked Eliot's *Finnish Grammar* out of the college library in an effort to learn enough Finnish to read the original. Though his attempt failed – he was "repulsed with heavy losses" (*Kullervo* 103), *Kalevala* "set the rocket off in story" (*Letters* 214). His own mythology for England would link the ideas of the two epigraphs we've been discussing, combining the myth-language symbiosis with the power of words to literally create what they purport to describe. The result would be the *legendarium* he came to call *The Silmarillion*, his so-called "mythology for England." Tolkien's reading of *Kalevala* fostered his own invention of languages and encouraged his creation of a world as a home for those languages. This, if you will, was his own personal version of romantic nationalism.

In the stories he wrote for *The Silmarillion* and its continuation in *The Lord of the Rings* is clearly to be found his fictive version of this reciprocal partnership between myth and language. Tolkien's Romanticism shared characteristics with its European and English counterparts. Like them, it eroded the barrier between the natural and super-natural. Like them, his greatest work *The Lord of the Rings* romantically elevated his hobbits, as 'little people', to the status of extraordinary folk-heroes. But at its most basic, Tolkien's Romanticism operated at the level of words and combinations of words. This operation was his making real and putting into practice of the dictum quoted above that mythology and language are indisseverable, that the latter provides the building-blocks of the former.

The method is laid out plainly in his allegory in '*Beowulf*: The Monsters and the Critics' which tells of the man who built a tower out of "old stone" from which he was able to "look out upon the sea" (*MC* 8). As I read the essay the old stones are the actual words from which the poem is made, time-engraved building-blocks shaped by past history which, in another *Beowulf* essay ('On Translating *Beowulf*'), Tolkien characterized as "tough builder's work of true stone" and described as "strong to stand" (*MC* 71). Ascent to the top of the tower leads to a higher awareness, the wider vision that is the sea. It is no great leap to move from the *Beowulf* poet and his poem to Tolkien and his work, to find a likeness in both in their use of words to communicate a vision.

The Power of Words

Tolkien's brand of Romanticism, centered on words and foreshadowed in the 'tower' allegory, has much in common with that of his fellow-Inkling Owen Barfield. I have written elsewhere about how Barfield's approach to language influenced Tolkien's, so I will only say here that even a brief look at the two men's own writing will show at once how both followed the same paths of thinking and came to the same conclusions. It was Barfield who wrote in an early collection of his essays, *Romanticism Comes of Age*, that the "face of nature, the objects of art, the events of history and human intercourse [betray] significances hitherto unknown as the result of [...] poetic or imaginative *combinations of words*" (Barfield 1944: 6, italics mine). The title of his book is the giveaway. *Romanticism Comes of Age* is a declaration that Romanticism has grown up. It has fulfilled its potential; it has become fully aware of its own process, which is what Barfield has called "a felt change of consciousness" (Barfield 1928: 48, 52) for which the evidence is an ever-increasing precision in the use of and differentiation among words and combinations of words.

It was Tolkien who wrote in his seminal essay 'On Fairy-stories':

> Anyone inheriting the fantastic device of human language can *say the green sun*. Many can then imagine or picture it. But that is not enough [...] To make a Secondary World in which the green sun will be credible will probably require labour and thought, and will certainly demand a special skill, a kind of elvish craft. (*TOFS* 61)

That "elvish craft," said Tolkien, was fantasy, and even as he wrote his essay, he was and had been for some time engaged in creating one. Barfield's thoughts about the power of words found a match in Tolkien's thoughts about the same thing. Tolkien's profession of philology, the study of the history of language, led him to explore the shifts and changes of words and meanings – therefore of consciousness – over time. Barfield's philosophic study of the history of consciousness led him to look for the evidence of it in those same shifts and changes of words and meanings – therefore of consciousness – over time.

Both men in their different ways were participating in a particular development of thought about the relationship between language and reality current in the mid-twentieth century. This was a time of great ferment in the study of language as it moved from historical philology to analytic linguistics, a ferment to which Barfield and Tolkien were responsive. There is a perceptible strain of Romanticism in the writings of philosophers of language like Ferdinand de Saussure, Edward Sapir, and Benjamin Whorf,[4] all of whom espoused the notion that words can create the reality they describe by expressing the perception of those who create the words and affecting the awareness of those who hear and repeat them.[5]

It was Barfield who declared that "the poetic or imaginative use of words enhances their meanings," and maintained further that "those enhanced meanings may reveal hitherto unapprehended parts of reality" (Barfield 1944: 6). Or to put it another way, words poetically and imaginatively used may create the things they purport to describe by causing the viewer to see new meanings in old images.

It was Tolkien, operating on the same wavelength, who wrote in 'On Fairy-stories':

> The human mind, endowed with the powers of generalisation and abstraction, sees not only *green-grass* [...] but sees that it is *green* as well as being *grass*. But how powerful, how stimulating to the very faculty that produced it, was the invention of the adjective: no spell or incantation in Faërie is more potent. And [...] such incantations might indeed be said to be only another view of adjectives, a part of speech in a mythical grammar. [...] When we can take green from grass, blue from heaven, and red from blood, we have already an enchanter's power – upon one plane. (*TOFS* 41)[6]

In that community of thought to which poets are drawn, Wordsworth, in his 'Preface to *Lyrical Ballads*', had made the same point two centuries ago when he advocated the use of

> language really used by men [... with] a certain colouring of imagination, whereby ordinary things should be presented to the mind in an unusual way; and, further, and above all, to make these incidents and situations interesting

4 The title of Whorf's most influential book, *Language, Thought, and Reality*, says it all.

5 I am not promoting the accuracy or inaccuracy of Sapir-Whorf, which has been called into question by competing scholars such as Ekkehart Malotki and Noam Chomsky. I am simply proposing that it was in play when Tolkien and Barfield were writing.

6 See also the matching quote from Tolkien's original 1939 draft which shows the enduring power of the words to the argument. "The human mind was endowed with powers of 'abstraction', of not only seeing green grass and discriminating it from other things, or of finding it good to look upon, but of seeing that it was green – as well as grass and hence of inventing a word green. But how powerful ~~and potent~~ even stimulating to the very faculty that gave birth to that invention is the adjective: no spell or talisman in a fairy story is more so/potent. [...] When we can take green from grass and paint the sky or a man's face with it, or blue from heaven and red from blood we have already an enchanter's power [...] Such fantasy is a new form, in which man is become a creator or sub-creator" (*TOFS* 181).

> by tracing in them, truly though not ostentatiously, the primary laws of our nature: chiefly, as far as regards the manner in which we associate ideas in a state of excitement. (Wordsworth 1880: 2-3)

What Wordsworth called "a state of excitement" Tolkien calls "Faërie". His use of the word, though it will be familiar to many of his readers acquainted with the Fairy-story essay, yet merits some explanation. It comes from Old French *fée* or *fay* meaning 'fairy', but can be traced back to Latin *fata*, meaning *fate*, from *fari*, 'to speak'. From this derivation comes Tolkien's association of the word with 'spell' and 'incantation'. Faërie embodies the power of the word. Like Barfield, like Wordsworth, Tolkien was describing the effect of language on perception, its "enchanter's power" to reveal "hitherto unapprehended" aspects of the world. His phrase "a part of speech in a mythical grammar" is the key to his thinking – not art, not yet even craft, but grammar, that most prosaic, most rule-bound of systems which yet underpins imagination and creates Fäerie. It is words that he is talking about, words understood in the way that Barfield describes, in the "the poetic or imaginative" use which enhances their meaning.

Unapprehended Aspects

Taking these statements at face value, we might suppose that the language – the grammar – referred to would be Tolkien's Elvish languages, specifically Quenya, which he called 'Elven Latin', and Sindarin, the more generally used language of the Elves of Middle-earth. We would be wrong, however, or at best only partially right, for those languages appear relatively rarely in the stories; they are invariably distinguished by being in italic and are used more to give flavor than to convey direct meaning. The study of Tolkien's invented languages is a discipline in its own right but sits slightly to one side of his more literary scholarship.[7] By and large, English is the language in which his mythos is written, and it is in common English words that Tolkien's mythmaking appears at its most effective. I want to take a close look at select passages from Tolkien's works that I think illustrate

7 Prominent journals in the field of Tolkien linguistics include *Vinyar Tengwar*, edited by Carl Hostetter and *Parma Eldalamberon*, edited by Chris Gilson. *A Secret Vice*, edited by Dimitra Fimi and Andrew Higgins, is a book-length study of Tolkien's essay of the same name and a history of his language-invention. A biennial meeting held since 2005 on Tolkien linguistics called *Omentielvo* attracts participants from many countries.

the same principles that the above statements offer. Some I have written about before in other contexts. All illustrate for me in one way or another the creative principles I have quoted by both Tolkien and Barfield.

The first passage describes Frodo experiencing his first sight of Lórien, the most enchanting, the most fantastic, the most Faërian realm in Tolkien's Middle-earth:

> Frodo stood awhile still lost in wonder. It seemed to him that he had stepped through a high window that looked on a vanished world. A light was upon it for which his language had no name. All that he saw was shapely, but the shapes seemed at once clear cut, as if they had been first conceived and drawn at the opening of his eyes, and ancient, as if they had endured forever. He saw no colour but those he knew, gold and white and blue and green, but they were fresh and poignant, as if he had at that moment first perceived them and made for them names new and wonderful. (*FR* 365)

The operative words here are 'gold' and 'white' and 'blue' and 'green', illustrating the stimulating power of the adjective, as in the passage from 'On Fairy-stories' cited above. It should be noted that this is not 'poetic diction' as the phrase is usually understood. The words – all of one syllable – conjure no vivid or striking images. They do not paint anything but themselves. But with them, Frodo and the reader are discovering the power of adjectives as parts of speech in the "mythical grammar" – that the process of naming is an act of creation.

Lórien, let us not forget, is Tolkien's Faërie at its purest and most distilled, a realm of enchantment that "cannot be caught in a net of words [... yet is a word that] may perhaps most nearly be translated by Magic" (*TOFS* 32). The perception-words in this passage about Lórien that try to capture its Fäerie – "it *seemed* to him", "he *saw*" (repeated twice), "as if he had first *perceived* them" – emphasize the subjective, Magical (therefore also Romantic with a capital 'R') nature of the experience.

If you are thinking here of Wordsworth's daffodils, you are on the right track. In both instances, the thing seen is made to appear by way of someone's subjective perception recreated in words. We don't apprehend the "Magic" directly, we see someone else seeing it and experience it through that person's experience. As with Wordsworth and the daffodils, all our response is tied to one individual's perception. Our consciousness merges with his as we look through his eyes. It's equally important that what Frodo sees for the first time he already knows.

Barfield's word 'unapprehended' is apposite here. Frodo is apprehending for the first time what has always been there, recreated by Tolkien "after the fashion of nature herself" (Barfield 1944: 19). This is the process Tolkien described in 'On Fairy-stories' as 'fantasy', writing that "in such 'fantasy' as it is called, new form is made; Faërie begins; Man becomes a sub-creator" (*TOFS* 42). Barfield says almost the same thing, declaring: "I think the true *differentia* of imagination is that the subject should be somehow merged or resolved into the object. Talent may copy nature, but genius claims to 'create' after the fashion of nature herself" (Barfield 1944: 19). Barfield's term 'create' and Tolkien's 'sub-create' seem interchangeable here, but the prefix added to the base verb creates in itself a new reality and deepens the romantic concept even further.

What Barfield tells us, Tolkien shows us – vividly and immediately. According to Barfield, "imagination involves a certain disappearance of the sense of 'I' and 'Not I'. It stands before the object and feels 'I am that'" (Barfield 1944: 19). Frodo feels he has made "names new and wonderful." He has done precisely what Tolkien described in the long passage from 'On Fairy-stories' quoted above; by enhancing the parts of speech in the mythical grammar, he has created a new reality. It takes a moment for a readerly consciousness to step back from this act of creation and remember that it is not Frodo but Tolkien who is using these words, this grammar, to do what Barfield describes, create the reader who becomes Frodo who merges with Lórien. My point is not that either Tolkien or Barfield is influenced by or paralleling the other. Rather, each is responding in a slightly different way to a then-current climate of thought that conjoined the principles of Romanticism with contemporary linguistic theory to say that language creates what it describes.

This reliance on secondary perception to create the thing perceived is a technique that Tolkien used again and again but never to better effect than in the episode wherein Gimli re-creates for Legolas his experience of the Glittering Caves of Aglarond. Gimli's account of the Caves is no less recollected emotion than was Wordsworth's account of seeing the daffodils. The lyrical description of "folded marbles, shell-like, translucent, columns of white and saffron and dawn-rose [...] fluted and twisted into dreamlike forms, wings, ropes, curtains fine as frozen clouds" mirrored in "still lakes" (*TT* 152) is hyper-romantic. It is Keatsian, over the top. It is Romanticism not just squared but cubed.

But the great reveal in this passage is not the beauty of the caves. It is the beauty of Gimli that we perceive for the first time. What distinguishes Gimli's description is not the poetic catalogue, the beauty-words like 'shell-like', 'dawn-rose', 'frozen clouds'. It is instead 'plink!', the child-like, onomatopoeic comic-book sound-effect uttered by Gimli to recreate the fall of "a silver drop" of water that wrinkles the lake and makes the towers "bend and waver like weeds and corals in a grotto of the sea" (*TT* 153). It is 'plink!' that anchors the whole speech and betrays the real Gimli. It is the surprise view of the gruff, taciturn, axe-brandishing Dwarf as a romantic poet, so unexpected that even Legolas is moved to say, "I have never heard you speak like this before" (*TT* 153). Neither have we, the readers, and now we feel the full force of Tolkien's sub-creative art.

Gimli the viewer is so persuasively recreated through his own words as the embodiment of Romanticism that it takes a while to remember that it is not Gimli's words to which we are responding but Tolkien's, whose "poetic or imaginative combinations of words" have created in us a felt change of consciousness. We have climbed his tower and seen the sea. The sea has many moods, as does Tolkien's power to alter through words his reader's consciousness. I intend my next example, considerably less lyrical than Frodo seeing Lórien or Gimli seeing the Caves, to shift into a higher gear, so to speak. It is my intention to extend the concept of Romanticism to an extreme, even a radical level, while still keeping faith with the familiar catchphrases cited above. The emotion recollected is not always a happy one; the human race would be bereft of empathy if it were. Nor is the overflow of feeling always positive. Negative feelings have their place in the spectrum and contribute as much to Romanticism as do their happier counterparts. We will, therefore, have to move beyond Wordsworth and the daffodils or Frodo and the colors of Lórien, beyond even Gimli and the caves, and turn to a grimmer experience.

Violent Death

I have chosen for this last example the passage in Chapter Four of *The Two Towers*, 'Of Herbs and Stewed Rabbit', in which Tolkien gives the reader Sam Gamgee's reaction to the death of the Man of Harad. This is the obverse face of Romanticism, its alter ego, not the gothic shiver of Hoffman and Poe but Barfield's "unapprehended reality" of the actual horror that human beings can inflict on one another. Neither Sam nor the reader is prepared for the shock when the idyllic setting of Ithilien, recalling the green world of Robin Hood's Sherwood and Shakespeare's Forest of Arden, becomes instead the backdrop for violent death.

Here is Tolkien's description:

> [...] suddenly straight over the rim of their sheltering bank, a man fell, crashing through the slender trees, nearly on top of [Frodo and Sam]. He came to rest in the fern a few feet away, face downward, green arrow-feathers sticking from his neck below a golden collar. His scarlet robes were tattered, his corslet of overlapping brazen plates was rent and hewn, his black plaits of hair braided with gold were drenched with blood. His brown hand still clutched the hilt of a broken sword.
>
> It was Sam's first view of a battle of Men against Men, and he did not like it much. He was glad that he could not see the dead face. He wondered what the man's name was and where he came from; and if he was really evil of heart, or what lies or threats had led him on the long march from his home; and if he would not really rather have stayed there in peace. (*TT* 269)

As with his treatment of Frodo in Lórien and Gimli at the Caves, Tolkien has implemented a two-stage perception by which to create the thing perceived. We do not see the man. We see Sam seeing the man, and at first glance this passage seems anything but romantic. The dry, wry words-of-one-syllable understatement of "he did not like it much" sounds more like Hemingway than Wordsworth, though we should not forget that Hemingway too has been called a romantic, his spare, elliptical prose the vehicle for suppressed emotion.

What happens to Sam in this scene is exactly that "felt change of consciousness" that Barfield described and that Tolkien's mythical grammar creates, like and yet unlike the felt change that so transported Wordsworth on seeing the daffodils. Barfield's word 'unapprehended' is no less apposite here than with Frodo in Lórien. We can contrast Frodo's color epiphany in Lórien with this second scene also marked with color – green feather, gold collar, scarlet robe, black hair, brown hand. These colors, a far cry from the freshness of Lórien, are all in the service of death. The green-feathered arrow – the killing device – protrudes incongruously from the man's neck just above the golden collar whose splendor is no longer of any use to him. The black hair "braided with gold" is drenched in blood whose implicit red color matches the scarlet robe to form a triad of red, black, and gold, ironic in its splendor and simplicity. This is not an accident.

As bright with color as Frodo's Lórien, the Southron still presents the tough other face of Romanticism, closer in imagery to Melville and Hawthorne than to Wordsworth. It is closer still to Tolkien's contemporary Wilfred Owen – at twenty-five, one year younger than Tolkien – who was killed in action in World War I, one week before the armistice. Owen's 'Dulce et Decorum Est', his savage re-vision of the Latin poet Horace's poetic tag *dulce et decorum est pro patria mori* ('It is sweet and fitting to die for one's country') was written while he was a convalescent at the rehabilitation hospital of Craiglockhart before he returned to France to be killed. It depicted the face of war for a whole generation in his merciless description of the dying victim of a gas attack:

> If in some smothering dreams you too could pace
> Behind the wagon that we flung him in,
> And watch the white eyes writhing in his face,
> His hanging face, like a devil's sick of sin;
> If you could hear, at every jolt, the blood
> Come gargling from the froth-corrupted lungs,
> Obscene as cancer, bitter as the cud
> Of vile, incurable sores on innocent tongues,–
> My friend, you would not tell with such high zest
> To children ardent for some desperate glory,
> The old Lie: *Dulce et decorum est*
> *Pro patria mori.*

If that isn't the spontaneous overflow of powerful feelings, emotion recollected (though not in tranquility but outrage), I don't know what is.

The bare-knuckled, explicit words of Owen's poem – 'writhing', 'gargling', 'froth-corrupted', 'obscene', 'vile', 'incurable' – challenge the conventional meaning of the term 'poetic', yet their raw power supports the idea of Romanticism as emotional reaction, the consciousness-raising process of heightened perception that Wordsworth was talking about. Owen's words are 'parts of speech' in an all-too-realistic grammar. This is not language used to portray heightened nature as with Keats or to create the supernatural as with Poe or Hoffman. Rather, it is language used to hammer home reality, language that is raw, unvarnished, and unsentimentalized. And unmediated. The reader is forced into the scene through the repeated words 'if' and 'you', through the phrase 'if you could', linked to the verbs 'pace', 'watch', 'hear' with the implied corollary 'as I did'. In the less explicit words of Wordsworth, it is a picture of "what man has made of man." This is Romanticism at its most intense, carried beyond epiphany to re-enactment not of inspiration but of horror.

Tolkien pushes the same phenomenon, death in battle, one stage further, transferring the same device of secondary perception – Owen's "if you could" – to Sam, enabling us to see through Sam's mind, as with Frodo in Lórien, the object in question. For sheer power of emotion, our re-living of Sam's experience in the death of the Man of Harad is far closer to Owen's than to Frodo's experience of Lórien or Wordsworth's moment with the daffodils. But it is equally consistent with the romantic sensibility. "A safe fairyland," wrote Tolkien to Stanley Unwin, "is untrue to all worlds" (*Letters* 24), and at this moment in this fairyland, we are not seeing beauty. We are seeing violent, bloody death. We are not emotionally transported, we are horrified. And with the horror comes, for us as for Sam, Barfield's "felt change of consciousness."

Sam's curiosity about the man's name suggests a wish to know the real person and is a reminder of the real-world Christmas truce of 1914, when Allied and German troops put down their guns to jointly celebrate Christmas, to sing carols and share family photographs, a detente that so outraged commanders on both sides that troops were henceforward ordered not to fraternize, lest familiarity should sap their willingness to kill men who were just like themselves. Sam also wonders what "lies or threats" had led the man on the long march from his home, a clear reference to the post-World War I revelation that commanders on both sides, England and Germany, had lied to their troops and to their countries about the actual conditions at the Front in order to sustain and promote the fighting.

Like Wilfred Owen and at about the same age, Tolkien learned in the war they shared all he needed to know about violent, unnecessary death. It touched him most personally in the deaths within months of one another of two of his closest friends, members of the TCBS. This was the fellowship whose nucleus was Tolkien and his friends Christopher Wiseman, G.B. Smith and Rob Gilson. It was formed in 1911 when they were schoolboys together at King Edward's School in Birmingham, sustained through their university years, cemented in a formative meeting in December of 1914 that they called 'The Council of London' – that resulted for Tolkien, as he later wrote, in his "finding a voice for all kinds of pent-up things" (*Bio* 73) – and carried on after, when as young men they went to war.

Rob Gilson and G.B. Smith were killed on the Somme in 1916. Gilson was machine-gunned in the first attack wave on the first day of battle, June 1, 1916. Smith was hit by stray shrapnel while walking behind the lines on November 29 of that year and died of gangrene four days later. Evidence for the far-reaching effect of those deaths can be found in the letters exchanged among the survivors. One, dated 15 July 1916 from Smith to Tolkien on learning of the death of Gilson, calls it "the worst of news" (*Bio* 84). Another, from Tolkien to Smith dated 12 August 1916, shows Tolkien trying without much success to find meaning in such death (*Letters* 9-10). A third, from Smith to Tolkien, shows a similar impulse and ends with the charge, "may you say the things I have tried to say long after I am not there to say them, if such be my lot" (*Bio* 86). And a later one from Christopher Wiseman said, "you ought to start the epic" (*Bio* 90).

It is not hard to see in these exchanges among young men in war the wellspring of Tolkien's writing ambitions – he had thought of the T.C.B.S. as "destined to testify for God and truth" as almost a pre-Raphaelite brotherhood (*Letters* 10), as well as the predictable mixture of grief, ambition, and survivor's guilt that impelled him to start the epic when he came home from France in 1916. Although unlike Sam, Tolkien did not witness either Gilson's or Smith's deaths first-hand, his imagined scene with Sam and the man of Harad can be read as his not-so-tranquil emotional re-collection of what their deaths might have been like, his most vivid depiction of the waste and destruction of war, re-created through the eyes of an unprepared civilian.

The shift of vision (though not of sensibility) from Frodo in Lórien to Sam in Ithilien is not a new phenomenon in Tolkien's work; it works both ways and can be traced back to the crucial period 1914 to 1916. It was this period in his life that brought about the sea-change from the Edwardian-romantic 'The Voyage of Earendel', dated to September 24 1914 (*LT II* 267-69), which he called the "first poem of my mythology" to the brutally realistic story of 'The Fall of Gondolin', the first prose narrative of his mythology, "written in hospital and on leave after surviving the Battle of the Somme in 1916" (*Letters* 220). And, we may add, after surviving the deaths of Gilson and Smith. 'The Voyage of Earendel' is a mythologized account of a celestial phenomenon, the apparent journey of the Evening Star from its appearance on the western horizon just after sunset to its reappearance in the east just before sunrise. John Garth calls it "a paean to imagination," and declares that the mariner's quest "is that of the Romantic individual who has 'too much imagination'." Earendel, says Garth, "overleaps all conventional barriers in a search for self-realization in the face of the natural sublime" (Garth 2003: 47). It is hard to conceive of anything more romantic, both with a small and a capital 'r'.

'The Fall of Gondolin' comes nearer in content and spirit to Owen's poem than to Frodo's Lórien epiphany. It is a realistic[8] account of the siege and sack of a great city and draws on Tolkien's personal and cultural experience as a soldier in World War I to create tank-like "serpents of bronze" with "great feet for trampling" (*FG* 85) and "dragons of flame" that gusts from their jaws (*FG* 85, 86). Such imagery forcibly recalls Wilfred Owen's searing diction. If the latter is Owen's Romanticism at its rawest and most direct, 'The Fall of Gondolin' must surely qualify as Tolkien's equivalent. This is Tolkien's own Barfieldian felt change of consciousness. It re-directed his word-choice but not his mythmaking impulse.

---

8 Or post-Tolkien's part in it at any rate. The actual conflict went on for another two years and ruined a generation but changed little else for Europe.

Conclusion

We do Tolkien a disservice if we look only at the sublime beauty of his words and combinations of words and not at their equally powerful realistic punch, if we allow the lyricism of his prose to overshadow the hard truths of much of his subject matter. For creative fantasy, as he stated in 'On Fairy-stories', is founded on "the hard recognition that things are so in the world as it appears under the sun" (*TOFS* 65). We should acknowledge that while Sam's dead warrior is no less the product of Tolkien's imagination than is Frodo's Lórien, he is also something more; he clearly represents – as that Faërie realm does not – Tolkien's hard recognition that things are "so" in the world under the sun. Both Frodo's vision of Lórien and Sam's view of the man of Harad are valid aspects of the world Tolkien saw around him, a world he recreated in all its variety to the end that others might share his vision.

But the man of Harad brings something to that vision that Frodo in Lórien does not – the "hitherto unapprehended" part of reality that is death in battle, unsought, unwelcome death. Tolkien describes other violent deaths in *The Lord of the Rings* – Théoden's and Denethor's are two – but in both those cases the dying man knows it is coming and in one way or another seeks it out. Furthermore, the details are omitted. The death of the man of Harad is the grim reminder forced on Sam and the reader that war is as constant an aspect of human life as is beauty and a far more prevalent one than any experience of the sublime, both of which it too often overshadows.

Tolkien's romantic spirit is to be found not just in the elven languages he invented to support and validate his mythology of Middle-earth, nor only in his descriptions of transcendent Faërie lands such as Lórien. It is also contained in the language in which he wrote his mythology for England – English. It is to be found in the plain, unadorned, almost always one-syllable, ordinary words he used to create the colors of Lórien, to conjure the effect of a drop of water on Gimli's experience of the Caves of Aglarond and to color in the death of the man of Harad. Tolkien's forthright portrayal of horror as well as enchantment lies not just the eerie gothic horror of his Black Riders or the overwhelming terror of monsters such as the Balrog or the frankly supernatural and unexplained

Eye of Sauron but in the all-too-familiar yet un-natural horror of war, the daily killing of ordinary people by other ordinary people, their shedding of blood and lonely deaths, the enormous impersonal personal insult that human beings can visit upon one another. It was this horror that shadowed the time of Tolkien's life and that he recalled and recreated not just in his elven languages nor, like the Romantic poets, in emotion-suffused poetic diction but in his "enchanters power" to use the romance of ordinary English words to create reality in the minds of his readers, in the plain, unadorned, "tough builder's work of true stone" (*MC* 71), the everyday words whose mythic significance is contained in their very ordinariness.

Like the *Beowulf* poet's, Tolkien's stones are "strong to stand" (*MC* 71). We may be grateful that he used them to build his tower and give us his vision of the sea.

Putting Words in Their Mouths

"Fantasy, of course, starts out with an advantage: arresting strangeness."
J.R.R. Tolkien, 'On Fairy-stories' (*TOFS* 60)

How to make the already strange even stranger. This was the problem Tolkien faced in *The Lord of the Rings* when he brought his monstrous Orcs on stage not just as masses in an army, as at Helm's Deep, but as individual players in the drama with lines of their own. As might be expected, he solved the problem linguistically by reversing the norms, juxtaposing incompatibilities of sight and sound, and having his most grotesque, monstrous, and exaggerated characters speak language more typical of fans at a football match than monsters in a secondary world fantasy. To propose as an alienating factor language which in its proper context is familiar, seems not just a far-fetched but a contradictory approach to alterity. Nevertheless, I will argue that it is just such alienation that readers of *The Lord of the Rings* experience when they encounter the speech of Tolkien's Orcs. The technique works. The more we recognize the Orcs by their speech as familiar types, the more they stand out as aliens among, and other than, the peoples of Middle-earth.

Tolkien gave his Orcs four scenes and a wealth of character portrayal starting in Book 3, Chapter 3 of *The Two Towers*, 'The Uruk-hai'; continuing at the end of Book 4, Chapter 10 of *The Two Towers*, 'The Choices of Master Samwise'; and again, in Book 6, Chapters 1 and 2 of *The Return of the King*, 'The Tower of Cirith Ungol' and 'The Land of Shadow'. In the vivid dialogue of these scenes Uglúk, Grishnakh, Shagrat, Gorbag, Snaga, and the anonymous Soldier and Tracker Orcs come to embody and exemplify what makes the Orcs among the most memorable of Tolkien's characters.

The question of racism is pertinent here, although it bears only tangentially on my main argument, which hinges on incongruity.[1] Orcs have long been targeted as a species of 'other' in *The Lord of the Rings*, their slant eyes and dark-to-sallow complexions invoking familiar western-inspired racial stereotypes. In addition to his fictional descriptions of them, Tolkien said, in a long commentary on the proposed screenplay of *The Lord of the Rings* that he meant them to be "corruptions of the 'human' form seen in Elves and Men. They are [...] in fact degraded and repulsive versions of the (to Europeans) least lovely Mongol-types" (*Letters* 274). Allowing him 'degraded', 'repulsive', and '(to Europeans)' as mitigating modifiers, it is still difficult not to see in this a reference to the conventional nineteenth-century European projections of the racially suspect East. Arguments rage pro and con, and it is not my intention here to enter the debate, except to say that in the above instance he was objecting to a screen treatment which had endowed the Orcs with beaks and feathers. Nevertheless, as Tolkien himself described them in the book, Orcs appear to be the objects of distinct racial bias.

The Solution

Racism notwithstanding, my purpose in discussing Orcs and alterity is to explore what happens (to the reader) when estranging characteristics are accompanied by language that is at once familiar and out of place. When this happens, alterity doubles back upon itself, and the result is radical estrangement through the incongruity of unexpected familiarities. Recognizable speech patterns and diction conventionally associated with familiar, even stereotypical character-types (lower-class, uneducated) fall strangely on the ear when put in the mouths of equally stereotypical monsters, and we realize with surprise that Orcs actually talk as much or more like real people than do the rest of the species that inhabit Middle-earth. After all the fantasy the reader has encountered in a pseudo-medieval world peopled by Wizards, Elves, Dwarves, dragons, and Hobbits – a world whose story settings include sentient forests and malevolent

1 For fuller discussion of Tolkien and racism see Chance 2005, Fimi 2008, Librán-Moreno 2011, Vink 2013, and Stuart 2022. Though his focus is not mine, Tom Shippey (2000) examines the six Orcish conversations in the novel, highlighting the jarring existence with their diction of a shared moral code with weight placed on cooperation, mistrust, and fear.

mountains and whose plot hinges on a Ring of power and invisibility – the Orcs' speech is so colloquially modern that it's jarring and is therefore counter, original, spare, and arrestingly strange in this fantastic world.

Tolkien's term for this estrangement (borrowed from Chesterton) is *Mooreeffoc* ("Coffee-room viewed from the inside through a glass door") or Chestertonian Fantasy. The word was used by Chesterton "to denote the queerness of things that have become trite when they are seen suddenly from a new angle" (*TOFS* 68). In an unfamiliar setting and context, the known becomes strange. This deliberate mismatch of appearance and language divides the Orcs not just from the reader but from their own identity as monsters. Their appearance is estranging. Their language is familiar, even trite, that of bullies in the locker-room or at the bus stop, petty and petty-minded individuals isolated from the society against which they stand out so clearly. Erupting into the secondary world Tolkien called Faërie, the primary triteness of Orc street-slang acts as *Mooreeffoc*, illustrating the queerness of monstrosity when seen suddenly from a new angle. To paraphrase Marianne Moore's call for "imaginary gardens with real toads in them" (Moore 1994: 267), it makes Orcs into real toads in an imaginary garden.

Setting aside for the moment Tolkien's invented languages (though they will reappear shortly), in the conventional English of the narrative, each of the species of Middle-earth can be recognized by speech, from Ted Sandyman at his most patronizingly ironic to Treebeard at his most mellifluous to Aragorn at his most declamatory. Tolkien might easily say, as fellow-writer Mark Twain said of the dialects in *Huckleberry Finn*, that "[t]he shadings have not been done in a haphazard fashion, or by guesswork; but painstakingly, and with the trustworthy guidance and support of personal familiarity with these several forms of speech" (Twain 1899: v). The narrative first introduces readers to the standard but relaxed English diction and usage of the middle-class Hobbits (both in Hobbiton and Bree), informal but governed by the conventions of written English orthography in which what is elided in actual speech is spelled out on the page. Of Bilbo's wealth, for example, it is said: "It will have to be paid for [...] It isn't natural, and trouble will come of it" (*FR* 29). There are few contractions, characters tend to say 'will not' instead of 'won't', 'does not' instead of 'doesn't', 'do not' instead of 'don't'. From the top of the scale, the somewhat poeticized cry of Frodo, "O Gandalf, best of friends, what am I do to?" (*FR* 68), to the hurried, breathless, run-on syntax of Barliman Butterbur, to the lower end of the scale with Sméagol's "Give us that, my love" and "I wants it" (*FR* 62), decorum, the fitting of the word to the speaker, is preserved. The slightly stilted English spoken by Gildor and his Elves – "Hail, Frodo!", "You do not know whither we are going", "Ask no more of me" – presages the plain but correct speech of Strider, as well as the more formal English used by Gandalf and Saruman and the multiple debaters at the Council of Elrond. At the very end of *The Fellowship* and the beginning of Book 3 of *The Two Towers*, we are given the very formal, archaic, and heroic inverted syntax of Aragorn, Éomer, and Théoden as well as the wheedling, whiney but correct diction of Wormtongue. Having read *The Fellowship*, the reader has become accustomed to such nuances in tone and diction.

Sight and Sound

Tolkien's invented languages enhance this experience. "*A Elbereth Gilthoniel/ silivren penna míriel*" sings a voice at Rivendell as Frodo and Bilbo leave the Hall of Fire. The song is described as "clear jewels of blended word and melody" (*FR* 150). Frodo has already heard the song, at his meeting with Gildor in the Woody End, and while he hears it in Elvish his thought re-shapes it into English as "*Gilthoniel! O Elbereth!/ Clear are thy eyes and bright thy breath!*" (*FR* 88), and the English translation does its best to match the Elven sound and appearance. This and other examples of Sindarin/English in the text invite the reader to expect sound matched not just to sense but to the outward appearance of the speaker. The language of the Elves matches their beauty, both in Sindarin and Common Speech. Likewise, we would expect the language of the Orcs to match their ugliness, and so it does but only halfway. Physically, Orcs are "yellow-fanged" (*TT* 48), "very broad" with "clawlike hands" (*TT* 50), "rending nails" (*TT* 51), and legs "made of wire and horn" (*TT* 55). These dehumanizing phrases compound their otherness, creating the image of a creature out of a bestiary.

Actual Orcish Black Speech is a good fit with Orcish appearance. It also is dehumanizing, harsh, and ugly in both explicit appearance and implicit sound, as the examples in the book will show. There's the Ring verse: *Ash nazg dur-*

batulûk, ash nazg gimbatul,/Ash nazg thrakatulûk agh burzum-ishi krimpatul (*FR* 59). There are a few scattered words: *gâsh* 'fire', *sharkû* 'old man', *snaga* 'slave', and *Uruk*, Orcish for 'Orc', which fit the Orcs' in both appearance and (presumed) sound. So far, so good. The monsters have a monstrous language. The Black Speech and the Orcs' appearance together have what Tolkien calls the "inner consistency of reality" (*TOFS* 59). The clashing consonants, gutturals, and dark vowels of Black Speech in the Ring inscription fit the Orcs' physical appearance just as the lyrical, melodious Elven language Sindarin fits the described beauty of Elves in Middle-earth.

It is just here, however, that Tolkien uses the familiar as double estrangement, for most of the Orc dialogue is not in Black Speech but in English of the most colloquial kind. The subsequent encounter with the actual barrack-room lingo of the Orcs in English creates culture shock for the hobbits (Pippin thinks it's "hideous") and dissonance for the reader, who experiences the confusion of meeting the familiar in an unfamiliar context. Tolkien uses several devices by which to enable such experience. In the first Orc-conversation in 'The Uruk-hai', the Orcs are presented as using a kind of lingua franca called "Common Speech" or "ordinary language" because they are from different tribes and cannot "understand each other's Orc-speech" (*TT* 48).[2] At the Tower of Cirith Ungol, the Ring enables Sam to understand the Orcs' language, and we are given a 'translation' of the actual Orc conversation, presumably conducted in Black Speech, into Sam's Common Speech and the reader's native English. By the time Frodo and Sam are caught by the Durthang Orcs in Mordor, this rationale has been abandoned, and Orc speech is rendered in English with no pretense at translation or enhanced hearing.

This is less carelessness on Tolkien's part than expediency. 'Appendix F' of *The Lord of the Rings*, 'Orcs and Black Speech', notes that while the Ring inscription "was in the ancient Black Speech", the curse of the Mordor-Orc and of Grishnakh was "in the more debased form used by the soldiers of the Dark

---

2 Tolkien got round this by way of 'Appendix F': "It is said that they [Orcs] had no language of their own, but took what they could of other tongues and perverted it to their own liking; yet they made only brutal jargons, scarcely sufficient for their own needs, unless it were for curses and abuse. And these creatures, being filled with malice, hating even their own kind, quickly developed as many barbarous dialects as there were groups or settlements of their race, so that their Orkish speech was of little use to them in intercourse between different tribes" (*RK* 409).

Tower" (*RK* 409-10). In other words, it is army slang, a patois far easier for Tolkien to reproduce in English than to try to invent in Black Speech. The one example in actual Orcish of what Tolkien called the "debased form" is the curse of the "yellow-fanged guard" (the Mordor-Orc) against Uglúk: *Uglúk u bagronk sha pushdug Saruman-glob búbhosh skaí* (*TT* 48). This is translated by Tolkien in a draft of 'The Appendix on Languages' in *The Peoples of Middle-earth* as "Uglúk to the cesspool, sha! the dungfilth; the great Saruman-fool, skai!" (*Peoples* 83). Carl Hostetter offers a variant translation as "Uglúk to the dung-pit with stinking Saruman-filth– pig-guts, gah!" (Hostetter 1992: 16).

The curse is effective in the Black Speech, but both translations fall strangely on the ear in the 'debased form', the Common Speech translation. Tolkien was probably wise not to include translation in the text, for it makes the strange both too strange and too familiar. He comes perilously close to tipping the balance as it is. Pippin's interior monologue at the opening of Chapter Three, reported by the narrator, has him hearing the Orcs' "abominable tongue", which when translated into the Common Speech of the narrative becomes in Pippin's mind "almost as hideous as [the Orc's] own language" (*TT* 48). Hideous and abominable it may be in both languages, but in the 'translation' into the Common Speech of the debased form the 'hideous' is immediately recognizable as slang, a mode that distinguishes it from the Ring verse as well as from the conventionally poetic English of the Elbereth hymn, with its 'thy' direct address and syntactic inversion. Elven Common Speech harmonizes with Elves' appearance, where Orcish Debased Common Speech clashes with the fantasy of their nature as monsters. It is as if in the middle of *Beowulf*, Grendel were to start talking like a rapper.

Much of this debased speech involves name-calling of one kind or another. While Orcs regularly curse one another as well as everybody else, and call each other names ("snotty", "sneakthief", "slugs"), as much as they do Éomer and his Rohirrim ("cursed Whiteskins"), their abuse is not couched in the language of fantasy but in the earthy realism of barnyard and gutter. Not just Merry and Pippin, and Frodo and Sam, but Snaga, Shagrat, Uglúk, and Grishnakh are regularly cursed and name-called, the last four by each other. *Snaga*, which means 'slave' in the Black Speech, may in fact be a contemptuous epithet and not a proper name or – even more typically Orcish – a contemptuous epithet turned into a proper name.

Orcs' debased barrack-room vocabulary – 'swine', 'guts', 'sties', 'maggots', 'slugs', 'dung', 'swag', 'dunghill rat' – chimes discordantly within its fantasy setting. Where the narrator refers to Sauron synecdochally as 'the Eye', or 'the Hand', or metonymically as 'the Tower', within the story proper, it is the Orcs whose formal name for Barad-Dûr is *Lugbúrz* (probably meaning 'Dark Tower' but listen to the effect of those gutturals and the buzz of that voiced fricative) and who more richly than the other inhabitants of Middle-earth use figures of speech. They refer to Sauron and/or the Nazgûl not just as "the Great Eye", but more familiarly as "the Big Bosses", "the Top Ones", "High Up", "He", "Himself", "Number One", a kind of definition by omission and/or circumlocution. Shelob is "Her Ladyship" and torture is "fun". Nobody else in the book talks this way.

'Personal Familiarity'

Where did a middle-class, university-educated inventor of languages find the 'debased', low-class street-slang he gave the Orcs, for he surely did not invent it as he did Black Speech? One possible answer is from books, for several dictionaries on such language were accessible to him, though it is not known if any was part of his personal library.[3] The earliest are *A New Dictionary of the Terms Ancient and Modern of the Canting Crew, in its Several Tribes of Gypsies, Beggars, Thieves, Cheats, &c.* by one B.E. (gent.), published in 1698 by W. Hawes, P. Gilbourne, and W. Davis and James Francis Grose's *A Classical Dictionary of the Vulgar Tongue*, published in 1785 by S. Hooper, which lists many of the same terms but expands the list. Grose's book was eventually superseded by John Camden Hotten's *Slang Dictionary* in 1859. In 1889, two multi-volumed slang dictionaries went on sale: *A Dictionary of Slang, Jargon and Cant* by Albert Barrere and Charles Leland and *Slang and its Analogues* by John Farmer and W. E. Henley; the latter was first published in a formidable set of seven volumes, later abridged to a single volume and released in 1905 as *A Dictionary of Slang and Colloquial English*. This book provided the major portion of Eric Partridge's

3 They need not have been. His work on the *OED* would have familiarized him with, and given him access to, an alphabet of dictionaries.

Dictionary of Slang and Unconventional English (1938). Given Tolkien's interest in language and languages, and his training in the history of their development, it seems reasonable that he might have availed himself of the opportunity to consult any one or several of these dictionaries, all of which fall comfortably within or before the timeframe of his composition.

But there is no proof. Moreover, he need not have relied on such academic sources, for he had a more personal and immediate one ready to hand. I suggest that here, as in so many instances, Tolkien could have been drawing on direct experience. Much has been made (not least by Tolkien himself) of his admiration for and sense of debt to the ordinary, working-class soldiers he met during his service in France in World War I. Sam, particularly, has been singled out at the prototypical batman (see Hooker 2004), the personal servant attached to an officer in the English army. As a batman, Sam is portrayed as talking low class but respectfully – "Mr. Frodo, sir" or "Mr. Pippin." Little has been said about the fact that since there is a range of behavior among and within all social classes, Tolkien would certainly also have heard from his fellow-soldiers less savory material in vocabulary and manner of speech, reflective of a different stratum of society and a different attitude toward authority.

Mark Twain's phrase, "personal familiarity" with the dialects used is apposite, and it is not unreasonable to imagine that Tolkien was drawing on a similar personal familiarity with the words and expressions he put into the mouths of his Orcs. In his landmark study, *Tolkien and the Great War*, John Garth observes that "English received an enormous jolt of electricity from […] the experiences of the Great War. Old words received new meanings; new words were coined; foreign phrases were bastardized" (Garth 2003: 124). Immersed as he was in army life, says Garth, "Tolkien was surrounded by wordsmiths […] soldiers' slang, which spanned death, drink, food, women, weapons, the battlefield, and the warring nations, grew out of irony and contempt for what was intolerable; it was a crude and unlovely as camp life itself" (Garth 2003: 124). A recent newspaper article on World War I concurred, describing World War I soldiers' slang as "privileging of the ordinary soldier's perspective […] a suspicion of authority and a tendency to mock those who wield it […] a taste for absurdity, sarcasm and black humor" (Scott 2014).

Christopher Tolkien, though he does not refer specifically to Orc speech, has noted that the initial drafting of the chapter in Book Three called 'The Uruk-hai', which gives the first close-up account of the Orcs was "astonishingly close to the final form" in *The Two Towers* as published (*Treason* 409). While Christopher is primarily referring to plot, the ease with which this chapter seems to have unfolded suggests that Tolkien had the personal familiarity of his army experience and was making good use of his well-known ear for language to create (in the most blatant example in the book) a species through its diction, through what the readers 'hear' as well as what they 'see'.

Words in Their Mouths

The obvious question is why Tolkien picked this particular kind of language for his Orcs, and I suggest that the answer is because it was the most jarring kind of language he had at his command. We can be sure his choice was not random. The Orcs are portrayed as talking even lower-class than Sam and anything but respectful. Their speech is 'vulgar' in both the literal and colloquial senses of the word, impolite, abusive, and liberally peppered with gutter-slang. Slang it may be, but as with other examples of colloquial 'folk' language, it is it is also precise, grammatical, rich in metaphor and vivid in imagery. Examination of the language of Uglúk, Grishnakh, Shagrat, Gorbag, Snaga, and the unnamed but sharply delineated soldier and tracker Orcs who follow Frodo, Sam, and Gollum as they approach Mount Doom, will show the skill with which Tolkien puts words in their mouths – street-slang, thieves' cant, gutter lingo – to otherize his Orcs and distance them from the rest of his two-legged creatures.

Here are examples. First, "absurdity, sarcasm and black humor" (Scott 2014), as seen, for example, in Grishnakh speaking to Merry & Pippin: "Enjoying your nice rest? Or not? A little awkwardly placed perhaps, swords and whips on one side, and nasty spears on the other" (*TT* 58). Or: "What do you think you've been kept alive for? My dear little fellows, please believe me when I say that it was not out of kindness: that's not even one of Uglúk's faults" (*TT* 59).

We get the message. It's Grishnakh who's "enjoying" the hobbits' exhaustion and discomfort, which is anything but a "nice rest." To be "awkwardly placed" better describes a social situation than whips and swords and spears, which are more than 'awkward'; they are physical, threatening, and dangerous. Spears are not "nasty", implying a psychological attitude; they are impersonal, lethal, killing tools. The hobbits have not been kept alive out of kindness but out of policy, implying that death would be preferable; moreover, in a reversal of the norm, kindness is a character flaw beyond even the capacity of the obviously flawed Uglúk. Grishnakh is not a student of rhetoric, but he's a whiz at absurdity, sarcasm and black humor.

Next, figures of speech:

> Grishnakh to Pippin: "Lie quiet or I'll tickle you with this." (*TT* 48)
>
> Grishnakh to Merry: "Untie your legs? I'll untie every string in your bodies." (*TT* 59)
>
> Shagrat to Frodo: "Keep your trap shut, see!" (*RK* 186)
>
> Soldier Orc: "I'll stick you if you don't shut it down!" (*RK* 202)
>
> Gorbag to Shagrat: "She's [Shelob] sat on a nail, and we shan't cry about that." (*TT* 346)
>
> Gorbag to Shagrat: "Who's stuck a pin into Her Ladyship?" (*TT* 349)
>
> Shagrat to Snaga: "I'll put red maggot-holes in your belly!" (*RK* 182)

And diction:

> Grishnakh to Merry and Pippin: "Curse you, you filthy little vermin!" (*TT* 59) and "I'll cut you both to quivering shreds!" (*TT* 59)
>
> Shagrat to Snaga: "Curse you, Snaga, you little maggot!" (*RK* 181) and "I'll squeeze your eyes out!" (*RK* 182)
>
> Shagrat to Snaga: "I'll eat you!" (*RK* 182)
>
> Snaga to Shagrat: "I'll put an arrow in your guts!" (*RK* 182)

And insult:

> Soldier Orc: "I reckon eyes are better than your snotty noses." (*RK* 202)
>
> Tracker Orc: "Garn!" "Nar!" "You cursed peaching sneakthief!" (*RK* 203)

It is clear from this and other dialogue that while all the Orcs use abusive slang, they do not all use it in the same way. Grishnakh's silky menace is quite different from the coarse bluster of Shagrat or the schoolboy venom of the soldier and tracker Orcs. His voice is described as "softer than the others, but more evil" (*TT* 49), and his elaborate sarcasm – "nice rest", "dear little fellows", "My dear tender little fools", "my little ones", "I'll tickle you", "quivering shreds" – has the effect of making him more dangerous by understatement. His language is proper English, but its very correctness implies a subtext of threat.

In this variegated litany of Orc abuse, from the aforementioned "maggot" and "guts" to the explicitness of "snotty noses" and "filthy vermin", the Tracker Orc's vocabulary is particularly worth attention. Both his expletives, 'garn!' (also used by Shagrat in the Tower) and 'nar!' are typical Cockney mispronunciations of standard English 'Go on!' and 'No'. Henry Higgins' judgment of Eliza Doolittle in *My Fair Lady* that "It's *aow* and *garn* that keep her in her place" ('Why can't the English teach their children how to speak?' Act One) says all that is needed about the separation of classes by diction and accent in Higgins' and by extension Tolkien's England. In addition, the word 'peaching' with which Tolkien modifies 'sneakthief' is a particularly nice touch. The soldier Orc has threatened to report the tracker to the Nazgûl, which provokes the Tracker to accuse him of 'peaching', a term which could have come straight out of the dictionary of Grose, who lists it as 'to impeach'. 'To peach' is London thieves' cant; it means 'to accuse, inform against, rat on'. Compare 'impeachment' (accusation, formal charge), as of a sitting president in American politics (Andrew Johnson, Bill Clinton, Donald Trump).

A major character in John Gay's *The Beggar's Opera*, set in the criminal underworld of 18th century London, is type-named Mr. Peachum (Peach 'em), an informer, fence, and receiver of stolen goods. In this world, for all its theatricality, Orcs would be at home. Orcish diction and usage when speaking among themselves, and to a lesser extent when speaking to non-Orcs (cf. Grishnakh to Pippin), marks them clearly as not just lower-class and ill-educated but as part of a criminal underworld right out of *Oliver Twist*, a seedy underworld that sets them off from the magic of the otherworld of Middle-earth. In a way, Orc dialogue is refreshing (once you get used to the fact that it's coming from monsters), and it can be a relief to read/hear colloquial modern English amid all the 'whither' and 'hither' and 'heed' and 'deem' and 'Hail!' and 'hath'. A little syntatic inversion goes a long way, and the Orcs offer a perhaps welcome break from a superabundance of medievalism.

Moreover, Orc speech alone of all the verbal patterns in Middle-earth seems to have the power to affect the speech of others. Grishnakh's behavior and mode of speech cause Pippin (and later Merry) to consciously abandon their own version of the Common Speech and enter into the Orcish mode of thought and behavior in order to bargain with him. When Grishnakh begins to paw them, Pippin infers from his physical actions what he wants: "The thought came suddenly into Pippin's mind as if caught directly from the urgent thought of his enemy" (*TT* 58), and he begins to bargain with his captor on Grishnakh's own terms and in Grishnakh's own idiom. First, and non-verbally, he imitates Gollum's guttural throat-sound "gollum, gollum." Merry picks it up: "Now's the time to do a deal" (*TT* 58), not usual Hobbit speech to one another or to anyone else but the right words to communicate with Grishnakh on his own terms.

Linguistic Conventions and Differentiations

It is, of course, not Merry but Tolkien who is consciously drawing on linguistic conventions, as shown by his response to an adapter preparing a script of *The Two Towers* for radio performance. To him Tolkien wrote,

> it would probably be better to avoid certain [...] features of modern 'vulgar' English in representing Orcs, such as the dropping of aitches (these are, I think, *not* dropped in the text, and that is deliberate). But of course, for most people, 'accent' [...] is confused with impressions of different intonation, articulation, and tempo. You will, I suppose, have to use such means to make Orcs sound nasty! (*Letters* 253-54)

The clear implication is that the adapter was proposing the use of dropped aitches as a way for actors to portray Orcs. As a linguistic marker the dropped aitch has, since the time of Dickens' Artful Dodger, Bernard Shaw's Eliza Doolittle, and their Cockney (or East End London) counterparts in British music hall, been standard shorthand for a cultural stereotype. Such pronunciation signals 'lower-class' and 'ill-educated', rather like the stage Irishman of the eighteenth and nineteenth centuries. Tolkien had used the dropped aitch (sparingly) for the Trolls in *The Hobbit*, but by the time of *The Lord of the Rings* he had refined his technique. Unlike the Trolls (and pursuant to Tolkien's opinion as expressed in the letter), his Orcs do not drop their aitches. Nonetheless, his comments to the adapter make it clear that their diction on the page implies the omission without the orthography and, even more than their squat, bow-legged appearance, singles Orcs out from the rest of the peoples of Middle-earth. Orcish usage as printed implies the accent, the "intonation, articulation, and tempo" to which Tolkien refers. In the same letter to the radio adapter, Tolkien went on to write,

> if this 'history' were real, all users of the C[ommon] S[peech] would reveal themselves by their accent, differing in place, people, and rank, but that cannot be represented when C.S. is turned into English – and is not, I think, necessary. (*Letters* 254)

Although he says the Common Speech would reveal its speakers by their accent, it is in fact only the Orcs whose speech does so, and the accent is only by implication. It is noteworthy that Tolkien singled out the Orcs as revealing themselves – i.e. sounding "nasty" – by their presumed accent.

In the same letter, he went on to say that he "paid great attention to such linguistic differentiation as was possible in diction, idiom, and so on." A revealing use of idiom which adds practical evidence of the importance of 'shadings' was noted by David Bratman in his essay on 'The Literary Value of *The History of Middle-earth*'. Bratman points out that in *The Return of the Shadow*, edited by Christopher Tolkien, the first draft of what became the 'Strider' chapter in *The Fellowship of the Ring* has Trotter (not yet Strider) say to Frodo at Bree: "I don't think somehow that you will be wanting to meet any of those Black-riders, if you can help it. They give me the creeps" (*Shadow* 153). With fastidious distaste and a discriminating ear Bratman (2000b: 87) comments: "They give him the *creeps*? Let us be grateful that Tolkien changed Trotter's speech as well as his name." Not only is Bratman right, Tolkien's own ear for "diction, idiom, and so on" allowed him to spot the discrepancy and rewrite the speech. In the published version Strider simply says: "Do you wish them to find you? They are terrible!" (*FR* 177). His face is "drawn with pain" (*FR* 177), while his hands clench the arms of his chair. This physical reaction speaks louder than any words and outpaces "the creeps" at every step.

Not only is the linguistic change from "you will be wanting" to "do you wish?" a shift to more correct, conventional literary language, the replacement of "They give me the creeps" by "They are terrible!" is both more dramatic and more in character. Strider with the creeps sounds more like a boy in the fifth form than the shadowed, mysterious stranger who arouses Sam's legitimate suspicions, much less the returning king with a line of distinguished ancestors behind him. What Bratman did not point out, but which rounds out the notion of Tolkien's sensitivity to language and caps the example, is how Tolkien found a way to re-use the idiom when he got to *The Two Towers*, changing the speaker, the addressee, and the immediate situation and bestowing the comment on the character most likely to use an expression like that. "Grrr!" says Gorbag, Captain of the Uruks to Shagrat, Captain of the Tower of Cirith Ungol, and one can almost hear the interjection, almost see the shudder: "Those Nazgûl give me the creeps" (*TT* 347). In this context the expression fits the character and at the same time reveals and distances him from Sam Gamgee (who is listening) as well as from the reader, by now accustomed to the usage of Tolkien's more conventionally-spoken characters.

We should not only be grateful for the change, as Bratman suggests, but observant of an author's growing awareness of how word-choice affects character and (in this case) creates alterity, alienating a character not just from the reader but from the other peoples of Middle-earth. A further bit of dialogue will illustrate. Not long after Gorbag has the creeps, he proposes to Shagrat: "What d'you say? – if we get a chance, you and me'll slip off and set up somewhere on our own with a few trusty lads, somewhere where there's good loot nice and handy, and no big bosses." "Ah," Shagrat replies, "Like old times" (*TT* 347). Not only does this establish the two Orcs as mafia-style petty criminals with a history of extortion if not worse, Gorbag's description of the "set up" offers a disturbing echo of Saruman and his parallel proposition that he and Gandalf join forces to work with Sauron, with the stated goal of ultimately overthrowing him and seizing power themselves. "Our time is at hand [...] And why not, Gandalf? [...] Why not? The Ruling Ring? If we could command that, then the Power would pass to us" (*FR* 272-73). The estrangement we feel from the Orcs' language and behavior, the assumption that such petty villainy is outside the norm, is overturned when we recognize the kinship between Gorbag and

Shagrat, Orcs of the Tower, and Saruman the White Wizard, a.k.a Sharkey, a.k.a the Chief, vandal-architect of the Shire's despoliation and its attempted ruination.

All that separates the White Wizard from the black Orcs is the way each talks, and that gap is closed in 'The Scouring of the Shire' when the former head of the White Council is reduced to Sharkey. The erstwhile Saruman reveals himself as having sunk to the level of the Orcs or – even worse – as having always been at that level, his true nature as Sharkey camouflaged behind his politician's use of a rhetoric as shifting as the colors of his white robe. While the surface of his diction is proper English – indeed rather elaborately proper – its correctness is undermined by its Orcian malice, understatement and irony. "Worm has been very hungry lately," Saruman tells the Hobbits with mock regret. He is – not very obliquely – implying that Wormtongue has not just killed but eaten Lotho, a monstrous act of cannibalism the likes of which up to now has only been attributable to Orcs. "No," Saruman says, "Worm is not really nice" (*RK* 299). "Not really nice" is putting it mildly. Such understatement is worthy of Grishnakh at his best, typical of the Grishnakhian penchant for "absurdity, sarcasm and black humor." That it is now equally typical of Saruman/Sharkey, who "was great once, of a noble kind" (*RK* 299) but is no longer either great or noble, is revealing. It's enough to give you the creeps.

Essay 14

The Fate of Free Will in Tolkien's World

In Chapter Two of J.R.R. Tolkien's *The Two Towers*, Éomer of Rohan confronts a group of strangers threatening his home turf. "What doom do you bring out of the North?" he asks suspiciously. The leading stranger, Aragorn, replies, "The doom of choice" (*TT* 36). Same word, different meaning. Éomer is using 'doom' in its negative sense of fate, destiny or in dictionary terms: "disaster, ruin, extinction" (*American Heritage Dictionary*, entry 4). Aragorn is using 'doom' in the legalistic sense of Old English *dom*: "judgment, judicial sentence, decree, law" or "ruling, command" (Bosworth-Toller, entries I, II). The contradictory phrase sounds like an ironic joke, but Aragorn is serious. So was Tolkien, who wrote the exchange between the two men to signal his deliberate inclusion of both forces – fate and free will – in his invented world. The tension created by pairing 'doom' with 'choice', not just as contrary forces but interactive ones as well, is a structural component built into the world of Middle-earth at the time of Creation. It is also a paradox, a self-contradiction, intentionally installed by its author in his process of creation.

I have written about this before,[1] examining the motives that drive Tolkien's characters when faced with impossible choices. I want now to take another approach, not as before from the inside out but from the outside in – that is to say, not examining whether the characters within the story might have thought they were fated or free to choose, but inquiring what their author, Tolkien, might have thought *he* was doing by having *them* do whichever they did. The words themselves – 'will' and 'fate' – are our best answers. The word 'will' comes from Latin *velle*, 'to wish' or 'to will' and refers to the exercise by human beings of volition, the freedom to choose. The word 'fate' means just the opposite. In grammatical terms, 'fate' is the past participle of the Latin verb *fari*, 'to speak', therefore 'spoken', and carries a sense of finality. Once uttered, a word can be

1 See Flieger 2009. See also Hostetter 2009 and Fornet-Ponse 2010.

repudiated or disavowed, but it cannot be unsaid. The word 'fate', then, conveys the power of words not just to communicate but to create the very reality they describe. As if saying could in truth make it so.

Tolkien had a model for this approach in the Icelandic Eddas, the prose and poetic accounts of the pagan Norse worldview. The Eddas personified fate as three deities, the Norns, goddesses whose names, Urth, Verthandi and Skuld, are parts of speech and thus can be understood as spoken words. *Urth* and *Verthandi* are respectively the past and present tenses of the verb *vertha*, which means 'to happen' thus 'Happened' and 'Happening'. The third deity, *Skuld*, whose name comes into English as the obligatory 'should' or the directive 'shall', is the preterite-present tense of the verb *skulu*, roughly translatable as 'to must'. The preterite present is a hybrid tense in which the present of a verb takes the form of the past tense. This produces two tenses in one but in reverse order, as if the past has traded places with the present, and the two work together to predict a completed future action. It is a grammatical device for showing that a future event is fated – bound to have happened though it has not yet been enacted. One of my former students described this concept as "has to will have happened." *Skuld* is a more economical way of saying it, but the result is the same. The spoken word creates the reality it names.

The 'Ainulindalë', the creation story of *The Silmarillion*, tells of a world conceived in and by music. The creator, Eru-Ilúvatar, presents a musical theme to a chorus of his angels/demigods and invites them to sing the world into being. When a rebellious chorister interposes his own theme, Ilúvatar combines the two and the resultant music comes out "beautiful, but slow and blended with an immeasurable sorrow" and "loud, and vain, and endlessly repeated" as well (*S* 16-17) – as a consequence, so does Arda, the world it creates. Tolkien described this as "a fall of Angels" (*Letters* 147), the Bible's original sin co-incident with creation rather than a consequence of it. To this, Ilúvatar adds an extra ingredient not in the Music: the independently created race of Men (by which is meant human beings) who thus inherit the Fall rather than causing it. Moreover, he gives them "a virtue to shape their life, amid the powers and chances of the world, beyond the Music of the Ainur, which is as fate to all things else" (*S* 41). An earlier version in *The Book of*

Lost Tales I describes the gift more plainly: "And he [Ilúvatar] devised that they [Men] should have free will and the power of fashioning and designing beyond the original music of the Ainu" (*LT* I 61).

The emendation of "free will" to "virtue" might look like a dodge to avoid philosophic controversy, but, whatever the words, the meaning is plain. I know of no other way to read "beyond the Music" and "all things else" than as describing the singular distinction of the capacity to choose among options as being unique to Tolkien's Men. I will take Tolkien's words as I think they were intended, as his enigmatic answer to the fate vs free will debate – that freedom to choose can itself be a doom, *a dom*, a decree or law. In a closed system – the Music is a symphony, not a jam session – this is a crucial distinction. Tolkien seems to have relished the contradiction, for he so arranged his world that the two conditions – fate and free will, doom and choice – are structurally interdependent, as interlocking as mortise and tenon. The entire architecture of his mythology rests on the tension between them.

It is world-building, of course, that exercise in imagination beloved by gamers and fantasy writers, that Tolkien has been credited with generating. But his fate & free will combo is more than world-building, more than a game. It has its origin in his own polarization between opposing literary types, the happily-ending fairy tales he loved and the defeatist ethos of *Beowulf* and the Icelandic Eddas and sagas to which he was drawn by temperament as well as professional interest. It has something to do also with his polarized emotional life, a lifelong seesaw between hope and despair. The hope was inherent in the Catholic faith given to Tolkien by his mother in her conversion from Protestantism when he was a boy of eight. The despair was caused by her death when he was twelve, a death he attributed to the hardship of estrangement from family caused by her adherence to her faith. This is old news in Tolkien studies, and I do not propose to dwell on it except to say that the two extremes taught him the doom of choice at a young age and set him up to see the close alignment – indeed the interdependence – of light and dark.

Tolkien's first biographer, Humphrey Carpenter, who had access to material other biographers have been denied, such as Tolkien's private diaries, called him "a man of antitheses" (*Bio* 95), whose "natural optimism was balanced by deep uncertainty" (*Bio* 129). Carpenter described him as someone for whom "nothing was safe. Nothing would last. No battle would be won forever" (*Bio* 31). He was not alone in this assessment. Some years after Tolkien's death, his friend Father Robert Murray commented in a letter to an inquiring student that "Tolkien was a very complex and depressed man and my own opinion of his imaginative creation [*The Lord of the Rings*] is that it projects his very depressed view of the universe at least as much as it reflects his Catholic faith" (West 2019: 135). The picture is of a dual sensibility, by faith cheerful and outgoing but schooled by early traumas to look on the dark side. The same duality is manifest in his interest in both the Happy Ending of fairy-story, which he equated with the Christian Gospels, and the doom-laden Icelandic Eddas whose Elves, Dwarves, trolls, sorcerers, and monsters inspired the *dramatis personae* of his Middle-earth.

That duality is at the core of two mirror-image statements that Tolkien planted in separate parts of the book, statements that both reflect and reverse one another. The first is Gandalf's pronouncement at the Council of Elrond that the escaped Gollum "must do what he will" (*FR* 269), i.e. that it is his destiny to act of his own volition. The second is Frodo's voluntary acceptance of the burden of the Ring after his last meeting with Boromir, when he says, "I will do now what I must" (*FR* 417). That is to say, he will freely choose what he is obliged to do. Both statements illustrate the preterite-present tense of *skuld*, and their mirroring is the doom of choice which is the fate of free will.

My next example is the Elf Fëanor from *The Silmarillion*, Tolkien's most explicit yet perplexing example of the intersection of fate and free will. As an Elf, Fëanor is bound by the Music. As a creator, he is tied to the things he has created, of which the most important are the jewels of light called Silmarils. These are one-of-a-kind artifacts whose making was a unique act never to be repeated. Fëanor loves the Silmarils "with a greedy love" and keeps them "guarded close, locked in the deep chambers of his hoard" (*S* 60). After the Two Trees that light Valinor are destroyed, all that is left of their light is in the Silmarils. When the vegetation goddess Yavanna asks Fëanor to give her the jewels to re-illuminate the Trees, essentially sacrificing his creation to save her creation, his answer is unequivocal: "This thing I will not do of free will" (*S* 79). Fëanor is no philosopher, and what he means by "free will" is his personal desire. What

Tolkien means by the same phrase is something bigger. The unwitting irony in Fëanor's use of the term is immediately revealed when the news is brought that the Silmarils are already gone, stolen by Melkor in that very hour. Fëanor's will to refuse has been forestalled by the fate of the Silmarils to be stolen.

But it is Tolkien, creator of all three characters – Fëanor, Yavanna, and Melkor – who has purposely brought the two concepts into collision. To understand fully this part of the narrative, we must look not at Feänor but at Tolkien, contriver of the entire situation. Why has he gone to such lengths to devise what seems like an elaborate game? I suggest it is precisely to illustrate how closely fate and free will can be intertwined, and how difficult it can be to distinguish one from the other. Like Fëanor, we go through life thinking that our decisions – not unlike his Silmarils – belong to us, little reckoning with what external circumstances may have a bearing on our internal ones.

This is analogous to Sam, who is a Hobbit and therefore a member of the human race and thus free to change the Music or doomed to the choice. Tolkien gives him the choice but also the dilemma in the chapter of *The Two Towers* called fittingly enough 'The Choices of Master Samwise'. After the attack by Shelob that leaves Frodo seemingly dead, Sam is in a quandary. He repeatedly asks himself, "What shall I do? What shall I do?" (*TT* 340). Sam doesn't know about *Skuld*, but Tolkien does, and knowing that, we can see that what he really has Sam asking is 'What am I *supposed* to do? What is my role in this drama?' Sam remembers his own spoken words at the beginning of the journey: "*I have something to do before the end. I must see it through*" (*FR* 96), but he has not yet caught up with what the "something" is. He agonizes over which is the 'right' choice among a list of bad options: 1) do nothing, 2) avenge Frodo by killing Gollum, 3) follow Frodo into death by killing himself, or 4) take the Ring to the Cracks of Doom.

Of course, he chooses the fourth and takes the Ring, but he also asks plaintively, "Why am I left all alone to make up my mind?" (*TT* 341). Good question. We should remember that the actual person both asking and (implicitly) answering it is not Sam but Tolkien, who has manoeuvered Sam into this position in order to raise the issue in the mind of the reader. So why is Sam left all alone? Aragorn could have told him, as he told Éomer, that choice is his doom, but Tolkien has arranged it so that Aragorn isn't there. There is a reason for that.

Sam's ignorance and confusion are Tolkien's depiction of the human condition as it really is: a foggy landscape in which the traveler is blind, without clear vision to guide choice. Sam's question – why me? – is the one asked by everyone faced with difficult choice – not between good and bad but between bad and worse without knowing which is which.

"Ah well," Sam concludes, "I must make up my own mind. I will make it up." Please notice both "must" and "will", *skuld* and 'choice'. Yet, he cannot help adding: "But I'll be sure to go wrong: that'd be Sam Gamgee all over" (*TT* 340-41). In case his readers haven't yet got the message, Tolkien has Sam carry it to conclusion: "I got it all wrong!" he cries upon learning belatedly that Frodo is alive and adds, "I knew I would" (*TT* 351). His confusion is Tolkien's point, but Tolkien's further point is that he didn't get it wrong after all. His choice of which action to take saves both the Ring and the Phial from being found by the Orcs who capture Frodo's body, although Tolkien takes care that neither Sam nor the reader will understand until afterward why it was essential that he perform those actions in this time and that place.

Leaving Fëanor to his fate and Sam to his choices, I turn now to Túrin Turambar. His story is nested within the larger frame of his father Húrin's imprisonment by Morgoth. Thus, Túrin's life is shaped by two external forces, two voices whose spoken words pronounce his doom. The first voice is that of Morgoth, who speaks a Curse on Túrin's father Húrin and his children: "Behold! The shadow of my thought shall lie upon them wherever they go, and my hate shall pursue them" (*UT* 66). The second voice is that of Morgoth's henchman, the dragon Glaurung, who misdirects Túrin's search for his family and casts a spell of forgetfulness on Túrin's sister Nienor. The word 'spell' is significant here. Tolkien defined it as meaning "both a story told and a formula of power over living men" (*MC* 128). In the case of Túrin, the spell is both the formula and the story.

Túrin's childhood is shadowed by his mother's disobedience of her husband's order to leave their home if danger threatens and her subsequent but belated decision to send only Túrin away. "Thus," says Tolkien as narrator, "was the fate of Túrin woven" (*S* 198), for her decision sets off the chain of events – his fostering by Thingol, his fight with and accidental killing of the Elf Saeros, and his unwitting incest with the sister he has never seen, that will ultimately destroy him. Tolkien has acknowledged the influence of Sophocles here, but the Oedipal association lies not so much in the brother-sister incest as in Túrin's utter lack of insight into his own nature, which is impulsive, stubborn, prideful, quick to take offence and quicker to act on it. Like Oedipus, Túrin is fighting an enemy who is himself. However much he tries to escape, he is a walking illustration of Heraclit's dictum: ἦθος ἀνθρώπῳ δαίμων (*ethos anthropos daimon*, 'Man's character is fate'). Like Oedipus, Túrin is doomed to make choices, but unlike Oedipus, all his choices are doomed. To escape his fate, with each new obstacle, each new turn of the screw, Túrin chooses a new name, and with it a new character, of which the most obvious are Neithan ('The Wronged'), 'Wildman of the Woods', Agarwain son of Umarth ('Bloodstained Son of Ill Fate'), and finally Turambar ('Master of Doom'). The names are Túrin's choices, but as with Fëanor, the irony is Tolkien's, and as with his treatment of Fëanor, it is fully intended.

Having established that Fate weaves a pattern throughout Túrin's life, Tolkien adds the free will thread of Túrin's own impulsive nature. The most traumatic moment in Túrin's trauma-filled life is his discovery that he has unknowingly killed his best friend, the Elf Beleg, who has come to rescue him from captivity. A look at how carefully Tolkien sets this up, how artfully he arranges apparently unconnected elements – a sword, a state of mind, a flash of lightning – for maximum effect, will make clear his intent to stir together fate and free will and leave the reader to wrestle with the mixture.

The first element is the sword carried by Beleg, originally called *Anglachel*, roughly "black sword" and then *Gurthang*, "iron of death". It is made by Eöl, the Dark Elf, and Melian warns him that "There is Malice in this sword" and that "it will not love the hand it serves" (*S* 202), a clear signal that it will bring bad luck to the user. Sure enough, when Beleg draws it to cut Túrin's bonds, the sword pricks Túrin's foot. The second element is Túrin's state of mind. Impulsive by nature, conditioned by torture, under extreme emotional stress, Túrin reacts to the pain by seizing the sword and killing his supposed attacker. The narrator's comment that "fate was that day more strong" (*S* 207) is intended to raise questions. More strong than what? Tolkien provides no gloss on this open-ended comparative. He has simply mixed free will with fate, entwining voluntary and involuntary actions so tightly that he might be challenging the reader to tell one from the other. The final element, the flash of lightning that reveals Beleg's face and shows Túrin what he has done, is a disinterested, wholly external weather event that yet plays into and underscores the fate-free will entanglement.

Túrin's opposite is Aragorn at the Falls of Rauros. All of Aragorn's speeches in this brief but crucial section of the book are predicated on the fate-and-free-will crux and that Aragorn knows there is a difference. When he hears the horn of Boromir signaling an attack by Orcs he cries: "Alas! An ill *fate* is on me this day, and all that I do goes amiss!" (*TT* 15; italics added). His subsequent debate with Legolas and Gimli about whether to follow Frodo and Sam or try to rescue Merry and Pippin is peppered with fate and free will references. He comments that "[a]n evil *choice* is now before us" (*TT* 17). In answer to Gimli's description of the signs they read as riddles, he comments that "we must guess the *riddles*, if we are to *choose* rightly" (*TT* 18, italics added).

And then Tolkien spells it out by having Aragorn pray aloud: "Now may I make a right choice, and change the evil fate of this unhappy day" (*TT* 21). Here, we have not just "choice" and "fate" but "may" and "change" and "unhappy" – mixing the concepts of fate, luck, and free will without value or preferment. But the key phrase in the sentence is "change the fate", a plain statement that Aragorn knows he has the power to go beyond the Music and thus to change it. His "may I make a right choice" is not a request for permission; the word 'may'– from Old English *magan*, 'be able' – is an invocation of Ilúvatar's gift. His curious word "unhappy" is not a pathetic fallacy ascribing emotion to natural phenomena, it simply adds a negative prefix to the archaic word 'hap' – 'hap-penstance', 'chance'. The day is un-*hap*-y, un-chance-y, but Aragorn's decision has the power to change its "evil fate." That he says it out loud to himself is Tolkien's way of saying it out loud to his reader.

No one says it out loud to Frodo. Yet, for him as much as for Aragorn, the power to change fate is complex. Frodo's battle with the Ring, or more properly, with his own desire to possess the Ring, is a primary motif running through *The Lord of the Rings*. Like Eru's theme in the Music, it comes up again and again in a variety of contexts, occurring so often, in fact, that we may properly ask if it is part of the

Singing of the Ainur and therefore his fate. But he has already questioned the fate that paired him with the Ring by asking Gandalf in their first meeting at Bag End: "Why was I chosen?" Gandalf's answer, "You may be sure it was not for any merit that others do not possess" (*FR* 70), assumes that Frodo was chosen while dodging the deeper "why" of the question. Many adventures and twelve chapters later, at the end of the Council of Elrond and after Frodo has volunteered to take the Ring, Elrond adds a rider to Gandalf's statement, telling Frodo that "this *task* is *appointed* for you [...] but if you take it *freely* I will say that your *choice* is right" (FR 284, italics added). Some of Elrond's words fit together comfortably – 'will', 'freely', 'choice' – and were clearly used by Tolkien for their philosophical implications. But two of his words – 'appointed' and 'task' – make his statement sound less like a prediction and more like a job description, which is in fact what it turns out to be.

Tolkien's use of such mundane words is worth examining. They first entered the mythology in an early draft of 'The Music of the Ainur' begun in 1918, where, according to a note from Christopher, the god-figure (there called Ilu) invoked them, declaring more explicitly that in the later *Silmarillion* text that "to Men I will *appoint* a *task* [my emphasis] and give a great gift. And he devised that they should have free will and the power of [...] designing beyond the original music of the Ainu" (*LT* I 61). The "great gift" is free will; the appointed task is to use that gift to go "beyond" the Music, left unfinished and in disarray through Melkor's rebellion. The echo of 'task' and 'appoint' in Elrond's words to Frodo at the Council is deliberate on the author's part, and this despite the fact that no one reading *The Lord of the Rings* when it first came out in 1954-55, or during the subsequent twenty-two years that passed before publication of *The Silmarillion* and the following *History of Middle-Earth* could possibly have seen the connection. Nevertheless, it is there, consciously placed by Tolkien in conformation with his larger design.

Armed with this retroactive information, we can now see numerous small moments in the narrative where Tolkien has built the motif of fate versus free choice into Frodo's story. Frodo's free announcement, "I *will* take the Ring" is preceded by his "dread" of "some *doom*", some inescapable end that he had hoped "might [...] never be *spoken*" (*FR* 284, italics added). Yet, in the end, it is Frodo himself who speaks, and his spoken words become his fate.

My last example for Frodo, and the one I suspect you can anticipate, comes in the heart-stopping scene at the Cracks of Doom, a placename meant not so much to be descriptive as terrifyingly literal. It is the site of Frodo's *dom*, his last judgment, his pronouncement of his own Doom. The text as published is clear enough. "I have come [...] But I do not choose now to do what I came to do. I will not do this deed" (*RK* 223). And he puts the Ring on his finger. The sequence of two phrases – "I do not choose" and "I will not" – is worth examining, for to abstain from choosing is to make a choice. One construction is passive – "I do not choose" – and the other is defiantly active – "I will not do." But the difference between both of those and what Tolkien originally wrote is greater than the difference between either and significant for the direction of the change. In the manuscript, Tolkien originally wrote "I cannot do what I have come to do." Written above it in pencil is the line as it appears in the published book (Marquette Archive LR05350, shelf mark for original paper page MS. Tolkien, 3/8/10/11b). The change moves Frodo from fate to free will and makes the moment infinitely more poignant – and infinitely more significant. The difference the words make to Tolkien's great story is both radical and profound. I cannot pretend to fathom what might have been going on in Tolkien's mind in the moment when he had Frodo change from "I cannot" to "I do not choose." All I know is the difference it made to the story, changing Frodo from a patient to an agent, giving him responsibility for his action while underscoring the enormity of the hold the Ring has on him. Sam has seen Frodo's act as "madness", and it's a safe bet that shocked and stunned readers for the last seven decades have been in agreement with Sam. To see Frodo lose his mind to the Ring after his long struggle is the final straw, more than the reader can bear. This reader, at any rate. I was shattered. I cannot think of another moment in literature that has had so powerful an effect on me.

In his essay 'On Fairy-stories', Tolkien described the *eucatastrophe*, the good catastrophe which brings about the "sudden joyous turn" from sorrow to joy that brings the Happy Ending. It isn't hard to see catastrophe in Frodo's capitulation to the Ring at the Cracks of Doom – or to see *eucatastrophe* in his restoration after Gollum's fall. But does the *eucatastrophe* bring a Happy Ending? My answer is both 'yes' and 'no'. It is 'yes' for Sam, whose fairy-story return to Rosie as she takes him in and sits him down by the fire is certainly a Happy

Ending. But it is 'no' for Frodo. Unlike Sam, Frodo has no Rosie to welcome him, and his return is temporary and haunted by his ordeal with the Ring, the "long defeat" that Tolkien found in his beloved *Beowulf*. What Tolkien said of the hero of that poem, that "*He is a man, and that for him and for many is sufficient tragedy*" (*MC* 18, italics in the original), could as well be said of Frodo as of Beowulf – or Túrin. In the final analysis, the success or failure of Tolkien's elaborate stratagem to intermix fate and free will in the lives of these his characters must be judged by the individual reader.

I'll leave it to you.

Essay 15

A Note on a Name

When I first learned, in Humphrey Carpenter's *Tolkien: A Biography*, that throughout the first complete version of *The Lord of the Rings*, Strider was "a queer-looking brown-faced hobbit" named Trotter (*Bio* 188), my initial reaction was not just surprise but disappointment, even bewilderment. As they do for any lover of Tolkien's work, the names of his characters comprised a large part of the enchantment of my first-reading experience. Not just the lyrical, polysyllabic Elven names on which he spent so much linguistic time and effort – *Nimrodel, Legolas, Galadriel* – but *Frodo, Wormtongue, Gaffer*, even the hyphenated *Sackville-Baggins*, with its nod to Bloomsbury aesthetes. *Frodo*, in particular, carried all kinds of mythic resonances from the Eddas of Norse mythology. There was King Froði, under whose reign a gold ring could lie on the ground and nobody would take it. There was the epithet *froðr* ('wise') for the fertility god Freyr. It is beyond doubt that Tolkien was fully conscious of the weight of these references when he changed his hero's name from Bingo to Frodo.[1] Granted, the references were pretty esoteric, and their impact required some knowledge of Old Icelandic literature. Still, they were there, and they were obviously intentional on Tolkien's part. Tolkien, I felt, had a gift for naming.

I particularly liked the name *Strider*. It was more accessible than *Frodo*, not dependent on mythological associations, besides being a perfect type-name for the mysterious hooded man I glimpsed in the common room at Bree. And like *Gaffer* and *Wormtongue, Strider* wasn't a proper name but an epithet, like Owen Wister's 'The Virginian', or 'The Lone Ranger' of my childhood cowboy fantasies. "What his right name is I've never heard," Butterbur says to Frodo, "but he's known round here as Strider. Goes about at a great pace on his long shanks" (*FR* 168). "Known" as Strider, this guy had a reputation and a name

1 On this and related themes, see also the chapter 'Names, Onomastics, and Onomaturgy' in Honegger (2023: 81-130).

to go with it. He didn't walk, he strode; he made great strides; he took things in his stride. All the idioms supported him as somebody who got around, who got things done, a mover and doer.

But what kind of hero 'trots'? The image simply did not fit the powerful, mysterious figure I glimpsed in the shadows at The Prancing Pony. Worse than just a poor fit, the name *Trotter* seemed jarringly inappropriate and dangerously close to cute. Like *Bingo*, it evoked games, or puppies, or pigs, if, like Leopold Bloom, you are into culinary treats. *Trotter* seemed an unsettling diminishment of a powerful character, hardly appropriate for the tall, sardonic authority figure who knows all about Frodo and his errand, is tight with Gandalf and crossways with Bill Ferny, who takes over the narrative with the wave of a finger and steers the quest to Rivendell. Of course, to my great, albeit retroactive relief, Tolkien did finally wise up – as he did with the change from Bingo to Frodo – and switch to the infinitely more evocative, powerful, name by which we all know Strider today. But how, I wondered, could Tolkien have made such a misstep in the first place? And stuck with it right to the end?

I learned the answer some years ago in a second-hand bookstore, where I picked up George MacDonald Fraser's *The Steel Bonnets*, a riveting account of the Scottish-English Border wars in the sixteenth and early seventeenth centuries. The book's endpapers were a map of the Scottish-English Border territory in the period, locating in their home territories the Riding Surnames – the perpetually feuding, raiding, cattle-rustling, barn-burning clans on both sides of the Border. And there – just north of the Tweed and inland from the English stronghold of Berwick, comfortably at home among the Dixons and Nixons, the Armstrongs, Grahams, Johnstones, Maxwells, and Elliots – were the Trotters, a Northern English and Scottish Border surname whose French origin, *trotier*, means 'messenger'.

This pushed my thinking in a new direction and opened up hitherto unimagined resonances for the name. It is not impossible possible that *Trotter* was a wholly Tolkien-invented Hobbit name and that it was intended to evoke and mimic the wooden shoes that, as Butterbur points out, clattered when he walked: "You can hear him coming along the road in those shoes: clitter-clap – when he walks on a path, which isn't often" (*RS* 138). It would also suit the presumed gait of someone with relatively short legs (unlike the final and much more appropriate "long shanks"). But given the pre-existence of the name, the choice seems more likely to have been the other way round, namely that the wooden shoes were meant to go with the name, in which case, it is also reasonable to suppose that, as turned out to be the case, my original reading of the name was wrong on all counts.

Trotter wasn't cute. It had nothing to do with games or puppies or pigs. It was a proper 'proper name'. And it carried historical baggage that fit with the character. I am not suggesting that Tolkien was influenced by *The Steel Bonnets*, which was first published in 1971, many years after the 1954-55 publication of *The Lord of the Rings*, and a scant two years before he died. But I do suggest that he, like any educated Englishman, had some knowledge of Border history, a history, moreover, that had a close resemblance to the immediate back-story of *The Lord of the Rings*, the unending guerilla action that we are told Strider/ Aragorn has been fighting for many years, riding under many different names with the Rohirrim and the Dûnedain in their struggle against Mordor.

Now *Trotter* is a British surname that, while not as common as Cooper or Thatcher or Webster or Wright, is nonetheless current in England and Scotland. It could have appealed to Tolkien for its sound alone. But I put it to you that no one as name-conscious as J.R.R. Tolkien, who once declared that "a name comes first and the story follows" (*Letters* 219), could have failed to be aware of the almost incantatory power of the surnames on the Scottish-English Border in the sixteenth century. I suggest that when he picked the name *Trotter* for his character, Tolkien was making a deliberate choice; he knew what he was doing; it was a conscious, albeit oblique, reference intended to evoke the toughness, endurance, tenacity, and dangerous history of the Border surnames and to honor his character's role as someone on the edge of a society at war, by choice an outsider and by destiny a messenger.

I would further suggest that Tolkien did not pick any of the better-known Border names for exactly the reason that they were better-known and would have given the game away by making a too-explicit reference to real-world history, which, like real-world mythology, Tolkien felt had no place in an invented world. *Trotter* was sufficiently obscure (even in the end-paper map it is printed in small caps, unlike the large caps of the – quite literally – big names that surround it) and sufficiently close to a real verb to be acceptable as a type-name for Tolkien's "queer-looking, brown-faced hobbit" (*RS* 137) who wears wooden shoes, walks a lot, and is also a Ranger.

It is not my purpose here to go into the checkered and diffuse history of Trotter/Strider/Aragorn as a character. Christopher Tolkien has explored this thoroughly, and his extended discussion in *The Return of the Shadow* is well worth reading as a roadmap of Tolkien's creative process at work in all its sprawling and overlapping glory. As part of that creative process, the character of Trotter went through many transformations and identities, at one point becoming Peregrin Boffin, a cousin of Frodo's whose name sounds too much like 'muffin', finally ending up not as a Hobbit but as a Man, though still called Trotter. I have no doubt (nor, I suspect, do most readers) that the last-minute change from *Trotter* to *Strider* was a wise decision on Tolkien's part. But his original choice of *Trotter* told us, as Tolkien meant it to, more than most readers (at least in America) were aware of at the time.

Essay 16

Credit Where it's Due

It is a great pleasure to be invited to speak about Christopher Tolkien, though I cannot help but wonder if there is anything to be said about him that hasn't been said already, more often and probably better than I can do. The most I can share with you is a look through the very narrow window of my own experience with this towering, yet curiously hybrid, figure. In the discipline of Tolkien studies, Christopher has been both a star and a supporting player, the sole purveyor of his father's works as well as their zealous guardian from exploitation. From the 1977 publication of the one-volume *Silmarillion* until his death in 2020, Christopher was the outstanding scholar, editor, transcriber, translator, and transmitter of his father's work. He was at once central and marginal, occupying center stage while at the same time hovering in the wings. He has left a body of son-to-father collaborative work that guards his father's legacy and preserves his father's vision, while keeping himself resolutely on the sidelines.

Even more than that, from the time his father died in 1973 until the day of his own death in 2020, he has been not just the custodian of the manuscripts but the keeper of the flame, standing foursquare against exploitation and potential misuse. In this respect as in so many others, we must be sorry that he is gone, for while he stood for his father in the eyes of the world, he also and just as staunchly stood between his father and the world. Today I want to talk about three major aspects of Christopher's work: first the inherent problem, second the scope of his achievement, and third the price he has had to pay for his scholarly integrity.

First: The Problem

The chief handicap to working with the Tolkien manuscripts is Tolkien's handwriting, which is notorious for both its calligraphic elegance and its impenetrable illegibility. It took the senior Tolkien over fifty years to create the world of Arda. It took his son another forty to decipher it. But because J.R.R. was not writing to be deciphered but to get his thoughts on paper as quick as he could, the results were sometimes indecipherable even to him but even more to those who had to read not just his handwriting but also his mind. This is an art as well as a skill. It demands a sleuth as well as a scholar. It means often having to rely on educated guess and equally often to requiring the humility to acknowledge that what you read is taxing to your capacity to understand.

I offer an instance from my own experience that bears witness to this, and I've picked this example because it's at once absurd and typical. Many years ago, when I was working with a then-unpublished manuscript, I encountered in a scribbled paragraph what looked like a complete anomaly – a word that just didn't belong. I was using xerox copies, not originals, but the copies were as clear and distinct as technology could make them. In the context in which it appeared, the word stuck out like a sore thumb. It had no relationship whatsoever to the text in which it was embedded. But there it was. The word was 'crabs', and it was in a passage that was emphatically not about seafood.

After trying to read it head-on, then side-ways, then upside-down, and finally with a magnifying glass, I gave up and consulted another Tolkien scholar, one I knew was experienced in deciphering Tolkien's handwriting. He agreed with my reading, which was reassuring but for that very reason of little help. Acknowledging defeat, I swallowed my pride and wrote to Christopher. The answer came by return post. The word was exile. That changed everything. Not only did the sentence now make sense, the surrounding paragraph took on a deeper meaning, and the narrative before and after it sprang into sharper focus.

Now compare my encounter with a single word to what Christopher faced every day and multiply that by the seventeen volumes of *The History of Middle-earth* that he produced and calibrate the ratio of raw data to editorial judgement. That will give you some idea of the sheer physical labor involved and will lead directly to the second of my three aspects, the scope of his achievement.

Second: The Scope

The scope is as vast as the subject itself. Christopher's contribution to the appreciation and understanding of his father's work is a scholarly tour de force in its own right, an accomplishment un-bettered so far as I know in the annals of modern scholarship. The labor has been one not just of love but a lot of very hard work, of high standards, and meticulous scholarship. It may not be unique – Boswell on Johnson comes to mind – but I think Christopher surpasses even Boswell in the depth of his understanding and respect for the works as well as for the man who wrote them, both of which he has served so well.

Christopher's life's work, the equal of his father's in its volume, has not only made available many unpublished works, it has connected them to one another to create a whole picture of a many-faceted vision and endeavor. He has mapped the geography of J.R.R. Tolkien's invented works world and traced its narrative and linguistic development, providing scholars and fans alike a look behind the scenes. Taken as a whole, Christopher's books are to Tolkien studies the equivalent of the *Oxford English Dictionary* and *Encyclopedia Britannica* combined.

The first volume, the stand-alone *Silmarillion* was published in 1977, the next, *Unfinished Tales*, not long after, in 1980, but with as far as I know no advance notice, in the United States at least. It just quietly, almost sneakily appeared in shops like my university bookstore where I saw it one day sitting casually on the shelf waiting to be noticed. No publicity, no advertising posters; it was just there. I once asked Christopher about this lack of fanfare, and he told me what I suspected – that it was a deliberate strategy. He was testing the waters to find out if there was an audience for Tolkien that went beyond *The Lord of the Rings*. He got his answer right away, and the rest is history – *The History of Middle-earth*. The work of two men given to the world by the one uniquely qualified to do it justice.

The titles of the books, always published as written by Tolkien and edited by Christopher, but whose appearance we owe entirely to the latter, ring like a litany – *The Silmarillion, Unfinished Tales, The Book of Lost Tales I* and *The Book of Lost Tales II, Lays of Beleriand, The Shaping of Middle-earth, The Lost Road, The Return of the Shadow, The Treason of Isengard, The War of the Ring, Sauron Defeated, Morgoth's Ring, The War of the Jewels, The Peoples of Middle-earth.*

And that's not counting the *Letters*, selected and edited by Humphrey Carpenter with Christopher as co-pilot, a work which gave us insight where the other books gave us the stories and their history. Even that was not enough, for then he turned to the so-called Great Tales and produced *The Children of Húrin*, *Beren and Lúthien*, and *The Fall of Gondolin*. This is not just a catalogue, it is a bibliography whose very titles are a history – again of two men's work, not just one. The texts themselves, the raw data, are testament not just to J.R.R. Tolkien's vision but to his prodigious output. That we have them is testament to Christopher's enormous labor in making himself the conduit for their transmission.

And Finally: The Price

The price for both authors has been high, costing nothing less than the whole inner consistency of the endeavour. As early as 1958, we find Tolkien writing, "It is now clear to me that in any case the Mythology must actually be a 'Mannish' affair. [...] What we have in the *Silmarillion* etc. are traditions [...] handed on by *Men* [...] blended and confused [...] with their own Mannish myths and cosmic ideas" (*MR* 370). This was sub-creation one step down, no longer a God-given right but an authorial strategy and one that furthermore undermined the original vision. The change that divided the legendarium into Mannish as opposed to other 'ishes' such as Elvish traditions widened the story by introducing the notion of point of view. But it also narrowed each approach to the particular point of view being held. This subverted the authority of the original myth and invalidated his commitment to preserving it, leading to what is, to me, the single saddest sentence in the whole collection: "you cannot do this anymore" (*MR* 370).

Christopher puts the date at "1958 or later" (*MR* 370) when Tolkien, creator of 'The Voyage of Eärendil', head arborist of the Two Trees, mythmaker of the Sun and the Moon and the edicts of Eru/Ilúvatar, wrote that "you cannot do this anymore," recording what was not just a rueful epiphany but a sacrifice of a whole vision on the altar of authorial integrity. To explore it, he wrote his most difficult work, the 'Athrabeth', the debate of Finrod, an Elf, and Andreth, a mortal woman.

'Most difficult' is my own opinion, but I don't think there are many who would disagree. The 'Athrabeth' is not only theologically experimental, it is deliberately a vehicle for conflicting and sometimes warring interpretations, for in it, Tolkien calls into question some of the most basic assumptions of his invented world, assumptions he had put in place in devising the Silmarillion and which Christopher had preserved in his *The Silmarillion* volume.

It is greatly to Christopher's credit that he had the courage to publish the 'Athrabeth' and the following essay by his father on 'Laws and Customs among the Eldar' to which he gave the title 'Myths Transformed'. Transformed is putting it mildly. The myths – the stories and their sources – were metamorphosed, their very nature changed from revelation to provenance, and the effect, as Christopher foresaw, was to change the whole tone and derivation of the mythology. In doing this, Tolkien had, whether deliberately or unconsciously, made it more like the mythologies and/or religions of the present day, where interpretation plays as important a part as revelation, and disagreements amounting to wars can arise over the same god, the same events, and the same story.

Christopher chose to publish the 'Athrabeth' but accompanied it with an essay in which he discussed his dismay at its contents as well as his reasons for making them public. That this was both a heartfelt and a difficult decision I can testify, for I was privileged to be a witness to both the dismay and the decision to go ahead. I can still remember the morning we talked about it and my vivid impression of his deep concern at the impact the publication would have on the existing canon. He was facing the very real risk that it would overturn the whole structure as it was currently understood and accepted.

In the event, as we all know, he did publish it in *Morgoth's Ring*, and it did overturn our assumptions. It did call into question what had been heretofore taken as authoritative. It did lead to the notion of beliefs, plural rather than belief singular, by introducing to the concept of 'versions' as over against a single story. Tolkien's realization that "you cannot say this anymore," led him to write the 'Athrabeth' and by so doing unleash a man-made earthquake, a seismic event that tumbled the edifice Tolkien himself had so laboriously constructed and replaced it with lesser structures conveying differing and often conflicting points of view.

It was an earthquake not just in the metaphoric but the actual sense as well, for at the same time Tolkien quite literally moved the earth of his invented world, putting it in a different relation to the sky that arched over it. While this could well have had the ruinous effect of overturning the sublime beauty of his Tolkien's original concept, my point here is that the beauty survived the earthquake in spite of the tremors. It is thanks to Christopher that the world of Tolkien scholarship now has both – the original, breathtakingly beautiful vision of the Light and the Two Trees, mythical in the best sense of that word, and the soberer and more rational revision that replaced it, growing out of its author's realization that "you cannot say this anymore," surely one of the most poignant farewell's to art in the history of literature.

The exciting thing about all this is that it is not merely a dry-as-dust, scholarly history of some manuscripts. It is a window into two men's minds – the processes, developments, contradictions, and unexpected changes of one, the academic honesty and filial as well as scholarly responsibility of the other. Both are worthy not just of our respect but of our admiration. For Christopher had the honesty to admit that with *The Silmarillion* he had made a mistake and the courage to start the whole process again from the beginning. The last volume to appear, *The Fall of Gondolin*, was published in 2019. Christopher died in 2020, leaving seventeen volumes created out of the welter of scribbled in haste, partially erased and overwritten, belatedly added manuscript material – not just sheets of paper, but bits and pieces, hastily jotted notes, old exams, and folded newspapers.

The world of Tolkien scholarship owes its very life to the courageous and highly-principled honesty of two different men in two widely separate times, one of whom invented a concept, the other of whom preserved it, both of whom eventually dismantled it. Our debt to both is incalculable, but without Christopher, we would have neither the original concept nor its subsequent undoing, much less the reasons for both, all of which are essential to our better understanding of both Tolkien's, their work, and their world.

Dear Reader,

A retrospective survey of the essays in this collection shows them to be a motley crew, as diverse as focus on a single subject will allow them to be. Tailored to the themes of this or that conference, book, Zoom gathering or podcast over the course of many years, they appear here to be a well-intentioned but disorderly bunch. This is due as much to the breadth and variousness of their overall subject as to the venues and/or occasions for their presentation. They are all about the same man and the same body of work, but beyond that they are as notable for their differences as their similarities. I find this exhilarating. I hope you do too.

Thanks for your patience,

Verlyn Flieger

Aotrou	Tolkien 2016
'Athrabeth'	Tolkien 1993b
Bio	Carpenter 1977
B&L	Tolkien 2017
C&G	Scull and Hammond 2017
Children	Tolkien 2007
FA	Tolkien 2013
FG	Tolkien 2018a
FR	Tolkien 1965a
H	Tolkien 1987b
Kullervo	Tolkien 2015
Letters	Tolkien 1981
LettersRev	Tolkien 2023
LB	Tolkien 1985
LR	Tolkien 1987a
LT I	Tolkien 1984a
LT II	Tolkien 1984b
MC	Tolkien 1983a
Morgoth	Tolkien 1993a
Peoples	Tolkien 1996
RK	Tolkien 1965c
RS	Tolkien 1988
SD	Tolkien 1992
S&G	Tolkien 2009
Shaping	Tolkien 1986
S	Tolkien 1999
Smith	Tolkien 2005
T&L	Tolkien 2001a
TOFS	Tolkien 2008
Treason	Tolkien 1989
TT	Tolkien 1965b
UT	Tolkien 1980

Bibliography

The American Heritage Dictionary of the English Language. 1969. Edited by William Morris. Boston: American Heritage Publishing Co. and Houghton Mifflin Company.

Apeland, Kaj André. 1998. 'On Entering the Same River Twice: Mythology and Theology in the *Silmarillion* Corpus.' In Nils Ivar Agøy (ed.). 1998. *Between Faith and Fiction. Tolkien and the Powers of His World. Arda Special 1.* Proceedings of the Arda Symposium at the Second Northern Tolkien Festival, Oslo, August 1997. Upsala: The Arda Society, 44-50.

Barfield, Owen. 1928. *Poetic Diction*. London: Faber and Faber.

1944. *Romanticism Comes of Age*. London: Anthroposophical Publishing Company.

Barrere, Albert and Charles Leland. 1889. *Slang and its Analogues*. London: Ballantine Press.

Bosworth-Toller. 1980. *An Anglo-Saxon Dictionary*. Based on the collections of Joseph Bosworth. Edited and enlarged by T. Northcote Toller. Oxford: Oxford University Press.

Bowman, Mary. 2010. 'Refining the Gold: Tolkien, *The Battle of Maldon*, and the Northern Theory of Courage.' *Tolkien Studies* 7: 91-115.

Bratman, David. 2000a. 'Top Ten Rejected Plot Twists from *The Lord of the Rings*: A Textual Excursion into the 'History of *The Lord of the Rings*'.' *Mythlore* 22.4: 13-37.

2000b. 'The Literary Value of *The History of Middle-earth*.' In Verlyn Flieger and Carl F. Hostetter (eds.). 2000. *Tolkien's Legendarium. Essays on The History of Middle-earth*. Westport, CT and London: Greenwood Press, 69-91.

Bunting, Nancy and Seamus Hamill-Keays. 2021. *The Gallant Edith Bratt. J.R.R. Tolkien's Inspiration*. Cormarë Series 46. Zurich and Jena: Walking Tree Publishers.

Carpenter, Humphrey. 1977. *Tolkien. A Biography*. Boston: Houghton Mifflin Company.

1979. *The Inklings. C.S. Lewis. J.R.R. Tolkien, Charles Williams and their Friends*. Boston: Houghton Mifflin.

(in conversation with Lyndall Gordon). 1995. 'Learning about Ourselves: Biography as Autobiography.' In John Batchelor (ed.). *The Art of Literary Biography*. Oxford: Clarendon Press, 267-79.

Catalogue of Books from the Library of J.R.R. Tolkien Held by the English Faculty Library Oxford. [n.d.]

CHANCE, Jane. 2005. 'Tolkien and the Other: Race and Gender in Middle-earth.' In Jane Chance and Alfred K. Siewers (eds.). 2005. *Tolkien's Modern Middle Ages*. (The New Middle Ages.) New York: Palgrave Macmillan, 171-88.

CILLI, Oronzo. 2019. *Tolkien's Library. An Annotated Checklist*. Edinburgh: Luna Press.

DE LA VILLEMARQUÉ, Hersart. 1846. *Barzaz-Breiz. Chantes Populaire de la Bretagne*. 2 vols. Fourth edition. Paris: A. Franck.

DROUT, Michael D.C. 2006. 'A Spliced Old English Quotation in '*Beowulf*: The Monsters and the Critics.' *Tolkien Studies* 3: 149-51.

2007. 'J.R.R. Tolkien's Medieval Scholarship and its Significance.' *Tolkien Studies* 4: 113-76.

2013. 'The Tower and the Ruin: The Past in J.R.R. Tolkien's Works.' In Helen Conrad-O'Briain und Gerard Hynes (eds.). *J.R.R. Tolkien. The Forest and the City*. Dublin: Four Courts Press, 175-90.

DUPLESSIS, Nicole M. 2019. 'On the Shoulders of Humphrey Carpenter: Reconsidering Biographical Representation and Scholarly Perception of Edith Tolkien.' *Mythlore* 37.2, Article 4.

DUNNE, John William. 1934. *An Experiment with Time*. London: Faber & Faber.

EDWARDS, Raymond. 2014. *Tolkien*. London: Robert Hale.

EKWALL, Eilert. 1960. *The Concise Oxford Dictionary of English Place-names*. 4th edition. Oxford: The Clarendon Press.

FARMER, John Stephen and William Ernest HENLEY. 1890-1904. *Slang and its Analogues Past and Present*. London: Printed for subscribers only.

FIMI, Dimitra. 2008. *Tolkien, Race and Cultural History. From Fairies to Hobbits*. New York and London: Palgrave Macmillan.

FLIEGER, Verlyn. 2005. *Interrupted Music. The Making of Tolkien's Mythology*. Kent, OH: The Kent State University Press.

2009. 'The Music and the Task: Fate and Free Will in Middle-earth.' *Tolkien Studies* 6: 151-81.

and Carl F. HOSTETTER (eds.). 2000. *Tolkien's Legendarium. Essays on The History of Middle-earth*. Westport, CT and London: Greenwood Press.

Fornet-Ponse, Thomas. 2010. '"Strange and free" – On Some Aspects of the Nature of Elves and Men.' *Tolkien Studies* 7: 67-89.

Frank, Anne. 1952. *The Diary of a Young Girl*. Translated by Susan Massotty. New York: Doubleday & Company.

Garth, John. 2003. *Tolkien and the Great War*. London: HarperCollins.

2014. *Tolkien at Exeter College*. Oxford: Exeter College.

2019. 'Ilu's Music: The Creation of Tolkien's Creation Myth.' In Dimitra Fimi and Thomas Honegger (eds.). 2019. *Sub-creating Arda. World-building in J.R.R. Tolkien's Works, its Precursors, and Legacies*. Cormarë Series 40. Zurich and Jena: Walking Tree Publishers, 117-51.

Gay, John. 1987. *The Beggar's Opera*. First performed 1728. London: Penguin Classics.

Gent, B.E. 1698. *A New Dictionary of the Terms Ancient and Modern of the Canting Crew, in its Several Tribes of Gypsies, Beggars, Thieves, Cheats, &c.* London: W. Hawes, P. Gilbourne, and W. Davis.

Glyer, Diana Pavlac. 2007. *The Company They Keep. C.S. Lewis and J.R.R. Tolkien as Writers in Community*. Kent, OH: The Kent State University Press.

Gordon, Eric Valentine (ed.). 1937. *The Battle of Maldon*. Reprinted 1968. London: Methuen.

Grimm, Jacob. 1835. *Deutsche Mythologie*. Göttingen: Dieterich.

and Wilhelm Grimm. 1812-15. *Kinder- und Hausmärchen*. 2 vols. Berlin: Realschulbuchhandlung.

Grose, James Francis. 1785. *A Classical Dictionary of the Vulgar Tongue*. London: S. Hooper.

Hammond, Wayne G., with the assistance of Douglas Anderson. 1993. *J.R.R. Tolkien. A Descriptive Bibliography*. Winchester: St Paul's Bibliographies.

Honegger, Thomas. 2004. 'A Note on Beren and Lúthien's Disguise as Werewolf and Vampire-Bat.' *Tolkien Studies* 1: 173-77.

2007. 'The Homecoming of Beorhtnoth: Philology and the Literary Muse.' *Tolkien Studies* 4: 189-99.

2011. 'The Rohirrim: "Anglo-Saxons on Horseback"? An Inquiry into Tolkien's Use of Sources.' In Jason Fisher (ed.). *Tolkien and the Study of His Sources. Critical Essays*. Jefferson, NC and London: McFarland, 116-32.

2023. *Tweaking Things a Little. Essays on the Epic Fantasy of J.R.R. Tolkien and George R.R. Martin*. Cormarë Series 50. Zurich and Jena: Walking Tree Publishers.

Hooker, Mark T. 2004. 'Frodo's Batman.' *Tolkien Studies* 1: 125-36.

Hostetter, Carl. 1991. 'Over Middle-earth sent unto Men: On the Philological Origins of Tolkien's Earendel Myth.' *Mythlore* 65 (Spring): 5-10.

1992. 'Uglúk to the dung-pit.' *Vinyar Tengwar* 26: 16.

(ed.). 2009. 'J.R.R. Tolkien: Fate and Free Will.' *Tolkien Studies* 6: 183-88.

Hotten, John Camden. 1859. *Slang Dictionary*. London. J.C. Hotten.

Lang, Andrew. 1885. *Custom and Myth*. New York: Harper & Brothers.

Lewis, Clive Staples 1938. *Out of the Silent Planet*. London: The Bodley Head.

1947. 'On Stories.' In C.S. Lewis (ed.). *Essays Presented to Charles Williams*. London: Oxford University Press, 90-105.

1954. 'The Gods Return to Earth.' *Time and Tide* (14 August 1954), 1082.

Librán-Moreno, Miryam. 2011. '"Byzantium, New Rome!" Goths, Langobards, and Byzantium in The Lord of the Rings.' In Jason Fisher (ed.). *Tolkien and the Study of His Sources. Critical Essays*. Jefferson, NC and London: McFarland, 84-115.

Lönnrot, Elias (ed.). 1907. *Kalevala*. Translated by W.F. Kirby. London: J.W. Dent.

(ed.). 1963. *The Kalevala*. Translated by Francis Peabody Magoun. Cambridge, MA: Harvard University Press.

(ed.). 1985a. *Kalevala*. Mikkeli: Suomallaisen Kirjallisuuden Seura.

1985b. *Kalevala*. Translated by W.F. Kirby. London: The Athlone Press.

Marie de France. 1900. *Die Lais der Marie de France*. Herausgegeben von Karl Warnke. Vergleichende Anmerkungen von Reinhold Köhler. Halle: Max Niemeyer.

1911. *French Medieval Romances from the Lays of Marie de France*. Translated by Eugene Mason. Everyman's Library. London: J.D. Dent & Sons.

1978. *The Lais of Marie de France*. Translated & introduced by Robert Hemming & Joan Ferrante. Foreword by John Fowles. New York: E.P. Dutton.

Moore, Marianne. 1994. *The Complete Poems of Marianne Moore*. London: Penguin.

Müller, Max. 1867-75. *Chips from a German Workshop*. 5 vols. London: Longmans, Green & Co.

Muir, Edwin. 1955. 'A Boy's World.' *Sunday Observer* 27 November 1955, 11.

Owen, Wilfred. 1920. 'Dulce et decorum est.' <http://literature.proquest.com/>

Parker, Douglass. 1957. 'Hwaet We Holbytla.' *Hudson Review* ix.4 (Winter 1956-57), 598-609.

Partridge, Eric. 1938. *A Dictionary of Slang and Unconventional English*. London: George Routledge & Sons.

Rateliff, John D. 2007. *The History of The Hobbit*. One-volume edition. London: HarperCollins.

Resnick, Henry. 1967. 'An Interview with Tolkien.' *Niekas* 18: 37-47.

Scott, A.O. 2014. 'A War to End All Innocence.' *New York Times* 20 June 2014. <https://www.nytimes.com/2014/06/22/arts/the-enduring-impact-of-world-war-i.html>

Scull, Christina and Wayne G. Hammond. 2017. *The J.R.R. Tolkien Companion and Guide. Volume 1: Chronology. Volumes 2&3: Reader's Guide*. First edition 2006. Revised and expanded edition. Boston, MA and New York: Houghton Mifflin.

Shaw, George Bernard and Alan Jay Lerner. 1956. *My Fair Lady*. Music by Frederick Loewe.

Shippey, Tom A. 2000. 'Orcs, Wraiths, Wights: Tolkien's Images of Evil.' In Clark, George and Daniel Timmons (eds.). *J.R.R. Tolkien and His Literary Resonances*. Westport, CT: Greenwood Press, 183-98.

2003. *The Road to Middle-earth*. Third edition. First edition 1982. Boston, MA: Houghton Mifflin.

2007. 'Tolkien and 'The Homecoming of Beorhtnoth'.' In Tom A. Shippey. 2007. *Roots and Branches. Selected Papers on Tolkien by Tom Shippey*. Cormarë Series 11. Zurich and Berne: Walking Tree Publishers, 323-39.

Stuart, Robert. 2022. *Tolkien, Race, and Racism in Middle-earth*. New York: Palgrave Macmillan.

Thomas, Paul Edmund. 2000. 'Some of Tolkien's Narrators.' In George Clark and Daniel Timmons (eds.). *J.R.R. Tolkien and His Literary Resonances*. Westport, CT: Greenwood Press, 161-81.

Tolkien, J.R.R. 1953. 'The Homecoming of Beorhtnoth, Beorhthelm's Son.' *Essays and Studies*, N.S. 6, 1-18. London: John Murray.

1965a. *The Fellowship of the Ring*. 2nd edition. Boston: Houghton Mifflin.

1965b. *The Two Towers*. 2nd edition. Boston: Houghton Mifflin.

1965c. *The Return of the King*. 2nd edition. Boston: Houghton Mifflin.

1980. *Unfinished Tales of Númenor and Middle-earth*. Edited by Christopher Tolkien. Boston: Houghton Mifflin Company.

1981. *The Letters of J.R.R. Tolkien*. Edited by Humphrey Carpenter, with the assistance of Christopher Tolkien. Boston: Houghton Mifflin Company.

1983a. *The Monsters and the Critics and Other Essays*. Edited by Christopher Tolkien: London: George Allen & Unwin.

1983b. '*Beowulf*: The Monsters and the Critics.' In *The Monsters and the Critics and Other Essays*. Edited by Christopher Tolkien: London: George Allen & Unwin, 5-48.

1983c. 'On Fairy-stories.' In *The Monsters and the Critics and Other Essays*. Edited by Christopher Tolkien. London: George Allen & Unwin, 109-61.

1984a. *The Book of Lost Tales I*. Edited by Christopher Tolkien. *The History of Middle-earth* 1. First published 1983. Boston: Houghton Mifflin Company.

1984b. *The Book of Lost Tales II*. Edited by Christopher Tolkien. *The History of Middle-earth* 2. Boston: Houghton Mifflin Company.

1985. *The Lays of Beleriand*. Edited by Christopher Tolkien. *The History of Middle-earth* 3. Boston: Houghton Mifflin Company.

1986. *The Shaping of Middle-earth*. Edited by Christopher Tolkien. *The History of Middle-earth* 4. Boston: Houghton Mifflin Company.

1987a. *The Lost Road*. Edited by Christopher Tolkien. *The History of Middle-earth* 5. Boston: Houghton Mifflin Company.

1987b. *The Hobbit*. 50th Anniversary Edition. London: Unwin Hyman.

1988. *The Return of the Shadow*. Edited by Christopher Tolkien. *The History of Middle-earth* 6. Boston: Houghton Mifflin Company.

1989. *The Treason of Isengard*. Edited by Christopher Tolkien. *The History of Middle-earth* 7. Boston: Houghton Mifflin Company.

1992. *Sauron Defeated*. Edited by Christopher Tolkien. *The History of Middle-earth* 9. Paperback edition 1993. London: HarperCollins.

1993a. *Morgoth's Ring*. Edited by Christopher Tolkien. *The History of Middle-earth* 10. Paperback edition 1994. London: HarperCollins.

1993b. 'Athrabeth Finrod ah Andreth.' In *Morgoth's Ring*. Edited by Christopher Tolkien. *The History of Middle-earth* 10. Paperback edition 1994. London: HarperCollins, 301-66.

1996. *The Peoples of Middle-earth*. Edited by Christopher Tolkien. *The History of Middle-earth* 12. London: HarperCollins.

1999. *The Silmarillion*. 2nd edition. Edited by Christopher Tolkien. London: HarperCollins.

2001a. *Tree and Leaf, including the poem Mythopoeia. The Homecoming of Beorhtnoth Beorhthelm's Son*. London: HarperCollins.

2001b. 'Mythopoeia.' In *Tree and Leaf, including the poem Mythopoeia. The Homecoming of Beorhtnoth Beorhthelm's Son*. London: HarperCollins, 85-90.

2001c. 'Leaf by Niggle.' In *Tree and Leaf, including the poem Mythopoeia. The Homecoming of Beorhtnoth Beorhthelm's Son*. London: HarperCollins, 91-118.

2004. *Sí Qente Feanor & Other Elvish Writings. Parma Eldalamberon* XV. Cupertino, CA: The Tolkien Trust.

2005. *Smith of Wootton Major*. Edited by Verlyn Flieger. Extended Edition. London: HarperCollins.

2007. *The Children of Húrin*. Edited by Christopher Tolkien. London: HarperCollins.

2008. *Tolkien On Fairy-stories*. Edited by Verlyn Flieger and Douglas A. Anderson. Expanded edition, with commentary and notes; first edition 1947. London: HarperCollins.

2009. *The Legend of Sigurd and Gudrún*. Edited by Christopher Tolkien. London: HarperCollins.

2013. *The Fall of Arthur*. Edited by Christopher Tolkien. London: HarperCollins.

2014. *Beowulf. A Translation and Commentary together with Sellic Spell*. Edited by Christopher Tolkien. London: HarperCollins.

2015. *The Story of Kullervo*. Edited by Verlyn Flieger. London: HarperCollins.

2016. *The Lay of Aotrou and Itroun*. Edited by Verlyn Flieger. London: HarperCollins.

2017. *Beren and Lúthien*. Edited by Christopher Tolkien. London: HarperCollins.

2018a. *The Fall of Gondolin*. Edited by Christopher Tolkien. London: HarperCollins.

2018b. 'Dragons.' In Christina Scull and Wayne G. Hammond. *J.R.R. Tolkien's The Hobbit 1937-2017*. London: HarperCollins, 39-62.

2023a. *The Letters of J.R.R. Tolkien*. Revised and expanded edition. Edited by Humphrey Carpenter, with the assistance of Christopher Tolkien. First edition 1981. London: HarperCollins.

2023b. *The Battle of Maldon together with The Homecoming of Beorhtnoth*. Edited by Peter Grybauskas. London: HarperCollins.

Tolkienlibrary.com/index.php

Twain, Mark (Samuel L. Clemens). 1899. *The Adventures of Huckleberry Finn*. New York and London: Harper & Brothers.

Vink, Renée. 2013. "Jewish' Dwarves: Tolkien and Anti-semitic Stereotyping.' *Tolkien Studies* 10: 123-145.

Walde, Alois and Julius Pokorny. 1927-32. *Vergleichendes Wörterbuch der indogermanischen Sprachen*. 3 vols. Berlin: de Gruyter.

West, Richard C. 2019. 'A Letter from Father Murray.' *Tolkien Studies* 16: 133-39.

Wilson, Edmund. 1956. 'Oo, those Awful Orcs!.' *Nation* 182 (14 April 1956): 312-13. Reprinted In Wilson, Edmund. 1965. *The Bit Between My Teeth*. New York: Farrar, Straus and Giroux, 326-32.

Wordsworth, William. 1880. 'Preface to *Lyrical Ballads*.' <https://faculty.csbsju.edu/dbeach/beautytruth/Wordsworth-PrefaceLB.pdf>

Zaleski, Philip and Carol Zalesky. 2015. *The Fellowship. The Literary Lives of the Inklings*. New York: Farrar, Straus and Giroux.

Walking Tree Publishers

Zurich and Jena

Walking Tree Publishers was founded in 1997 as a forum for publication of material related to Tolkien and Middle-earth studies.

www.walking-tree.org

Cormarë Series

The *Cormarë Series* collects papers and studies dedicated exclusively to the exploration of Tolkien's work. It comprises monographs, thematic collections of essays, conference volumes, and reprints of important yet no longer (easily) accessible papers by leading scholars in the field. Manuscripts and project proposals are evaluated by members of an independent board of advisors who support the series editors in their endeavour to provide the readers with qualitatively superior yet accessible studies on Tolkien and his work.

News from the Shire and Beyond. Studies on Tolkien
Peter Buchs & Thomas Honegger (eds.), Zurich and Berne 2004, Reprint, First edition 1997 (Cormarë Series 1), ISBN 978-3-9521424-5-5

Root and Branch. Approaches Towards Understanding Tolkien
Thomas Honegger (ed.), Zurich and Berne 2005, Reprint, First edition 1999 (Cormarë Series 2), ISBN 978-3-905703-01-6

Richard Sturch, *Four Christian Fantasists. A Study of the Fantastic Writings of George MacDonald, Charles Williams, C.S. Lewis and J.R.R. Tolkien*
Zurich and Berne 2007, Reprint, First edition 2001 (Cormarë Series 3), ISBN 978-3-905703-04-7

Tolkien in Translation
Thomas Honegger (ed.), Zurich and Jena 2011, Reprint, First edition 2003 (Cormarë Series 4), ISBN 978-3-905703-15-3

Mark T. Hooker, *Tolkien Through Russian Eyes*
Zurich and Berne 2003 (Cormarë Series 5), ISBN 978-3-9521424-7-9

Translating Tolkien: Text and Film
Thomas Honegger (ed.), Zurich and Jena 2011, Reprint, First edition 2004 (Cormarë Series 6), ISBN 978-3-905703-16-0

Christopher Garbowski, *Recovery and Transcendence for the Contemporary Mythmaker. The Spiritual Dimension in the Works of J.R.R. Tolkien*
Zurich and Berne 2004, Reprint, First Edition by Marie Curie Sklodowska, University Press, Lublin 2000, (Cormarë Series 7), ISBN 978-3-9521424-8-6

Reconsidering Tolkien
Thomas Honegger (ed.), Zurich and Berne 2005 (Cormarë Series 8), ISBN 978-3-905703-00-9

Tolkien and Modernity 1
Frank Weinreich & Thomas Honegger (eds.), Zurich and Berne 2006 (Cormarë Series 9), ISBN 978-3-905703-02-3

Tolkien and Modernity 2
Thomas Honegger & Frank Weinreich (eds.), Zurich and Berne 2006 (Cormarë Series 10), ISBN 978-3-905703-03-0

Tom Shippey, *Roots and Branches. Selected Papers on Tolkien by Tom Shippey*
Zurich and Berne 2007 (Cormarë Series 11), ISBN 978-3-905703-05-4

Ross Smith, *Inside Language. Linguistic and Aesthetic Theory in Tolkien*
Zurich and Jena 2011, Reprint, First edition 2007 (Cormarë Series 12), ISBN 978-3-905703-20-7

How We Became Middle-earth. A Collection of Essays on The Lord of the Rings
Adam Lam & Nataliya Oryshchuk (eds.), Zurich and Berne 2007 (Cormarë Series 13), ISBN 978-3-905703-07-8

Myth and Magic. Art According to the Inklings
Eduardo Segura & Thomas Honegger (eds.), Zurich and Berne 2007 (Cormarë Series 14), ISBN 978-3-905703-08-5

The Silmarillion – Thirty Years On
Allan Turner (ed.), Zurich and Berne 2007 (Cormarë Series 15), ISBN 978-3-905703-10-8

Martin Simonson, *The Lord of the Rings and the Western Narrative Tradition*
Zurich and Jena 2008 (Cormarë Series 16), ISBN 978-3-905703-09-2

Tolkien's Shorter Works. Proceedings of the 4th Seminar of the Deutsche Tolkien Gesellschaft & Walking Tree Publishers Decennial Conference
Margaret Hiley & Frank Weinreich (eds.), Zurich and Jena 2008 (Cormarë Series 17), ISBN 978-3-905703-11-5

Tolkien's The Lord of the Rings: Sources of Inspiration
Stratford Caldecott & Thomas Honegger (eds.), Zurich and Jena 2008 (Cormarë Series 18), ISBN 978-3-905703-12-2

J.S. Ryan, *Tolkien's View: Windows into his World*
Zurich and Jena 2009 (Cormarë Series 19), ISBN 978-3-905703-13-9

Music in Middle-earth
Heidi Steimel & Friedhelm Schneidewind (eds.), Zurich and Jena 2010 (Cormarë Series 20), ISBN 978-3-905703-14-6

Liam Campbell, *The Ecological Augury in the Works of JRR Tolkien*
Zurich and Jena 2011 (Cormarë Series 21), ISBN 978-3-905703-18-4

Margaret Hiley, *The Loss and the Silence. Aspects of Modernism in the Works of C.S. Lewis, J.R.R. Tolkien and Charles Williams*
Zurich and Jena 2011 (Cormarë Series 22), ISBN 978-3-905703-19-1

Rainer Nagel, *Hobbit Place-names. A Linguistic Excursion through the Shire*
Zurich and Jena 2012 (Cormarë Series 23), ISBN 978-3-905703-22-1

Christopher MacLachlan, *Tolkien and Wagner: The Ring and Der Ring*
Zurich and Jena 2012 (Cormarë Series 24), ISBN 978-3-905703-21-4

Renée Vink, *Wagner and Tolkien: Mythmakers*
Zurich and Jena 2012 (Cormarë Series 25), ISBN 978-3-905703-25-2

The Broken Scythe. Death and Immortality in the Works of J.R.R. Tolkien
Roberto Arduini & Claudio Antonio Testi (eds.), Zurich and Jena 2012 (Cormarë Series 26), ISBN 978-3-905703-26-9

Sub-creating Middle-earth: Constructions of Authorship and the Works of J.R.R. Tolkien
Judith Klinger (ed.), Zurich and Jena 2012 (Cormarë Series 27), ISBN 978-3-905703-27-6

Tolkien's Poetry
Julian Eilmann & Allan Turner (eds.), Zurich and Jena 2013 (Cormarë Series 28), ISBN 978-3-905703-28-3

O, What a Tangled Web. Tolkien and Medieval Literature. A View from Poland
Barbara Kowalik (ed.), Zurich and Jena 2013 (Cormarë Series 29), ISBN 978-3-905703-29-0

J.S. Ryan, *In the Nameless Wood*
Zurich and Jena 2013 (Cormarë Series 30), ISBN 978-3-905703-30-6

From Peterborough to Faëry; The Poetics and Mechanics of Secondary Worlds
Thomas Honegger & Dirk Vanderbeke (eds.), Zurich and Jena 2014 (Cormarë Series 31), ISBN 978-3-905703-31-3

Tolkien and Philosophy
Roberto Arduini & Claudio R. Testi (eds.), Zurich and Jena 2014 (Cormarë Series 32), ISBN 978-3-905703-32-0

Patrick Curry, *Deep Roots in a Time of Frost. Essays on Tolkien*
Zurich and Jena 2014 (Cormarë Series 33), ISBN 978-3-905703-33-7

Representations of Nature in Middle-earth
Martin Simonson (ed.), Zurich and Jena 2015, (Cormarë Series 34), ISBN 978-3-905703-34-4

Laughter in Middle-earth
Thomas Honegger & Maureen F. Mann (eds.), Zurich and Jena 2016 (Cormarë Series 35), ISBN 978-3-905703-35-1

Julian Eilmann, *J.R.R. Tolkien – Romanticist and Poet*
Zurich and Jena 2017 (Cormarë Series 36), ISBN 978-3-905703-36-8

Binding Them All. Interdisciplinary Perspectives on J.R.R. Tolkien and His Works
Monika Kirner-Ludwig, Stephan Köser, Sebastian Streitberger (eds.), Zurich and Jena 2017 (Cormarë Series 37), ISBN 978-3-905703-37-5

Claudio Testi, *Pagan Saints in Middle-earth*
Zurich and Jena 2017 (Cormarë Series 38), ISBN 978-3-905703-38-2

Music in Tolkien's Work and Beyond
Julian Eilmann & Friedhelm Schneidewind (eds.), Zurich and Jena 2019 (Cormarë Series 39), ISBN 978-3-905703-39-9

Sub-creating Arda: World-building in J.R.R. Tolkien's Works, its Precursors, and Legacies
Dimitra Fimi & Thomas Honegger (eds.), Zurich and Jena 2019 (Cormarë Series 40), ISBN 978-3-905703-40-5

"Something Has Gone Crack": New Perspectives on J.R.R. Tolkien and the Great War
Janet Brennan Croft and Annika Röttinger (eds.), Zurich and Jena 2019 (Cormarë Series 41), ISBN 978-3-905703-41-2

Tolkien and the Classics
Roberto Arduini, Giampaolo Canzonieri & Claudio A. Testi (eds.), Zurich and Jena 2019 (Cormarë Series 42), ISBN 978-3-905703-42-9

José María Miranda Boto, *Law, Government, and Society in J.R.R. Tolkien's Works*
Zurich and Jena 2022 (Cormarë Series 43), ISBN 978-3-905703-43-6

Middle-earth, or There and Back Again
Łukasz Neubauer (ed.), Zurich and Jena 2020 (Cormarë Series 44), ISBN 978-3-905703-44-3

Tolkien and the Classical World
Hamish Williams (ed.), Zurich and Jena 2021 (Cormarë Series 45), ISBN 978-3-905703-45-0

Nancy Bunting and Seamus Hamill-Keays, *The Gallant Edith Bratt. J.R.R. Tolkien's Inspiration*. Zurich and Jena 2021 (Cormarë Series 46), ISBN 978-3-905703-46-7

Nólë Hyarmenillo: An Anthology of Iberian Scholarship on Tolkien
Nuno Simões Rodrigues, Martin Simonson, and Angélica Varandas (eds.), Zurich and Jena 2022 (Cormarë Series 47), ISBN 978-3-905703-47-4

The Songs of the Spheres: Lewis, Tolkien and the Overlapping Realms of their Imaginations
Łukasz Neubauer and Guglielmo Spirito (eds.), Zurich and Jena 2024 (Cormarë Series 48), ISBN 978-3-905703-48-1

Richard Z. Gallant, *Germanic Heroes, Courage, and Fate: Northern Narratives of J.R.R. Tolkien's Legendarium*. Zurich and Jena 2024 (Cormarë Series 49), ISBN 978-3-905703-49-8

Thomas Honegger, *Tweaking Things a Little. Essays on the Epic Fantasy of J.R.R. Tolkien and G.R.R. Martin.* Zurich and Jena 2023 (Cormarë Series 50), ISBN 978-3-905703-50-4

The Romantic Spirit in the Works of J.R.R. Tolkien
Will Sherwood and Julian Eilmann (eds.), Zurich and Jena 2024 (Cormarë Series 51), ISBN 978-3-905703-51-1

Nancy Bunting, Seamus Hamill-Keays, and Toby Widdicombe, *Celebrating Tolkien's Legacy. Essays by Nancy Bunting, Seamus Hamill-Keays, and Toby Widdicombe.* Zurich and Jena 2024 (Cormarë Series 52), ISBN 978-3-905703-52-8

Tolkien among the Theologians
Austin M. Freeman (ed.), Zurich and Jena 2025 (Cormarë Series 53), ISBN 978-3-905703-53-5

Verlyn Flieger, *A Real Taste for Fairy-stories. Essays by Verlyn Flieger.* Zurich and Jena 2025 (Cormarë Series 54), ISBN 978-3-905703-54-2

Arda Notebooks. The Best of "I Quaderni di Arda"
Roberto Arduini, Claudio A. Testi, and Wu Ming 4 (eds.), Zurich and Jena 2025 (Cormar Series 55), forthcoming

Beowulf and the Dragon

The original Old English text of the 'Dragon Episode of Beowulf is set in an authentic font and bound i hardback as a high quality art book. Illustrated by Ank Eissmann and accompanied by John Porter's translation Introduction by Tom Shippey. Limited first edition of 50 copies. 84 pages. Selected pages can be previewed on: www.walking-tree.org/beowulf

Beowulf and the Dragon, Zurich and Jena 2009 , ISBN 978-3-905703-17-7

Tales of Yore Series

The *Tales of Yore Series* provides a platform for qualitatively superior fiction that will appeal to readers familiar with Tolkien's world:

The Monster Specialist

Sir Severus le Brewse, among the least known of King Arthur's Round Table knights, is preferred by nature, disposition, and training to fight against monsters rather than other knights. After youthful adventures of errantry with dragons, trolls, vampires, and assorted beasts, Severus joins the brilliant sorceress Lilava to face the Chimaera in The Greatest Monster Battle of All Time to free her folk from an age-old curse. But their adventures don't end there; together they meet elves and magicians, friends and foes; they join in the fight to save Camelot and even walk the Grey Paths of the Dead. With a mix of Malory, a touch of Tolkien, and a hint of humor, The Monster Specialist chronicles a tale of courage, tenacity, honor, and love.

The Monster Specialist is illustrated by Anke Eissmann.

Edward S. Louis, *The Monster Specialist*
Zurich and Jena 2014 (Tales of Yore Series No. 3), ISBN 978-3-905703-23-8

Tales of Yore Series (earlier books, presently unavailable)

Kay Woollard, *The Terror of Tatty Walk. A Frightener*
CD and Booklet, Zurich and Berne 2000 (Tales of Yore Series No. 1), ISBN 978-3-9521424-2-4

Kay Woollard, *Wilmot's Very Strange Stone or What came of building "snobbits"*
CD and booklet, Zurich and Berne 2001 (Tales of Yore Series No. 2), ISBN 978-3-9521424-4-8

Information for authors

Authors interested in contributing to our publications can learn more about the services we offer on the "services for authors" section of our web pages.

www.walking-tree.org/authors

Manuscripts and project proposals can be submitted to the board of editors:

Walking Tree Publishers
e-mail: info@walking-tree.org

www.ingramcontent.com/pod-product-compliance
Ingram Content Group UK Ltd.
Pitfield, Milton Keynes, MK11 3LW, UK
UKHW021828190726
13853UKWH00003B/1251